MARX, METHOD,
AND THE DIVISION OF LABOR

MARX, METHOD,
AND THE
DIVISION OF LABOR

Rob Beamish

UNIVERSITY OF ILLINOIS PRESS
Urbana and Chicago

This book is printed on acid-free paper.

Library of Congress Cataloging-in-Publication Data

Beamish, Rob.
    Marx, method, and the division of labor / Rob Beamish.
       p.   cm.
    Includes bibliographical references and index.
    ISBN 0-252-01878-8 (alk. paper)
    1. Marx, Karl, 1818-1883—Views on division of labor.   I. Title.
D51.M38B43   1992
306.3'68—dc20   91-24213
                                                      CIP

For Nada, Travis, and Ryan

CONTENTS

ACKNOWLEDGMENTS

This book is a significantly revised version of the doctoral dissertation I completed at the University of Toronto. Despite many changes to the manuscript, I would like to acknowledge the assistance, critical commentary, and encouragement that Richard Gruneau, Cyril Levitt, and Miguel Murmis made to that earlier project. During my residency as a doctoral student in sociology, I received financial support from the Social Sciences and Humanities Research Council in Canada, and I wish to acknowledge its assistance.

While working on the book manuscript over the past few years at Queen's University, Hart Cantelon, Roberta Hamilton, Vinnie Mosco, and Ester Reiter all contributed, in their own ways, to the creation of a working environment that was extremely supportive, educational, and enabling. I am truly fortunate to have them as friends.

While preparing the book's final draft in Berlin, Carl-Erich Vollgraf and Jürgen Jungnickel of the Berliner Verein zur Förderung der MEGA-Edition were extremely generous with their time and assistance. Access to the library at the Institut für Geschichte der Arbeiterbewegung and the Marx-Engels Lesesaal at Wilhelm-Pieck-Strasse, where numerous editions of Marx's and Engels's works as well as their entire personal libraries are housed, significantly eased the final checking of sources. At the same time, Toni Niewerth and Chrisi Pabst-Niewerth ensured that the time my family and I spent in Berlin ranks among the best times in our lives.

Three people in particular must be recognized for the roles they played in publication of this book in its present form. I discussed this project with Richard Martin long before it was ever completed as a dissertation. His advice at that time, and his assistance and insight years later as I prepared the book manuscript, were essential in improving the content and quality of the study. I would like to thank him for doing far more than his job description of editor ever included.

Second, Bertell Ollman, who served initially as an anonymous reviewer, forwarded an encouraging assessment of the project as well as questions and commentary that have improved the quality of my presentation. I thank him for taking the time to assess the manuscript carefully and for indicating so clearly and perceptively points that needed further work.

Third, Mary Giles undertook the tedious task of copy editing the entire manuscript. I sincerely appreciate her expertise, assistance, and good nature.

My greatest debt, however, is to Nada, Travis, and Ryan, who have given me sustained support, love, and friendship even when this project greatly curtailed my involvement in our family's various activities. I thank them and love them for their understanding and their continued belief that scholarly work is an important element in the constitution of a more just society.

Due to the nature of my particular personality and work habits, I must accept full responsibility for the arguments herein. Working with texts is a slow, labor-intensive, and solitary undertaking that yields, in the long run, a product that almost takes on a life of its own as subject and object dialectically engage. Incorporating constructive ideas from outside into this relationship meets with greater resistance, I suspect, than in most collaborative and social forms of research. Those whose advice I have not followed will, I trust, understand on the basis of this book that the context of the intellectual labor process plays a decisive role in the results an author produces; this study is no exception.

INTRODUCTION

One of the few aspects of Karl Marx's work on which all scholars can agree is the unfinished state in which he left it. Marx did not even bring the first volume of *Das Kapital* to a point that satisfied him fully, and he left the manuscripts for "*the circulation process of capital (Book II) and the configurations [Gestaltungen] of the total process (Book III)*" as well as "the closing *[abschliessende] third volume (Book IV), the history of the theory,*" in a less developed state than even Friedrich Engels had anticipated.[1] In addition to these texts, there are the remaining five parts to the six-part project that Marx outlined in the opening sentence of *Zur Kritik der politischen Ökonomie*—that is, works on "*landed property, wage labor; the state, foreign trade, world market.*"[2] Finally, in any inventory of works that Marx did not complete, one must note the absence of a systematic statement on method.

This latter text is important for two reasons. First, Marx himself recognized the need for a systematic presentation of method even though he ranked its priority and utility below the completion of his work on political economy. Thus, in his correspondence, on the two occasions in which he completed—or neared completion—of a major undertaking in his critique of political economy, Marx indicated a desire to complete a text on the dialectic. "If there is ever time for such labors," Marx wrote to Engels while working on the seven notebooks of 1857–58, "I have a great longing to make accessible to common sense, in 2 or 3 printer's sheets [thirty-two to forty-eight pages], the *rational* in the method which H[egel] discovered, but at the same time mystified."[3] A decade later, following the publication of *Das Kapital*'s first volume, Marx informed Joseph Dietzgen that "when I have shaken off this

1

economic burden, I will write a 'Dialectic.' The correct laws of the dialectic are already contained in Hegel, although in a mystical form. It must be stripped of this form."[4]

In addition to these indications Marx actually dealt with the issue briefly within the afterword to the second German edition of *Das Kapital,*[5] and he drafted a longer segment on method within his discarded 1857 introduction to the *Critique of Economic Categories.*[6] Finally, in 1880, Marx felt compelled to correct Adolf Wagner's misunderstandings of the dialectical method when preparing study notes to Wagner's *Lehrbuch der politischen Ökonomie.*[7] Thus, for Marx, although a statement on method was not his highest priority, there is no doubt that he appreciated its significance for a complete understanding of the critique of political economy.

The second reason one should not overlook the absence of a systematic statement on method concerns the role it could play in the continued systematic study of capitalist societies. Bertell Ollman is only one of many who have argued that Marxists must "give priority to questions of method over questions of theory.... For it is only upon grasping the assumptions and means, forms, and techniques with which Marx constructed his explanations of capitalism that we can effectively use, develop, amend, and even evaluate them."[8]

As late as 1967, this was not a wide-spread sentiment. At a centenary conference for *Das Kapital,* Roman Rosdolsky pointed out that "there is hardly an aspect of Marx's theory which has been treated more negligently than the method of *Das Kapital.*"[9] Since then, researchers have increasingly recognized the importance of understanding Marx's method, and the early neglect of method has turned into an abundance of work in the area. The resulting volume of research has brought forth considerable insight into Marx's work as well as how to apply it to contemporary analysis. Nevertheless, despite the intensive efforts of many researchers during the 1970s and 1980s, work on the question of method is far from complete.

Following Ollman's idea that "method exists on five levels, representing successive stages in its practice: (1) ontology; (2) epistemology; (3) inquiry; (4) intellectual reconstruction; and (5) exposition,"[10] it is clear that the bulk of research has concentrated on some elements and relationships far more than others. Because researchers have drawn so heavily from "Marx's most renowned methodological text,"[11] the section on "The Method of Political Economy" within the 1857 introduction, the first two dimensions Ollman enumerates have received the most attention. The latter two elements have fared less well, but researchers have examined them to some degree. It is the actual, concrete procedures of inquiry and their relationship to intellectual reconstruction, exposition, ontology, and epistemology that analysts have studied least.

The major objective of this book is to explore systematically the much neglected set of issues related to how Marx actually carried out his inquiry into political economy. To do this, I have narrowed my focus to a detailed study of how Marx developed his conception of the division of labor, how he internalized that conception during the intellectual labor process involved in the development of his critique of political economy and then, finally, how Marx employed that conception in the production of his critique. To accomplish this task, I begin with Marx's first reading notes on political economy in 1844 and proceed through the publication of *Das Kapital*'s first volume in 1867.

There are two main reasons for undertaking this project. The first is to correct an imbalance in the study of Marx's method. Given the thrust of the current literature, there is the very real danger that the actual nature and development of the process will not be fully understood. For example, even though Ollman's own work and his actual discussion of Marx's method are sensitive to the relational unity that exists between the five aspects of method that he identifies, it is easy to think of Marx's method in linear terms. When Ollman, for example, notes that Marx's method "exists on five levels, representing *successive stages*" [my emphasis], it is clear that even he is not immune to an occasional slip on this question. Such an understanding, as I will document throughout this book in general and in chapter 1 in particular, is erroneous because the development of Marx's ontology and epistemology themselves was dependent on early inquiry, intellectual reconstruction, and exposition. Furthermore, Marx was still refining his epistemology and ontology while he worked on *Die Grundrisse*.[12] In the case of a particular concept, such as the division of labor, it is not true that Marx produced it at the culmination of his movement through the five aspects of method that Ollman notes. Marx produced his concepts through a complex interrelation of the elements Ollman identifies, but this is not readily apparent from the bulk of what has been written about Marx's methodology.

The second reason is that some schools of neo-Marxist thought, particularly the structuralists, have shown a marked tendency toward turning his method into an abstract formalism. Although a number of commentators have criticized this tendency on largely logical grounds, or by showing how it apparently contradicts Marx's ontological and epistemological assumptions, no one has based their critique on an intensive study of Marx's actual mode of inquiry.[13] This book rectifies that situation.

3

My central thesis is that a major dimension to Marx's method is located within the actual concrete processes of inquiry, elaboration, and intellectual reconstruction. No attempt to comprehend his method will be satisfactory unless it deals with the fundamental, dialectical relationship between abstract and concrete in Marx's intellectual labor process—that is, the dialectic between Marx's conceptions (the abstract) and his interaction with a variety of textual materials, plus the practical activities involved in the writing and indexing of his texts (the concrete).

The corollary to my major thesis is that Marx's method does not support the practice of abstract, formalistic theorizing that Louis Althusser suggested some time ago. On the contrary, as Marx's theoretical comprehension of the underlying structures of capital advanced—as his intellectual apprehension of capital became a more fully developed, synthetically logical construct—he had to turn to a more intensive use of detailed, empirical research to develop his critique further rather than to retreat progressively into abstract formalism.

Marx's continued collection of empirical material in the 1860s, for example, was not for purely illustrative purposes; his empirical work was decisive in building his concepts and enabling him to present his 1867 critique of the production process in capitalist society. As I will document throughout this study, any approach to Marx's method that ignores the dialectic of abstract and concrete—that overlooks the actual intellectual labor process Marx used to produce his concepts—necessarily fails to grasp a central component to his methodological legacy to modern social science. Before outlining the development of my arguments, the selection of the division of labor conception as the focus of this analysis merits some explanation.

Marx and the Division of Labor Question

I have chosen to examine the production of a single concept in Marx's work and relate it to questions of method because this approach represents a necessary complement to the research already completed in the area. Most researchers have used the full text of *Das Kapital* and the support of others such as Volumes 2 and 3, *Theorien über den Mehrwert, Die Grundrisse, Misère de la philosophie,* or *Die Deutsche Ideologie,* to "exemplify" selected aspects of Marx's methodology.

Jindrich Zeleny draws extensively from *Das Kapital* and *Die Grundrisse,* for example, to indicate the "structural-genetic" logic Marx employed, the relation of form and substance, the relation of theory and history, the question of causality, and finally, the relation of appearance and essence.[14] Rosdolsky primarily uses *Das Kapital* and *Die Grun-*

drisse to discuss logic and history, Marx's relational epistemology, the mediation between appearance and essence, and Marx's procedure for abstraction and the status of those abstractions.[15] Derek Sayer emphasizes the relations of phenomenal forms and real relations (appearance and essence), Marx's relational philosophy, and the process of abstraction in Marx's method, by drawing extensively from *Das Kapital, Theorien über den Mehrwert,* and *Die Deutsche Ideologie.*[16]

Stuart Hall centers his discussion of what is essentially an analysis of Marx's method on the 1857 "Introduction" and illustrates his points about the abstraction process, Marx's relational philosophy, appearance and essence, determination, abstraction, logic and history, and Marx's "synchronic/diachronic" mode of conceptualization by quoting extensively from *Das Kapital, Die Grundrisse, Misère de la philosophie,* and *Die Deutsche Ideologie.*[17] Finally, Althusser refers to a broad range of Marx's texts to illustrate his conception of Marx's theoretical practice.[18]

All of these studies have made the important contribution of establishing fundamental dimensions of Marx's method, especially his final position on ontology and epistemology. At the same time, however, because these authors have sought to present a number of aspects to Marx's method, some aspects—most notably, Marx's "means of investigation"[19]—have not received the detailed treatment they deserve. Furthermore, because researchers have treated Marx's method in an extensive manner, they tend to cite textual material that illustrates their points, but this does not necessarily establish that Marx used his method in a systematic fashion throughout his intellectual career as he progressively developed his critique of political economy.

To overcome the first problem, I have chosen to concentrate on the single most neglected aspects of Marx's method: those aspects related to his procedures for inquiry, intellectual reconstruction, and exposition. To overcome the second problem, I have chosen to focus on the production of a single concept and follow it through Marx's work to document how his method was developed and applied across the corpus of his inquiries.

The Significance of the Division of Labor
for Marx's Method

A number of reasons related directly to Marx's work indicate why the division of labor is a significant theme upon which to focus. Marx's primary modus operandi for the assimilation of new material was to record, in notebooks, excerpts from a text that he was reading. He also attempted to set out a critique of political economy on a number of occasions between 1844 and 1867. The division of labor is significant in this context for two reasons. First, it is a question Marx dealt with from his entry into political economy through to 1867—a recurrent issue in his work throughout the twenty-four-year production process of *Das Kapital*. Second, the editors of the new Karl Marx and Friedrich Engels *Gesamtausgabe* (*MEGA*) project and some independent scholars have published significant portions of Marx's literary estate dealing with the division of labor issue, thus making the material available to a wide readership. Consequently, not only does the issue have a lengthy history in Marx's work with political economy, but there is also an extensive, relatively complete, accessible public record of that history. Thus, the division of labor provides an excellent forum for studying how Marx actually worked with a particular issue in political economy.

Second, aside from the length and completeness of the record associated with the division of labor, the issue itself is an important one for Marx's work. The flow of *Das Kapital* centers around a number of important transitions; some are logical and build concepts synthetically, some are empirical, and others develop exclusively as a dialectical unity of both. The division of labor falls into the last of these three categories and at the same time is involved in one of the major transitions in the first volume of *Das Kapital*.

The first edition of *Das Kapital* is comprised of six chapters. Marx began with the commodity to indicate that commodities are exchanged on the basis of the abstract, socially necessary labor time that is objectified in their production and that money emerged as the universal medium of exchange. Chapter 2 follows money as it becomes capital, and this introduces the purchase and sale of labor power. In chapter 3, Marx differentiated between the labor process in general and the valorization process in particular, which led into his analysis of how surplus value was created. Following from that discussion, Marx examined the concept of absolute surplus value associated with the length of the working day. Because absolute surplus value is limited by the length of the day, chapter 4 enters into one of the major considerations for the growth and development of capital: the increased extraction of relative surplus value that accrues to the capitalist as he or she increases the portion of surplus labor time relative to necessary labor time. This is achieved by increasing productivity per unit time. Cooperation and the division of labor present and develop the most basic forms for increasing productivity. In fact, they—especially the division of labor—create the basis for the emergence of capitalism's major period of revolutionary transformation: the emergence of machine-based, large-scale industry. Without the industrial revolution, the growth of capitalism

6

would have been drastically curtailed, and it is within the division of labor that Marx located a pivotal development that created the possibility for such a transformation. On this basis, I view the dynamic inherent in the division of labor, which Marx ferreted out and analyzed in some detail, as one of the major transitions set forth in his magnum opus.[20]

Some transitions in *Das Kapital* are logical, some are shown through empirical examples, and some involve an essential dialectical unity to develop. An example of a logical transformation is the movement from the immediate appearance of the wealth of bourgeois society (the commodity) to its constituent parts (use value and exchange value) and the final distinction between exchange value and value. An empirical transition is seen in the chapter on the accumulation process of capital. The division of labor section presents a perfect example of the unification of a synthetically logical framework and empirical history in a dialectic that advanced Marx's grasp of the concept.

To move from absolute to relative surplus value required a mechanism for increasing productivity. This mechanism also had to have within it a dynamic that would lead beyond itself. This developmental flow has a certain logical dimension that Marx grasped throughout the course of his work on the division of labor issue. The problem was that he could never specify exactly how the division of labor led beyond itself to large-scale industry until 1863, very late in his work on the critique of political economy. In January 1863, while working with empirical material related to machinery, Marx finally drew out of it the conceptual framework needed to present the division of labor as a transitional dimension of production that led to machine production. This transition simultaneously possesses a logical and an empirical dimension and thus provides an excellent opportunity to see how Marx's concepts evolved both logically, and in conjunction with empirical evidence.

A third reason why the division of labor issue in and of itself is important for Marx's work concerns Adam Smith's *An Inquiry into the Nature and Causes of the Wealth of Nations*. Smith was one of the first political economists to identify productive labor in general as the source of social wealth.[21] According to Smith, labor was so bountiful because of the tremendous productivity gains that arose through the division of labor. In his treatment of the division of labor issue throughout the twenty-four-year period under consideration in this study, Marx had to determine how labor could remain as the central source of wealth while the division of labor itself could not be used as the explanation for the creation of surplus value. Resolving that problem was almost as important for Marx's theory of value as his overturning of David Ricardo's theory of rent.[22]

The fourth reason for choosing the division of labor issue returns to the theme of completeness. In developing the conceptual framework for *Das Kapital,* Marx continually mediated his concepts with an empirical referent. The division of labor issue affords insight into three different dimensions of that abstract yet concrete relation. First, the theme of alienation, which was far more conceptual than concrete in 1844, was progressively transformed into an empirically situated concept by 1867. In this case, a related abstract concept (that is, alienation) was progressively materialized through the division of labor. Second, when Marx began to work with the division of labor concept as presented by Smith, it was virtually a transhistorical concept. To come to grips with it critically, Marx incorporated a much more realistic sense of empirical history into the concept. In this case, a concept is simply located more accurately in empirical history. Finally, the transition from manufacture to large-scale industry is a significant transition for capitalism, and Marx had to understand the mechanism behind that transition. The solution came when Marx was working through empirical material on machinery. Consequently, this empirical work influenced more than Marx's discussion of large-scale industry; it also altered and refined Marx's concept of the division of labor. In this instance, a concept (the division of labor) was refined through the use of related empirical material (material on machinery). Thus, for all of the reasons noted in this section, I have chosen to produce an intensive analysis of Marx's development of the division of labor issue within the critique of political economy.

Before presenting an overview of the argument I will develop, it is worth mentioning how this volume differs from Ali Rattansi's earlier, rather extensive treatment of the division of labor theme.[23] In many ways this book and Rattansi's complement each other. Even though both focus on the division of labor issue, they do so with very different objectives. Rattansi points out that he has "chosen to analyse Marx's conception of the division of labor through a consideration of one significant interpretational issue: the idea of the abolition of the division of labor."[24] To be sure Rattansi discusses the historical development of Marx's conception of the division of labor, but he relies exclusively upon English translations of Marx's work, which necessarily limits the materials upon which he can draw. Rattansi does not, for example, use any of Marx's study notebook material, the first five notebooks of Marx's 1861–63 manuscripts, or the indexes to *Die Grundrisse.* Despite this limitation, there are important and interesting parallels in our arguments as well as significant differences that access to the study notebook material used herein allow.

Although our projects share some similarities, my main focus is quite different from Rattansi's. I am not only interested in the development of Marx's conception of the division of labor, but I am also interested in presenting that developmental history to bring important and new insight to discussions of Marx's method. In this study, I will use the developmental history of the division of labor concept to detail how Marx combined all five aspects of method outlined by Ollman and how Marx's method influenced his conception of the division of labor as it developed over the twenty-three-year period separating his first entry into the study of political economy and the publication of the first edition of the first volume of *Das Kapital*.

Outline of the Argument

Chapter 1 focuses on Marx's study notebooks, the most valuable primary material related to his method and intellectual labor process. Because one of Marx's primary procedures for mastering new ideas was to excerpt material from various sources and then keep those excerpts as a permanent record to which he frequently referred, it is important to consider this concrete dimension of Marx's intellectual activity. It is in the transition between his study notebooks and his particular writing projects that Marx appears to have made some important conceptual developments. As a result, one must consider the notebooks carefully in any intensive analysis of Marx's method. Because it is on the basis of previously unavailable study notebook material that I am able to develop key parts of my theses, the study notebooks merit some individual consideration as a source of information.

Chapter 2 chronologically follows through Marx's development of the division of labor concept from his entry into political economy in 1843 until 1860, just before he drafted the twenty-three notebooks that represent the intended third chapter to *Zur Kritik der politischen Ökonomie* and the text that has subsequently been entitled *Theorien über den Mehrwert*. [25] Chapter 2 demonstrates Marx's early movement between theoretical analyses of the division of labor and concrete historical questions related to this topic. The chapter illustrates various stages of the concept's development as Marx attempted to grasp it more comprehensively and make it a part of his own slowly emerging comprehension of the production process in capitalist society.

Between August 1861 and March 1862, Marx filled five notebooks with a draft manuscript that he intended as the third chapter to *Zur*

Kritik der politischen Ökonomie. In chapter 3, I proceed through the section of this draft manuscript concerned with the division of labor. Chapter 3 illustrates Marx's grasp of the concept at this point in his critique, but more importantly, it allows one to see how the actual composing and writing process played a role in sharpening and focusing insight into the concept. This becomes apparent when the 1861–62 analysis is contrasted with earlier formulations, and the 1861–62 draft is set as a reference point for the ensuing discussion of the division of labor in *Das Kapital.*

In January 1863, Marx spent considerable time and energy pursuing empirical information pertaining to large-scale industry. This research, however, affected more than his discussion of machinery in *Das Kapital;* it had a decided impact on the analysis of the division of labor. Chapter 4 documents how Marx not only carried specific parts of the 1863 material directly into *Das Kapital,* but also how his conception of the division of labor was recast in some major ways by his 1863 excursus into study notebooks relating to the history of technology and large-scale industry.

Chapter 5 proceeds chronologically through the discussion of the division of labor found in the first German edition of *Das Kapital.* The chapter presents Marx's final grasp of the concept as the culmination of a lengthy, concrete production process. In the final chapter, I review the stages Marx worked through in the production of his conception of the division of labor and relate this material to the question of method.

NOTES

1. Karl Marx, *Das Kapital,* 1st ed. (Hamburg: Otto Meissner, 1867), p. xii. Unless otherwise noted, all emphases are in the original. If one compares the German text to that of the first French edition (*Le Capital,* trans. Joseph Roy, and revised by author [Paris: M. Lachtre, 1875], p. 12), then the potentially ambiguous meanings for *Gestaltungen* and *abschliessende* are clarified. *Gestaltungen* is specified as "diverse forms," and *abschliessende,* which also carries the connotation of definitive, is translated as "the third and final" volume.

2. Karl Marx and Friedrich Engels, *Gesamtausgabe: Werke, Artikel, Entwürfe* [hereafter cited as *MEGA*] (Berlin: Dietz Verlag, 1975ff), II, 2.1 p. 99:3–5. Throughout this text, in addition to indicating the part, volume number, and page for references to the *MEGA,* I have also included line references because the volumes permit such precision. As a result, the preceding reference refers to material between lines 3 and 5 inclusive on page 99 of the first half volume of vol. 2 of part II. A reference such as *MEGA* II, 2.2, pp. 18:33–19:7 refers to material in the second half volume of vol. 2, part II beginning on line 33 of page 18 and continuing to line 7 on page 19.

3. This letter is dated January 16, 1858; see also Marx to Ferdinand Lassalle, May 31, 1858. Karl Marx and Friedrich Engels, *Werke* [hereafter cited as *MEW*], (Berlin: Dietz Verlag, 1956–90), pp. 29: 260, 561.

4. This letter is dated May 9, 1868, *MEW* 32:547. See also Marx to Ludwig Kugelmann, March 6, 1868, *MEW* 32:538.

5. Karl Marx, *Das Kapital,* 2d ed. (Hamburg: Otto Meissner, 1873), pp. 813–22. Unfortunately, these comments are in the form of an excerpt from a review written by the Russian economist Illarion Kaufman, *MEW* 23:25 n2*, so this is not a statement formulated exclusively by Marx. Marx must have considered these comments on method important because in the French edition of *Das Kapital,* even though he omitted parts of the afterword to the German edition from *Le capital* (pp. 349–51), Marx retained the excerpts on method.

6. See *MEGA* II, 1.1, pp. 35:34–43:14 for this well-known discussion on method. I have used the title *Critique of Economic Categories* rather than *Grundrisse der kritik der politischen Ökonomie (Rohentwurf) 1857–58*—the title for the notebooks supplied by the editors who first published Marx's 1857–58 notebooks—because that is the title that Marx gave the text when writing to Ferdinand Lassalle in 1858—"The work, which is also its chief concern, is the *Critique of Economic Categories* [*Kritik der ökonomischen Kategorien*] or, if you like, the system of bourgeois economy critically presented." Marx to Lassalle, February 22, 1858, *MEW* 29:550. The editors (Karl Marx, *Grundrisse der Kritik der politischen Ökonomie (Rohentwurf) 1857–58* [Berlin: Dietz Verlag, 1953], p. xiv) who supervised the first publication of the notebooks drew their title from a statement that Marx made to Engels on December 8, 1857—"I am working like crazy throughout the night on the condensation [*Zusammenfassung*] of my economic studies so that I can at least have the outlines [*Grundrisse*] ready before the deluge." *MEW* 29:225. Although I will refer to it throughout the remainder of this study as *Die Grundrisse,* it is important to realize that Marx cast the 1857–58 notebooks at such an abstract level that the text does indeed represent a critique of economic categories. The editorially supplied title—*Die Grundrisse*—fails to convey that tendency in the 1857–58 notebooks. I will consider the abstract nature of the 1857–58 notebooks further in chapters 2 and 6.

7. Karl Marx, "Randglossen zu Adolf Wagners' *Lehrbuch der politischen Ökonomie,*" *MEW* 19:364–76.

8. Bertell Ollman, "Marxism and Political Science: Prolegomenon to a Debate on Marx's Method," *Politics and Society* 3, no. 3 (1973):493.

9. Roman Rosdolsky, "Einige Bemerkungen über die Methode des Marxschen *Kapital* und ihre Bedeutung für die heutige Marxforschung," in *Kritik der politischen Oekonomie Heute: 100 Jahre Kapital,* ed. Walter Eucher and Alfred Schmidt (Frankfurt/M.: Europäische Verlaganstalt, 1968), p. 9.

10. Ollman, "Marxism and Political Science," 495. This statement suggests an almost linear relationship among these five stages, but Ollman's discussion of method conveys a much more relational unity among them; see also Bertell Ollman, *Alienation: Marx's Conception of Man in Capitalist Society* (Cambridge: Cambridge University Press, 1971), pp. 3–42, 62–74. Indeed, among all those who have written on Marx's method, Ollman is among the strongest advocates

for a relational understanding of Marx's method. Thus, when someone as aware as Ollman writes a statement about method in linear terms, it becomes clear how difficult it is to grasp the dialectical nature of Marx's method.

11. Derek Sayer, *Marx's Method* (Atlantic Highlands: Humanities Press, 1979), p. x.

12. See, for example, Carol Gould, *Marx's Social Ontology* (Cambridge: MIT Press, 1978); and Alfred Schmidt, *Der Begriff der Natur in der Lehre von Marx* (Frankfurt/M.: Europäische Verlaganstalt, 1962).

13. For general criticisms of the structuralist position, see Henri Lefebvre, "Forme, fonction, structure dans *Le capital,*" *L'homme et la société* 7 (1968):69–81; Lefebvre, "Réflections sur le structuralisme et l'histoire," *Cahiers internationaux de sociologie* 35 (1963):3–24; André Glucksmann, "A Ventriloquist Structuralism," *New Left Review* 72 (1972):68–92; or Leszek Kolakowski, "Althusser's Marxism," in *Socialist Register,* ed. Ralph Miliband and David Saville (London: Merlin Press, 1971), pp. 111–28.

14. Jindrich Zeleny, *The Logic of Marx,* trans. Terrell Carver (1962, repr. Oxford: Basil Blackwell, 1980), pp. 113–17, 21–31, 35–46, 71–88, 103–8.

15. Rosdolsky, "Einige Bemerkungen über die Methode," passim; Rosdolsky, *The Making of Marx's Capital,* trans. Peter Burgess (1968, repr. London: Pluto Press, 1977), pp. 25–55.

16. Derek Sayer, "Method and Dogma in Historical Materialism," *Sociological Review* 23, no. 4 (1975):779–810; Sayer, *Marx's Method,* passim.

17. Stuart Hall, "A 'Reading' of Marx's 1857 Introduction to the *Grundrisse,*" occasional paper distributed by the University of Birmingham through the Center for Contemporary Cultural Studies, 1973.

18. Louis Althusser, "On the Materialist Dialectic," in *For Marx,* trans. Ben Brewster (London: New Left Books, 1977), pp. 161–218.

19. In the afterword to the second German edition of *Das Kapital* (p. 821), Marx noted that "[t]o be sure, the means of presentation must be distinguished formally from the means of investigation. Investigation has to appropriate the material in detail, to analyze its different forms of development and to trace out their inner association. Only after this work has been done can the actual movement be appropriately represented."

20. In 1919, Julian Borchardt, the first to translate volumes 2 and 3 of *Das Kapital* into French, developed the first digested, single-volume edition of the three volumes: *Das Kapital: Kritik der politischen Ökonomie,* (Berlin-Schöneberg: Neuzeitlicher Buchverlag, 1919). In this single volume of 322 pages, Borchardt also seems to have felt that the division of labor was a significant part of the entire three volumes because he reproduced far more of the material from this single section of *Das Kapital* than any other section; see pp. 49–89, esp. 58–78, which deal exclusively with the division of labor.

21. Adam Smith, *An Inquiry into the Nature and Causes of the Wealth of Nations,* vol. 2 of the Glasgow Edition of the *Works and Correspondence of Adam Smith,* ed. Roy Hutcheson Campbell and Andrew S. Skinner (Indianapolis: Liberty Press, 1976). There is no doubt that Marx held Smith in high regard. For example, Marx recognized Smith as the main economist of the manufacture

period. *Das Kapital,* 1st ed., p. 332 n44; see also *MEGA* II, 3.1, p. 249:13–19. In correspondence with Engels, Marx frequently commented on Smith's significance. On April 2, 1851, for example, Marx noted that political economy, as a science, had made little progress after Smith and David Ricardo. *MEW* 27:228.

22. In January 1851, Marx and Engels exchanged letters over the theory of rent, upon which Marx was working. Marx to Engels, January 7, 1851, ibid., pp. 157–62; Engels to Marx, January 29, 1851, ibid., pp. 157–62, 170–72. In his reply to Marx, Engels noted (p. 171) that "there is no doubt that your solution [to the problem of absolute rent] is correct and that you have thus acquired a new claim to the title of the economist of ground rent." The study notebooks on Ricardo's *Principles* compiled by Marx at that time were published in *Die Grundrisse,* pp. 769–80; *MEGA* IV, 7, pp. 316–28.

23. Ali Rattansi, *Marx and the Division of Labour* (London: Macmillan Press, 1982).

24. Rattansi, *Marx and the Division of Labour,* p. xii.

25. Karl Kautsky was the first to edit Marx's massive 1861–63 notebooks thereby producing the first version of *Theorien über den Mehrwert.* The text was published by J. H. W. Dietz Verlag in Stuttgart as a three-volume collection comprised of four books. Half the set appeared in 1905 (vol. 1 and the first book of vol. 2) and the other half in 1910 (the second part of vol. 2 and vol. 3). Not until the second Russian edition of Marx's and Engel's collected works, the *Sochineniia* (Moscow: Idsatelstvo Politiceskoi Literatury, 1955–81), was a more complete transcription and publication of the contents of notebooks 6 to 15, 18, and selected sections from 20 to 22 undertaken. The Russian edition was soon followed by an independently standing, three-volume German edition of *Theorien über den Mehrwert* (Berlin: Dietz Verlag, 1956, 1959, 1962), which contained the same material as the earlier Russian edition. These volumes were subsequently included in the Marx-Engels *Werke* as vols. 26.1, 26.2, and 26.3 (Berlin: Dietz Verlag, 1965, 1967, 1968). Notebooks 1 to 5 of the 1861–63 manuscripts were first published in Russian as vol. 47 of the *Sochineniia,* then in 1976 as *MEGA* II, 3.1 and in 1990 as vol. 43 of *MEW. MEGA* II, 3.1 to 3.6 (Berlin: Dietz Verlag, 1976, 1977, 1978, 1979, 1980, 1982) represents the entire contents of the twenty-three notebooks that Marx drafted between 1861 and 1863.

ONE

Marx's Study Notebooks

One of Marx's primary methods of critically addressing the work of other scholars was to record excerpts from their texts in notebooks that he kept for short- and long-term reference. The practice was a long-standing one that began in Marx's second year at university in Berlin. In a November 10, 1837 letter, he informed his father that he had "adopted the habit of making excerpts from all of the books I read . . . [and] . . . from time to time scribble down my reflections."[1] Marx continued this practice for the rest of his active intellectual life, kept most of his copious study notebooks throughout his peripatetic lifetime, and referred to them frequently.[2]

As a result of Marx's study habits, and the publication of more and more of his study notebooks, scholars have at their disposal a lasting record of his initial reaction to the material he was reading at any particular moment and under specific intellectual conditions, as well as a lasting record of how Marx would later selectively draw from that material as he developed particular writing projects. As a result, Marx's study notebooks represent one of the most fundamentally important—and significantly underused—sources in understanding his method at the level of inquiry, intellectual reconstruction, and exposition.[3]

General Considerations

Marx's study notebooks, as Rainer Winkelmann has argued, are essential sources of information for the application of the materialist conception of history to the development of the materialist conception of history itself.[4] Winkelmann's work and discussion of the study notebooks shows that a detailed analysis is a complex undertaking. For example, he notes that Marx's reading of a text can be viewed from two vantage points—one is what Winkelmann terms Marx's "reading interests" and the other is Marx's "knowledge interests."[5] Marx's reading interests relate to the specific problems and issues raised by the text itself. These interests are particular in focus, relate immediately to the text, and provide a set of data that a researcher can pursue more or less inductively in order to trace the development of Marx's critico-theoretical project. Marx's knowledge interests, on the other hand, represent more general, overarching interests which, on the basis of *Das Kapital,* for instance, a researcher can determine deductively and then employ in an analysis of the study notebooks to see Marx's referent as he excerpted and commented on various texts.

Naturally, these two interests are part of a dialectical process; Marx never read totally passively, and his excerpts from each text were never fully centered only on the text in the total absence of a larger framework of knowledge interests. In addition, Marx's knowledge interests were not static sets of ideas. They changed as new material was absorbed, and it would be misleading to always use *Das Kapital,* for example, as the sole vantage point for his knowledge interest framework (especially in the study of some of Marx's early works). A careful reading of the notebooks must deal with the two moments of reading interests and knowledge interests not only analytically and then synthetically, but also in terms of when Marx read a text and what knowledge-interest reference is used to compare with the study notebook material.

The complexity of Marx's study notebooks does not end with the interaction of his reading interests and his knowledge interests. The form and content of the notebooks is also an important consideration. He frequently excerpted without commentary.[6] In his 1844 study notes on Jean-Baptiste Say's *Traité d'économie politique,* for example, Marx excerpted in a chronological fashion for fifteen and a half notebook pages with virtually no commentary.[7] In such cases, the excerpts themselves are important because what Marx excerpted and paraphrased means something. Similarly, the material he omitted also has potential hermeneutic meaning. It is the researcher who must retrospectively try to determine that meaning as fully as possible, as I have tried to do in several places throughout this study.

Marx, however, did not always merely excerpt in a more or less chronological fashion. In the last section of manuscript page 15 of the Say notes, Marx made a series of comments on the right-hand side of the page opposite some of Say's statements about "Principles with Respect to the Circulation of Wealth," which Marx had recorded on the left-hand side of the page.[8] This practice of excerpting and commenting occurs throughout Marx's study notebooks and provides the most direct information about his position concerning many thinkers.

A final variation in Marx's study notebooks is also exemplified in the Say study notes. From notebook page 16 on, Marx did not excerpt chronologically. As he wrote down terms and Say's definitions, Marx established his own order to the material.[9] This part of the text is arranged under four of Say's major headings: "I Principles Relating to the Circulation of Wealth," "II Principles Relating to the Phenomenon of Production" (which included three subsections entitled "Agents of Production," "Process of Production," and "Different Classes of Producers"), "III Source and Distribution of Revenues," and "IV Principles Relating to the Phenomenon of Consumption."[10]

Aside from Marx's technique for producing excerpts and commentary, three other points about his study notebooks should be considered. First, the notebooks establish how systematic Marx was in his reading. Following his arrival in London, and upon securing a reader's permit to the British Museum in July 1850, Marx read intensively on the question of currency and banking theory.[11] For example, he read and excerpted in his first notebook John Fullarton's *On the Regulations of Currencies; Being an Examination of the Principles, on which It Is Proposed to Restrict, within Certain Fixed Limits, the Future Issues on Credit of the Bank of England and the Other Banking Establishments Throughout the Country* (1844) and Thomas Tooke's *A History of Prices and the State of the Circulation, from 1839–1847 Inclusive: With a General Review of the Currency Question, and Remarks on the Operation of the Act 7 and 8 Vict. C. 32. Being a Continuation of the History of Prices from 1793–1839* (1848).[12]

This work was followed in the second study notebook with further work on Tooke's *A History of Prices*, Robert Torrens's *The Principles and Practical Operation of Sir Robert Peel's Bill of 1844. Explained and Defended Against the Objections of Tooke, Fullarton and Wilson* (1848), Lord Ashburton's *The Financial and Commercial Crisis Considered* (1847), and William Blake's *Observations on the Principles which Regulate the Course of Exchange; and on the Present Depreciated State of the Currency* (1810) to which Fullarton had referred.[13] This pattern continues throughout the study notebooks.

The reading of Torrens's, Ashburton's, and Blake's works suggests a second dimension to Marx's systematic reading. He followed up on sources used in one book to see exactly what was written in the referenced work. His reading appraised him of several sides to the debates in political economy, and he pursued the debates through the primary sources while the ideas were fresh in his mind.

Finally, Marx also concentrated his work by reading, where appropriate, more than one work by a single author. Thus, for example, in the first six London study notebooks one can see that Marx read three works by Gavin Mason Bell, as well as Johan Georg Büsch, two works by Sir Archibald Alison, James Taylor, and "Gemini"—a pseudonym some thought to belong to John Harlow and Thomas Barber Wright although Marx believed it to be Thomas Atwood's.[14] While this sort of systematic analysis is not uncommon to any scholar of merit, it is useful to have the practice documented because it indicates several important features of how Marx worked throughout the production of *Das Kapital*.

First, one can see how much Marx relied on the work of others to build his critique. Marx rarely collected data himself; he almost always worked as a critic of others' theoretical positions or reinterpreted their findings within a different theoretical framework.[15] Second, although this mode of investigation poses certain limitations to what one can confirm empirically, because the researcher must rely on the information gathered by other sources and may be limited by the data, it is also apparent that Marx read widely in the pursuit of information so that he had access to considerable material when formulating his critique.

This latter point confirms not only Marx's 1859 preface to *Zur Kritik der politischen Ökonomie* about the wealth of information on political economy available in the British Museum but also the fact that he took advantage of that wealth of information.[16] In addition to the preceding material, Marx also listed references to such anonymous essays as *An Examination of the Currency Question and of the Project for Altering the Standards of Value* (1840) and *The Three Prize Essays on Agriculture and the Corn Law* published by the Anti-Corn Law League in 1842.[17] He excerpted extensively from the *Economist* and listed many references to such relatively obscure works as Henry Parnell's *Observations on Paper Money, Banking, and Overtrading, Including Those Parts of the Evidence Taken Before the Committee of the House of Commons, which Explain the Scotch System of Banking* (1827) or Robert Montgomery's *China; Political, Commercial and Social; in an Official Report to Her Majesty's Government* (1847).[18] These titles indicate not only how many resources Marx drew upon while in London, but also how much empirical information he consumed when developing his ideas on money, currency, and value.

The third relevant point about the notebooks is that Marx referred back to them several times during his intellectual career. Thus, in the case of the London study notebooks, he made up a list of contents to assist later referencing. In addition, when Marx compiled his so-called citation notebooks during 1859 and 1860, he reexamined his twenty-four London study notebooks of the 1850s, as well as the Paris, Brussels, and Manchester notebooks of the 1840s.[19] As a result, it is apparent that these study notebooks served more than the immediate purpose of establishing ideas in Marx's mind as he read each author's work; the notebooks were also enduring references although, as in the case of Smith and Ricardo, Marx read and excerpted from some works on more than one occasion.[20] It will become apparent throughout the course of this book just how influential Marx's return to various study notebooks was in terms of his overall conception of the division of labor.

Marx's Study Notebooks on Smith's *La richesse des nations*

Marx's study excerpts from Smith's *Recherches sur la nature et les causes de la richesse des nations* are found in two study notebooks. The first one is six folio sheets (twenty-four pages), of which Marx used and paginated the first twenty-three.[21] In these twenty-three pages, Marx excerpted material up to Book 3—"Of the Different Progress of Opulence in Different Nations."[22] In another study notebook of seven folio sheets (twenty-eight pages), Marx continued his excerpts on Smith. In this particular study notebook, the first six pages—which Marx did not paginate—contained excerpts from René Levasseur's *Mémoires* (volumes 1 to 4, 1829–33), which Marx had read when planning to write a history of constitutional assemblies.[23] Marx paginated the next eleven pages, 24 to 34, and left the following one without a number even though it contains two lines of writing. In this part of the notebook, Marx wrote excerpts from Books 3 and 4 of *La richesse des nations*.[24] The last ten pages of the notebook are blank. Unlike many of Marx's study notebooks, the majority of material on Smith's work is excerpted chronologically with minimal commentary. Finally, Marx did not excerpt from Book 5, although he would later note that Smith made some critical observations about the social consequences of the division of labor in that section.[25]

There is one major exception to the chronological excerption. When Marx finished the section on natural price and market price in chapter 7 of Book 1, he made only two excerpts from chapter 8, "Of the Wages of Labor." Marx excerpted the first, single-sentence-long paragraph of the chapter: "That which constitutes the natural recompense or the *wages* of labor, is the *product of labor.*"[26] He then excerpted the next paragraph in full: "In the primitive state which precedes the ownership [*propriété*] of land and accumulation of stock [*capitaux*], the entire product of labor belongs to the worker. He has neither landlord nor master with whom he must share."[27]

Marx then left this section of *La richesse des nations* and proceeded into a short excursus on chapter 2 of Book 2: "Of Money Considered as a Particular Branch of the General Stock of the Society, or the Expense of Maintaining the National Capital." Marx excerpted from only eight pages of the chapter,[28] and then returned to chapter 8 of Book 1, "Of the Wages of Labor."[29] He wrote the heading "Der Arbeitslohn (des salaires du travail)," Smith's chapter title, and then proceeded to excerpt and paraphrase chronologically from the entire chapter. He continued excerpting and paraphrasing chapter 9 under the heading "II Der Gewinn der Capitalien (des profits des capitaux)," which essentially duplicated Smith's title "Of the Profits of Stock."[30]

Under the heading "III Salaire und Gewinne in den verschiedenen Anwendung von Arbeit und Capital," Marx excerpted much more intermittently than before from Smith's chapter 10 of Book 1, "Wages and Profit in the Different Employments of Labor and Stock."[31] He excerpted from chapter 11, "Of the Rent of Land," under the heading "IV de la rente de la terre Grundrente."[32] In this section, Marx closely excerpted the first eight pages of the Germain Garnier translation and then skipped twenty-five pages of historical examples to excerpt some theoretical points on rent and population at the end of the chapter's first section.[33] He made a few excerpts from the chapter's second section and then skipped over a lengthy discussion of the role of rent in the price of metals and a long digression on silver.[34] He also excerpted from the concluding section of the chapter.[35]

This reading led Marx into the introductory section of Book 2.[36] After reading and excerpting from chapter 1 of Book 2, Marx proceeded to chapter 3 because he had already excerpted from chapter 2 in the excursus noted previously. From this point on, Marx's excerpts are less detailed and proceed chronologically through the remainder of Book 2, Book 3, and the first eight of the nine chapters in Book 4. Marx's excerpts from Books 3 and 4 are easier to follow than those in Books 1 and 2 because he duplicates the chapter numbers and titles from Books 3 and 4 as sections in his notebook, which was not his practice in the first two books.

Among the more striking features of Marx's excerpts from *La richesse des nations* are the headings for chapters 8, 9, and 11 of Book 1; "I. Der Arbeitslohn. (des salaires du travail.)," "II. Der Gewinn der Capitalien. (des profits des capitaux.)," and "IV. de la rente de la terre.

Grundrente."[37] Marx subsequently used these, or similar, titles for each of the three columns under which he wrote in the first twenty-one pages of the first manuscript of his Paris notebooks of 1844.[38]

Before Smith, it appears from the existing study notebooks that Marx had only read Say's *Traité d'économie politique* and his *Cours complet d'économie politique pratique,* possibly Frédéric Graf von Skarbek's *Théorie des richesses sociales,* as well as Carl Schüz's *Grundsätze der National-Oekonomie,* Heinrich Osiander's *Entäuschung des Publikums über die Interesses des Handels, der Industrie und der Landwirtschaft,* and Osiander's *Ueber den Handelsverkehr der Völker.* None of these authors made the threefold division "wages of labor," "profits of stock," and "rent of land" as Smith did. To be sure, Ricardo noted in his preface to *On the Principles of Political Economy and Taxation* that the objective of political economy was to determine the laws that regulate the distribution of the earth's produce among the "three great classes of the community; namely, the proprietor of the land, the owner of the stock or capital necessary for its cultivation, and the laborers by whose industry it is cultivated." He also noted that distribution allotted to each class came under "the names of rent, profit and wages."[39] It is also apparent from the study notebooks that Marx read Ricardo shortly after finishing with Smith. But the separation of the three classes and categories of allotment are not developed by Ricardo to the extent they are in Smith, and Marx directly transferred the translations of Smith's headings found in the study notebooks to his 1844 draft manuscript. Thus it appears that Marx's reading interests relating to *La richesse des nations* provided considerable influence over the form he used to set out his first draft text for the critique of political economy as well as over some of the content of that critique.

This idea is supported further by the role Smith plays in the first twenty-one pages of the 1844 draft text. In each of the three columns Marx cites Smith extensively. At the same time, however, it is apparent that a developing set of knowledge interests, based in part on Marx's initial exposure to some of the French socialists while living in Paris, influenced how he reread and culled material from his study notebooks on Smith. Rather than merely repeating material from Smith that he had placed under each of the headings, Marx subsumed under those column headings more quotations from other areas of *La richesse des nations* than he had excerpted from those three specific chapters in Smith's text.[40]

All of this is important because Marx's first sojourn into a critique of political economy was cast at a largely theoretical level. He essentially used Georg Wilhelm Friedrich Hegel's conceptions of the philosophy of history and alienation to examine political economy critically. The sources of political economy that Marx used, however, were basically theoretical treatises like Smith's *Richesse des nations,* Ricardo's *Des principes de l'économie politique et de l'impôt,* Say's *Traité,* and James Mill's *Élémens d'économie politique.* While there are many solid grounds for supporting such an approach and selection of material, it is important to note why Marx began in this theoretical fashion—his reading had prepared him for little else—and that he could not stay at this level for very long if he hoped to make an exhaustive critique.[41]

The Division of Labor in *La richesse des nations:* Marx's Excerpts

Marx began his study notes on Smith with a direct quotation of the first single-sentence paragraph of chapter 1.[42] He omitted the next long paragraph and summarized the famous pin-making example by focussing on the number of pins produced while totally ignoring each of the distinct operations Smith outlined.[43] Marx then quoted from Smith, translating the French text into his own German. "The division of labor, insofar as it can be brought about [*getrieben*], occasions a proportionate increase in the productive capacities [*Vermögen (facultés)*] of labor."[44] Marx omitted the remainder of paragraph 4 which explains how the effects of the division of labor are the same in all industries and carried farthest in the most advanced countries.[45]

Next Marx paraphrased the three reasons for the increased quantity of work attributable to the division of labor.[46] Although he made several direct excerpts from Smith's analysis, Marx did not address Smith's comments on the emergence of an intellectual class.[47] Apparently Marx's primary focus was, at this time, upon the more or less technical side of the division of labor issue. Although he would later address the technical division of labor in conjunction with the emergence of science, he did not see that as an important relation during this reading of *La richesse des nations.*

Marx's final excerpt from chapter 1 is a paraphrase. "In a civilized country the smallest private man cannot be dressed or furnished without the assistance of over a thousand people."[48] This summarizes a lengthy concluding paragraph of the chapter that Smith filled with examples to establish his point.[49]

To introduce chapter 2, Marx wrote, "To whom is one indebted for the origin of this division of labor?"[50] "Not human wisdom [*Weisheit*] says Smith. It is much more 'the necessary, although long and gradual [*stufenweise*] consequence, of a certain natural propensity of men, namely the propensity to traffic [*handeln*] and [barter] in order to exchange one thing against another'" Marx paraphrased and quoted.[51] He also noted that according to Smith this propensity was most likely not "fortuitous [*zufälligen*]," but rather "a necessary consequence of the use of reason and speech."[52]

In a series of quotations and paraphrases, Marx covered Smith's argument that the propensity to truck, barter, and exchange is found only in the human species. Concerning Smith's conclusions that it is the propensity to truck that gives rise to the division of labor—a point Smith substantiated with examples drawn from a tribe of hunters— Marx criticized the circular nature of the argument. "In order to explain the division of labor, he [Smith] imputes exchange. But in order that exchange is possible, he must already assume the division of labor, the difference of human activity. Although he has shifted the problem to the primitive condition, he has not become free of it [that is, his problem]."[53] This comment is important for two reasons. First, it signals a reading interest that focussed on an issue Marx would deal with a number of times over the next twenty-three years while sharpening his analysis of the division of labor. The issue of causality surfaced in a number of contexts before he finally dealt with it systematically in *Das Kapital*.

The second point about the observation is more general in nature. In 1845 and 1846, Marx began to develop the idea of historical specificity. The critique of Smith's failure to see the circularity in his argument, and the absence of criticism elsewhere in the study notebook, suggests that, for the most part, Marx lacked much of a knowledge-interest framework to gauge the quality of Smith's arguments; a strong historical background is Marx's most obvious lacuna. Consequently, he did not criticize many of Smith's vague and broadly sweeping historical generalizations.

To complete his work on the second chapter, Marx made five excerpts that covered the remainder of the chapter in some detail. He noted Smith's arguments about how exchange and the division of labor promote specialization and the development of one's talents. "Then the certainty of being able to exchange all the products of his work which exceeds his own consumption, against an identical surplus of the products of the labor of others, of which he has need, encourages each man to undertake a particular occupation and to cultivate and perfect everything that he is able of his talent and intelligence for this type of labor." He then recorded: "The difference of natural talents among individuals is not so much the cause as the result of the division of labor."[54]

The next two excerpts restate, in slightly different ways, Smith's position on exchange producing the division of labor and thus the development of specific talents. "Without the disposition of men to traffic and to exchange, everyone was bound to supply himself with all the necessities and conveniences [*Bequemlichkeiten*] of life. Everyone had to accomplish the same daily work [*Tagwerk*] and the great difference of occupations which alone can produce a great difference of talents, had not taken place." Marx's second excerpt was as follows: "Just as it is this disposition to exchange which produces the difference of talents among men, it is also the same disposition which renders this diversity useful."[55]

Marx's last excerpt is a lengthy combination of quotation and paraphrasing of the remainder of the chapter's last paragraph. In essence, the section presents Smith's view that the division of talents among animals is of no consequence to the species as a whole because the diversity is not drawn together via exchange. With men, on the other hand, "the most disparate talents are useful to one another because the products of each of their respective diverse sorts of industry, by means of the universal propensity to truck and trade, find themselves, so to speak, in a common stock where each man is able to purchase, following his needs, whatever portion of the produce of the industry of others."[56]

Marx made only one excerpt from chapter 3, "That the Division of Labor Is Limited by the Extent of the Market." Marx excerpted the first paragraph in full from Smith's work by copying out the quotation in French.

> Since it is the *power of exchange* which gives occasion to the division of labor, the growth [*accroissement*] of this division must as a consequence always be limited by the extent of the power of exchange, or, in other words, by the *extent of the market*. If the market is very little, no one is encouraged to dedicate himself entirely to a single occupation, for want of being able to exchange all the surplus product of his labor which exceeds his necessary consumption, against an identical surplus of the products of the labor of others which he wishes to obtain.[57]

Marx omitted the remainder of chapter 3, which essentially provided examples to confirm this position, and moved into chapter 4, paraphrasing most of the chapter's closing paragraph. Smith argued that once the division of labor was established, each person produces only a very small part of his or her own wants. "Thus *every man* lives by exchange or becomes a type of *merchant*, and the society itself is properly a *commercial society*."[58] Smith then began to analyze the origin and use of money in a commercial society.

In these excerpts on the division of labor, Marx's reading interests focussed upon issues that he would examine from a number of different angles—drawing different conclusions—over the next twenty-three years. The idea of talent emerging from the division of labor is dealt with critically as early as the Paris draft manuscript although much more so in later discussions. The scope of the market, the nature of the division of labor, and what commercial society led to in terms of how and why men and women labored also become major themes in Marx's later analyses.

Marx, of course, omitted material such as Smith's comments on the creation of a class of scientists since he did not view it as significant at the time. More surprising, however, is the absence of any notations on Smith's famous discussion of pin-making. Marx did not refer to this aspect of Smith's work at all until *Das Kapital,* where the example is used clearly and explicitly to differentiate between the two ways in which the division of labor arose. The pin-making example represented how the division of labor arose from within an organic process, as opposed to the making of a watch, which drew together previously unrelated trades and was thus an example of a heterogeneous process. There were earlier occasions where Marx might have made use of the pin-making example, but he did not.

In this chapter, I have considered a number of general features concerning Marx's study notebooks and some of the particular contents of his study notes for *La richesse des nations.* I have done this to increase familiarity with this concrete dimension of Marx's method as well as to list some of the most important material he had at his disposal when he engaged in his first critique of political economy. It is obvious from the study notebooks on *La richesse des nations*—Marx's major source of information for the division of labor which he used when drafting his Paris manuscripts—that he had little concrete information with which to construct a far-reaching critique of political economy in 1844. What will become apparent, however, is that in drafting his 1844 critique, Marx developed a basis upon which he would then increase the historical and empirical content of his conception of the political economy in general and the issue of the division of labor in particular. Thus, the study notebooks of 1844 represent the first step in what became a very long trek through political economy. Furthermore, Marx's first entry into political economy was centered almost exclusively on theoretical treatises, which contained little, if any, empirical substantiation even though his interest in political economy had been first kindled by his work as an editor for *Die Rheinische Zeitung,* where he first had to take into account "the so-called material interests."[59]

Put another way, although Marx's interest in political economy was first aroused by actual concrete, historical events and conditions, his introduction to political economy did not entail the study of political economy through detailed historical accounts of the concrete conditions that capitalism ushered in and how the newly emerging political economy impacted upon the lives of the proletariat. His initial exposure was almost totally confined to theoretical treatments of political economy. Marx's movement to concrete, historical material, as I will indicate in the next chapter, arose out of the interrelation between his study notebook material and his own draft attempts to develop a critique of political economy on the basis of the material that he had at hand in 1844. In setting out his own critique of political economy, Marx created the conditions from which he would begin to seek out an increasingly historical and empirical grasp of the division of labor issue.

NOTES

1. See Karl Marx and Friedrich Engels, *Historisch-kritische Gesamtausgabe* [hereafter cited as *MEGA*[1]], ed. David Ryazanov and Vladimir Adoratsky (Berlin: Marx-Engels Verlag, 1927–32; Moscow-Leningrad: Verlagsgenossenschaft Ausländischer Arbeiter in der UdSSR, 1935), I, 1.2, p. 218:4–7. Marx also noted in the same letter that he had developed other work habits that were to characterize much of his later work. He had read through J. G. Heineccius' *Elementra iuris civilis secundum ordinem Pandectarum, commoda auditoribus methodo adornata* and A. F. J. Thibaut's *System des Pandekten-Rechts* (ibid., p. 215:6–15), and translated the first two books of the Pandect—a compendium of Roman civil law—into German (ibid., p. 215:6–15). Finally, Marx attempted to develop a philosophy of law covering the whole field, a work, no longer extant, which ran to almost three hundred pages by his own account. This work led Marx into a massive undertaking in jurisprudence and philosophy—detailed in the remainder of the letter—which delivered Marx "into the arms of the enemy," the idealist philosopher Georg Wilhelm Friedrich Hegel.

The *MEGA*[1] project was initiated by Ryazanov in 1927 and continued under his supervision until 1930. While editor, Ryazanov saw vols. 1.1, 1.2, and 2 of part I plus vols. 1, 2, and 3 of part III come before the public. Adoratsky edited the project from 1930 to 1935, supervising the publication of vols. 3 to 7 of part I, vol. 4 of part III, and a special volume of Engels's work to commemorate the fortieth anniversary of his death. All of the volumes except *MEGA*[1] I, 7 and the commemorative work were published in Berlin. Following the rise of Adolph Hitler and the Nationalsozialistische Deutsche Arbeiterpartei to power in January 1933, the *MEGA*[1] project was moved to the Soviet Union, where its last two volumes were published by the Verlagsgenossenschaft Ausländischer Arbeiter in der UdSSR in Moscow and Leningrad.

2. Lawrence Krader, ed., *The Ethnological Notebooks of Karl Marx* (Assen: Van Gorcum, 1976); and Maxamilien Rubel, "Les cahiers d'étude de Marx," *Marx, critique du marxisme* (Paris: Payot, 1974), p. 303.

3. Because Marx's excerpt notes represent such a crucial source for understanding the development of his ideas, it is remarkable that few scholars studying his work—especially his method—have referred extensively to the notebooks. Although there is some justification to the claim that many notebooks were not available until the publication of the new Marx-Engels *Gesamtausgabe* (*MEGA*), this is not completely satisfactory; see Karl Marx and Friedrich Engels, *Gesamtausgabe: Werke, Artikel, Entwürfe* [hereafter cited as *MEGA*] (Berlin: Dietz Verlag, 1975ff). In addition, valuable notebook material appears in *Arkhiv K. Marxsa i F. Engel'sa,* vols. 1–5, ed. David Ryazanov (Moskva: Gosudarstvennoe Isdatelstvo, 1924–30) and *Arkhiv Marxsa i Engel'sa,* vols. 1–5, ed. Vladimir Adoratsky (Moscow: Partijnoje Istatelstvo, 1932–33, Partisdat zK VKP, 1934–35, Gosudarstvennoe Isdatelstvo Politiceskoj, 1938) although scholars have made little use of even this material. Finally, Ryazanov published the first two volumes of the *Arkhiv K. Marxsa i F. Engel'sa* in a German edition; see *Marx-Engels Archiv,* vols. 1–2 (Frankfurt/M.: Marx-Engels-Archiv Verlag, 1926–27).

4. Karl Marx, *Exzerpte über Arbeitsteilung, Maschinerie und Industrie,* trans. and ed. Rainer Winkelmann (Frankfurt/M: Verlag Ullstein, 1982), pp. iv–v.

5. Marx, *Excerpte über Arbeitsteilung,* pp. viii–ix.

6. See, for example, any of the "Kreuznach Study Notebooks" of 1843, *MEGA* IV, 2, pp. 9–278, or any of the first six "London Study Notebooks" of 1850–51, *MEGA* IV, 7, pp. 35–604.

7. *MEGA* IV, 2, pp. 201:1–316:22.

8. Ibid., pp. 316:29–317:24. See also the notes on James Mill's *Élemens d'économie politique,* where Marx excerpted chronologically but made two very lengthy—and now well-known—commentaries on the text; ibid., pp. 428–79, 447:13–459:8, 462:6–466:18. The most one-sided example of Marx's own commentary surpassing the amount of material he excerpted is found in the study notes to Guillaume Prevost's *Réflections du traducteur sur le système de Ricardo;* ibid., pp. 480–84.

9. Ibid., pp. 320:10–327:36. My discussion of Smith will show another example of this practice.

10. Ibid., pp. 316:29–33, 322:27–28, 323:34, 324:15, 324:27, 325:32, 326:10, and 327:15–16.

11. Maximilien Rubel, *Marx Chronology* (London: Macmillan Press, 1980), p. 24.

12. *MEGA* IV, 7, p. 691.

13. Ibid., p. 692.

14. The three works by Bell are *The Philosophy of Joint Stock Banking* (1840), *The Currency Question: An Examination of the Evidence on Banks of Issue Given Before*

a Select Committee of the House of Commons (1840), and *The Country Banks and the Currency: An Examination of the Evidence on Banks of Issue, Given Before a Select Committee of the House of Commons in 1841* (1842); ibid., pp. 571–79, 585–87, 591–99. The three works of Büsch's are *Abhandlung von dem Geldlauf in anhaltender Rücksicht auf die Staatswirtschaft und Handlung,* 2 parts (1840), *Theoretische-praktische Darstellung der Handlung in ihren mannigfältigen Geschäften,* 2 vols. (1808), and *Sämtliche Schriften über Banken und Münzwesen* (1801); ibid., pp. 277–91, 292–303, 329–43, 361–72. The last two references apply to the *Sämtliche Schriften.* The works by Alison are *Free Trade and a Fettered Currency* (1847) and *England in 1815 and 1845: Or, a Sufficient and a Contracted Currency* (1845); ibid., pp. 112–14, 150–54. Taylor's works were *A View of the Money System of England, from the Conquest, with Proposals for Establishing a Secure and Equable Credit Currency* (1828), which was interspersed with a reading of *A Letter to His Grace the Duke of Wellington on the Currency* (1830); ibid., pp. 155–74, 176–79, 175. From Gemini, Marx read and excerpted from *The True Character and Certain Consequences of Our Present Currency System Shown by Sir James Graham, Bart., in His "Corn and Currency"* (1843) and *The Currency Question: The Gemini Letters* (1844); ibid., pp. 146, 147–49.

15. Marx's most noted undertaking in data collection was related to his so-called "Enquête Ouvrière," a questionnaire published in the *Revue Socialiste* on April 20, 1880, with an additional twenty-five thousand copies distributed to various workers' societies and other interested parties. See Marx to Friedrich Sorge, November 5, 1880, Karl Marx and Friedrich Engels, *Werke* [hereafter cited as *MEW*] (Berlin: Dietz Verlag, 1956–90), 34:475 n570, p. 616. The questionnaire was first published in English by Bottomore and Rubel. See Tom Bottomore and Maximilien Rubel, eds., *Karl Marx: Selected Writings in Sociology and Social Philosophy* (London: Watts and Company, 1956), pp. 203–212. It had appeared much earlier in German translation; Helde Weiss, "Die 'Enquête Ouvrière' von Karl Marx," *Zeitschrift für Sozialforschung* 5 (1936):76–98; *MEW* 19:230–37. The response to the questionnaire, as Weiss explains, was disappointingly small.

16. *MEGA* II, 2, p. 102:22–23.

17. *MEGA* IV, 7, pp. 182–83, 29:3.

18. See ibid., pp. 273:12, 345:4, for references to Parnell's work and p. 315:5 for the reference to Martin's report. Other works one might list within this section are two works by John Holland: *The Directors of the Bank of England, Enemies to the Great Interests of the Kingdom; and Also Not Just to the Trust Reposed in Them by the Adventurers, Who Chose Them to Do Their Best Endeavours, by All Honest Means, for the Advantage of the Joint Stock* (1715) and *The Ruine of the Bank of England and All Publick-credit, Inevitable: and the Necessity, in a Short Time, of Stopping the Payments upon the Several Funds to the Bank, South Sea Company, Lotteries etc. if the Hon. House of Commons Will Not Themselves Be Judges of the Means That May Be Offer'd to Prevent It* (1715); ibid., p. 191:22.

19. See *MEGA* II, 2, pp. 414–42, 264–71 for information on Marx's citation notebooks. Essentially, the citation notebooks, begun no earlier than 1859, represent a collection of citations that Marx excerpted from all of his economic

study notebooks dating to the 1840s and 1850s. Marx apparently began by listing selected excerpts from his ten London economic study notebooks of 1851–53 (see *MEGA* IV, 7 and 8), followed by material from his 1840 study notebooks—that is, the Paris, Brussels, and Manchester study notebooks—followed by excerpts from notebook VII of a second set of London study notebooks that date between 1859 and 1862.

20. For example, Marx excerpted from Ricardo's work in French translation in 1844 (see *MEGA* IV, 2, pp. 392–427, 549–50) and then from *Principles of Political Economy and Taxation* twice during the 1850s; see Karl Marx, *Die Grundrisse der politischen Ökonomie (Rohentwurf) 1857–58* (Berlin: Dietz Verlag, 1953), pp. 764–80, 781–839.

21. *MEGA* IV, 2, p. 747.

22. Ibid., pp. 332:1–364:7.

23. The *MEGA* editors indicate that Marx had corresponded with Arnold Ruge about this project in 1843. They also note that Bruno and Edgar Bauer published a series of essays under the title *Reminiscences of the History of Recent Ties Since the French Revolution.* Three of the essays dealt with the French Revolution itself, with Bruno Bauer also writing a piece entitled "June 20 and August 10, 1792 or the Last Struggle of the Monarchy in France with the People's Party," which the *MEGA* editors feel may have incorporated many of Marx's ideas on assemblies; ibid., pp. 725–26.

24. Ibid., pp. 364:8–386:32.

25. Karl Marx, *Das Kapital,* 1st ed. (Hamburg: Otto Meissner, 1867), pp. 347–48 n70.

26. *MEGA* IV, 2, p. 344:32–33, Marx's emphases. My translation here, as in all cases throughout this section where Marx uses Germain Garnier's translation of Smith, is from the French supplied by Marx. The actual English text is only marginally different. "The produce of labor constitutes the natural recompense or wages of labor." Adam Smith, *An Inquiry into the Nature and Causes of the Wealth of Nations,* vol. 2 of the Glasgow Edition of *The Works and Correspondence of Adam Smith,* ed. Roy Hutcheson Campbell and Andrew S. Skinner (Indianapolis: Liberty Press, 1976), p. 82.

27. *MEGA* IV, 2, p. 344:34–36. The English is different from the French in this case. "In that original state of things, which precedes both the *appropriation* [my emphasis] of land and the accumulation of stock, the whole produce of labor belongs to the laborer. He has neither landlord nor master to share him." Smith, *The Wealth of Nations,* p. 82. Marx would no doubt have regarded the English term appropriation used by Smith as more historically and technically correct.

The term *stock* used by Smith was translated by Garnier as *capitaux* and thus by Marx as *Capitalien.* This change of terminology encompasses the meaning of *stock* but also suggests the cognate capital very clearly. Here, Garnier, and thus Marx, have interpreted Smith and altered his vocabulary slightly to make it more consistent with the emerged capitalist market; Smith kept some terms from the precapitalist era in his text.

The translation of the second sentence is more consistent with the first sentence than is Smith in his original English text. Smith's English text implies a nearly slavelike dependence upon a master, which introduces a different form of exploitation than the surplus *product* extraction indicated in the first sentence.

28. *MEGA* IV, 2, pp. 344:1–346:2; cf. Smith, *The Wealth of Nations,* pp. 286–92, or *Recherches sur la nature et les causes de la richesse des nations,* 5 vols., trans. Germain Garnier (Paris: H. Agasse, 1802), pp. 218–27.

29. Smith, *The Wealth of Nations,* p. 82, *La richesse des nations,* p. 129.

30. *MEGA* IV, 2, p. 349:12; cf. Smith, *The Wealth of Nations,* p. 105.

31. See *MEGA* IV, 2, p. 351:33–34 for the heading. The excerpts are found on pp. 351:35–353:2; cf. Smith, *The Wealth of Nations,* pp. 116–59.

32. Smith, *The Wealth of Nations,* p. 160; *MEGA* IV, 2, p. 353:3.

33. The material Marx omitted is found in Smith, *The Wealth of Nations,* pp. 163–77.

34. The material Marx omitted is from Smith, ibid., pp. 185–264. See *MEGA* IV, 2, p. 355:25–27 for Marx's excerpt from this large section of *La richesse des nations.*

35. Ibid., pp. 355:27–357:27.

36. Ibid., pp. 357:30–359:41.

37. Ibid., pp. 346:5–351:33, 353:5–355:25.

38. Marx placed the three headings derived from Smith on almost all of the pages of the first manuscript. He wrote in columns for the first twenty-one pages and then on the next six pages wrote across the columns, ignoring the headings, on material most editors of the manuscripts entitled "Die ent-fremdete Arbeit" (Alienated Labor) following the first *MEGA* edition, see *MEGA*[1] I, 3, pp. 81–97. On manuscript pages xiii, xiv, and xv, Marx had only two columns: "Arbeitslohn" (Wages of Labor) is paired respectively with "Gewinn des Capitals" (Profit of Capital) on page xiii; "Gewinn der Capi-talien" (Profit of Stock) is on page xiv, and "Grundrente" (Ground Rent) is on page xv. On page xvi, Marx paired "Grundrente" with "Gewinn des Capitals." See Jurgen Rojahn, "Marxismus—Marx—Geschichtswissenschaft: Der Fall der sog. 'Ökonomische-philosophischen Manuskripte aus dem Jahre 1844'," *International Review of Social History* 28, no. 1 (1983):48.

39. David Ricardo, *On the Principles of Political Economy and Taxation,* vol. 1 of *The Works and Correspondence of David Ricardo,* ed. Piero Sraffa and Maurice Dobb (Cambridge: Cambridge University Press, 1951), p. 5.

40. Looking at only the columns "Arbeitslohn" and "Gewinn der Capi-talien," the following material was employed by Marx in the Paris draft manu-script of 1844. Marx did not draw any quotations for the draft manuscript from the section "Wages of Labor" in his own study notebook per se. He placed one section from Smith's "Profits of Stock" (*MEGA* IV, 2, p. 350:10–16) within the column "Arbeitslohn" in the Paris draft text; *MEGA* I, 2, p. 202:4–23.

From the section "Der Gewinn der Capitalien. (Profits des capitaux.)" in the study notebook, Marx transplanted several excerpts into the Paris draft under essentially the same headings. In 1844, under the heading "Capital-gewinn" (ibid., pp. 208:31–37, 213:32–214:7, 197:23–198:3, 211:2–16, 195:18–

196:3) Marx drew material from *MEGA* IV, 2, pp. 349:13-15, 349:27-34, 349:34-350:2, 350:23-28, and 350:28-36. Under "Profit des Capitals" (*MEGA* I, 2, pp. 193:15-194:15, 194:40-195:17, 194:15-35), Marx transferred material from *MEGA* IV, 2, pp. 349:15-25, 350:17-22, and 350:36-351:2. Marx also included considerable material not found under the heading "Gewinn der Capitalien" in his study notebook to the Paris draft text under the columns related to the profit of capital. Under "Profit des Capitals" (*MEGA* I, 2, pp. 190:8-25, 192:29-193:6, 191:13-18, 191:31-192:25) Marx drew material from *MEGA* IV, 2, pp. 339:12-16, 341:26-31, 360:8-9, 341:32-39; under "Capitalgewinn" (*MEGA* I, 2, pp. 198:5-199:3, 196:15-197:19, 215:6-21, 201:31-203:16, 211:17-25, 211:29-212:25, 213:25-31, and 209:1-17) Marx used material from *MEGA* IV, 2, 342:5-15, 344:14-24, 345:32-39, 356:31-357:27, 360:19-23, 360:33-361:13, 361:13-15, and 361:33-39; under "Gewinn des Capitals" (*MEGA* I, 2, pp. 199:32-200:2, 200:2-16, 222:24-223:3, and 200:29-201:14) Marx drew upon *MEGA* IV 2, pp. 352:29-31, 352:24-27, 363:29-33, and 364:1-6; finally, under "Gewinn der Capitalien" (*MEGA* II, 2, pp. 223:15-225:3, and 223:3-15), Marx used *MEGA* IV, 2, pp. 358:5-32, and 360:24-29.

41. I will return to this in detail in chapter 3.

42. *MEGA* IV, 2, p. 332:4-7; Smith, *The Wealth of Nations*, p. 13.

43. *MEGA* IV, 2, p. 332:8-16; cf. Smith, *The Wealth of Nations*, pp. 14-15 (paragraphs 2 and 3).

44. *MEGA* IV, 2, p. 332:17-19. Marx's use of *Vermögen* to render *facultés*, which Garnier had used for Smith's term *productive powers* of labor, is significant insofar as Marx later relegated the term *Vermögen* to minor status in favor of *Kraft* in *Das Kapital:* that is, he almost stopped using the term *Arbeitsvermögen* in *Das Kapital* even though he had used it extensively up to the mid-1860s. The term *Arbeitsvermögen* has an important history. It was not until 1857 that Marx first grasped what the worker actually sold to the capitalist. Within the context of *Die Grundrisse,* Marx noted that the use value that the worker exchanged with capital "is not materialized in a product, does not exist generally outside him, thus not actually, rather only as a possibility [*Möglichkeit*], as his ability [*Fähigkeit*];" *MEGA* II, 1.1, p. 189:30-34, see also pp. 196:21-38, 198:1-201:9, and 204:36-205:32. "Thus the use value which he offers, exists only as possibility, capacity of his corporality; it has no existence outside of these"; ibid., p. 205:32-34. A few manuscript pages later, Marx abbreviated the commodity sold by labor to *Arbeitsvermögen*. "One has termed labor capacity [*Arbeitsvermögen*] as the capital of the worker, since it is the fund which he does not consume in an individual exchange, rather he can return constantly anew during his *life's duration as a worker."* Ibid., p. 212:3-6.

The term *labor capacity* is far richer in terms of meaning than *Arbeitskraft* and suggests much more explicitly the creative, mediate relation of labor as an activity. Marx continued to use the term right up to the writing of *Das Kapital,* where the term still exists but is rarely used; see *Das Kapital,* 1st ed., pp. 130, 137. The reason for the reduction is related to the context of Marx's critique.

The production process Marx described in *Das Kapital* is characterized by large-scale industry in which the worker, for the most part, sells only physical power to capital. The worker's skills—or *Virtuosität,* as Marx often termed it— are almost insignificant. The reduced use of labor capacity, however, does not mean that Marx changed his view of the labor process, only that he recognized that in industrial capitalist work processes it was power, and not ability and capacity, that capitalists purchased.

45. Smith, *The Wealth of Nations,* pp. 15-17. In the August 1861 to March 1862 manuscripts, Marx cites from the material omitted in the study notebook at this time; cf. *MEGA* II, 3.1, p. 247:27-41. His citation is from *La richesse des nations,* showing that he had returned to Smith's text after his 1844 study notebook. Marx also referred to the *The Wealth of Nations* in English in the August 1861 to March 1862 notebooks using material from a notebook written in 1851; ibid., pp. 135:31-32, 266:23-28, and *MEGA* II, 3.1, p. 2867.

46. *MEGA* IV, 2, pp. 332:20-335:29; Smith, *The Wealth of Nations,* pp. 17-21.

47. Compare Smith to Marx on this point. Smith (*The Wealth of Nations,* p. 21) wrote that "All the improvements in machinery, however, have by no means been the inventions of those who had occasion to use the machines. Many improvements have been made by the ingenuity of the makers of the machines, when to make them became the business of a particular trade; and some by that of those who are called philosophers or men of speculation, whose trade it is not to do anything but to observe everything; . . . In the progress of society, philosophy or speculation becomes, like every other employment, the principal or sole trade and occupation of a particular class of citizens." Although Marx enclosed the following statement within quotation marks, it is obviously a hurried mixture of quotation and paraphrase of the preceding that leaves the expression of some ideas totally incomplete. "In that the division of labor benefits not only by way of the discovery of machines in which the immediately engaged worker discovers [things], rather first a particular branch of labor comes about from *machinery* and second a theory, the *erudition* comes about which knows to discover remote combinations, first to a particular life-task and divides itself into many parts and branches which become fruitful also with respect to mechanics, etc." *MEGA* IV, 2, p. 335:30-36.

48. Ibid., p. 335:37-39.

49. Smith, *The Wealth of Nations,* pp. 22-24.

50. *MEGA* IV, 2, p. 335:40. Smith entitles the chapter "Of the Principle which Gives Rise to the Division of Labor," *The Wealth of Nations,* p. 25.

51. "This division of labor from which so many advantages are derived, is not originally the effect of any human wisdom, which foresees and intends that general opulence to which it gives occasion. It is the necessary, though very slow and gradual, emergence of a certain propensity in human nature which has in view no such extensive utility; the propensity to truck, barter and exchange one thing for another." Smith, *The Wealth of Nations,* p. 25. Following Marx's excerpt and paraphrase, which I have given in the text, Marx excerpted, in French, Smith's final clause—"C'est ce penchant à tra-

fiquer, à faire des troc et des échanges d'une chose pour une autre." *MEGA* IV, 2, p. 336:3–4.

52. Ibid., p. 336:5–7. Marx's paraphrase slightly alters Smith's position. Smith wrote, "[w]hether this propensity be one of those original principles of human nature, of which no further account can be given; or whether, as seems more probable, it be the necessary consequence of the faculties of reason and speech, it belongs not to our present subject to enquire." *The Wealth of Nations,* p. 25. By using the term *fortuitous,* Marx essentially sidestepped the problem of human nature that would occupy him in *Die Deutsche Ideologie* and his so-called "Thesen über Feuerbach." Marx was apparently more interested in Smith's explanation of what actually determined the division of labor than he was in what Smith ignored on the question, and thus allowed Smith's questionable idea of a human nature to slip by unquestioned and unnoted. See Andrew Gamble and Paul Walton, "Marx, Adam Smith and Political Economy," in *From Alienation to Surplus Value* (London: Sheed and Ward, 1972), pp. 143–57 for a detailed comparison of the view of human nature found in each thinker.

53. *MEGA* IV, 2, p. 336:29–32, 33–38.

54. Ibid., p. 336:39–40. Marx presented this statement as a quotation in the study notebook even though it omits a large segment of the sentence. Smith's text reads: "The difference of natural talents in different men is, in reality, much less than we are aware of, and the very different genius which appears to distinguish men of different professions, when grown up to maturity, is not upon many occasions so much the cause, as the effect of the division of labor." *The Wealth of Nations,* p. 28. In his August 1861-March 1862 manuscripts, Marx used this full quotation plus the last sentence in the paragraph to show how Smith's conceptions of the effects of the division of labor were drawn from Adam Ferguson. *MEGA* II, 3.1, p. 248:28–36.

55. *MEGA* IV, 2, p. 336:41–337:5–9. In this citation, Marx again designated it as a direct quotation although the wording varies from Smith's text. The differences in wording, however, are not essential to the meaning; cf. *The Wealth of Nations,* p. 29.

56. *MEGA* IV, 2, p. 337:27–32.

57. Ibid., p. 337:33–40, Marx's emphases.

58. Ibid., p. 338:3–5, Marx's emphases.

59. *MEGA* II, 2.1, p. 99:24–26.

TWO

DEVELOPING A CONCEPT

In the preface to *Zur Kritik der politischen Ökonomie,* Marx noted that while editor of *Die Rheinische Zeitung* in 1843, he found that for the first time he "had to take part in discussions over so-called material interests." Following a change in editorial policy, he willingly left the paper and "returned to the study desk" to examine some of the fundamental issues he had confronted as an editor. Marx's first work, a critical study of Hegel's *Rechtsphilosophie,* "led to the conclusion that the relations of law, as well as the forms of the state, are not to be grasped in themselves, nor by the so-called general development of the mind [*Geistes*], rather they are rooted in the material relations of life whose totality Hegel, following the lead of the English and French of the 18th century, gathered together under the name 'bourgeois society' [*bürgerliche Gesellschaft*], [and] that the anatomy of bourgeois society is to be sought in the political economy."[1] It was on this basis of these particular events, coupled with Marx's appreciation for Engels's contribution entitled "Umrisse zur Kritik der politischen Ökonomie" to the *Rheinische Zeitung,* that Marx began what became a life-long study of political economy.[2] Based on his reading of various works in political economy, and against the background of his experiences as an editor, it was not long before Marx felt he was ready to write such a critique.[3]

On February 1, 1845, Marx signed a contract with Carl Leske to publish a two-volume study—*Kritik der Politik und Nationalökonomie*—that would examine the anatomy of bourgeois society.[4] Although Marx never published either volume—Leske cancelled the contract in 1846—the proposal led Marx to work through both political economy itself and the premises underlying his own approach to human history. Thus, the contract with Leske was Marx's prime motive for drafting two of the most important texts for his early intellectual development: the Paris manuscripts of 1844 and *Die Deutsche Ideologie*. Moreover, these two texts enabled Marx to discover the weaknesses of the overly theoretical viewpoint that dominated his work in the 1844 study notebooks and led him to a more serious confrontation with concrete history. Consequently, the contract with Leske set in motion a twenty-three-year-long research and writing project in which Marx continually moved between abstract and concrete until he could finally produce the text of the first volume of *Das Kapital.*

The objective in this chapter is to trace some of the most important factors and events that shaped Marx's conception of the division of labor between the drafting of the Paris manuscripts of 1844 through to the completion of *Die Grundrisse* in 1858. Among the most significant aspects is how the actual concrete process of reflectively writing a critique of political economy moved Marx from his original abstract, theoretically informed position to one in which material history played an increasingly dominant role. At the same time, Marx's digestion of concrete historical events sharpened and redirected his theoretical conceptions in significant ways.

In terms of the division of labor, the Paris draft is actually a disappointing treatment of the subject. In comparison with Marx's overall success in linking political economy to a thoroughly revised conception of labor inspired by Hegel's *Phänomenologie des Geistes,* Marx's analysis of the division of labor fails to make the same integration successfully. Drawing his ideas from a limited number of treatises in political economy, Marx began his analysis of the division of labor by presenting Smith's ideas. He then attempted to develop a critique by presenting material from James Mill, Frédéric Graf von Skarbek, and Jean-Baptiste Say that showed that political economists could not agree on the nature and causes of the division of labor. Marx also attempted to link his critique of the division of labor with the alienation problematic that dominates much of the Paris manuscripts, but he ended his analysis before developing the connection in more than a cursory and highly unsatisfying fashion.

When working through the Paris manuscripts, Marx became aware of the need to separate his own approach to a critique of political economy from the prevailing critical work found in Germany at the time. Through a critique of the *Phänomenologie des Geistes* that was formulated from the more concrete reference point of political economy, Marx began to distance himself from the so-called Left-Hegelians.[5]

This segment of the 1844 manuscripts suggested the potential for a substantial volume, and Marx, it seems, wanted to establish his own social ontology based on his 1844 work. This became the main objective in *Die Deutsche Ideologie.*

Setting out his materialist premises in *Die Deutsche Ideologie* led to three major developments in Marx's conception of the division of labor. First, by setting out the importance of material history, Marx had to examine a number of issues, including the division of labor, within a concrete historical context that concentrated on the production process. As a result, the treatment of the division of labor in *Die Deutsche Ideologie* contrasts markedly with Marx's 1844 treatment in terms of empirical content and the relative absence of theoretical material included in the presentation. Consequently, Smith, who was the predominant figure in the 1844 analysis, is virtually absent from the analysis presented in *Die Deutsche Ideologie.* Nevertheless, Smith remains as an implicit foil in the development of Marx's argument. Thus it appears that on the basis of his conceptual grasp of the division of labor, Marx went to the concrete detail of history to examine its adequacy. The interaction of concrete and abstract, as Marx's account of the development of production in general and the division of labor in particular indicates, led to a considerably revised conception of the division of labor in society, which Marx then carried through to the 1850s.

Second, in studying the empirical development of the division of labor, Marx's Hegelian background and the knowledge interests developed within the Paris manuscripts enabled him to focus upon a number of internal contradictions, tensions, and conflicts associated with both the social division of labor and the technical division of labor although he did not use these terms at this time. These conflicts became a major source of critique in his treatment of the division of labor in *Die Deutsche Ideologie.* Finally, Marx was able to use his concrete historical material to link his critique of the division of labor more successfully with the alienation framework.

Marx next dealt with the division of labor in *Misère de la philosophie,* in which he drew his empirical work and his theoretical understanding of the division of labor into a single text. In terms of theoretical material, he criticized Pierre-Joseph Proudhon's transhistorical conception of the division of labor, and he used material by Pierre Lemontey and Adam Ferguson to indicate that other political economists had seen the negative side of the division of labor question. The concrete, historical material Marx used in *Misère de la philosophie* was virtually the same as that contained in *Die Deutsche Ideologie,* although somewhat less detailed.

Surprisingly, *Die Grundrisse der Kritik der politischen Ökonomie (Rohentwurf)* contains very little material directly concerned with the division of labor. Nevertheless, within *Die Grundrisse* there are a few major developments in Marx's critical treatment of the division of labor itself. For example, it was the first time that Marx fully addressed the production process, and thus the division of labor, within the context of an analysis of value and surplus value. Second, *Die Grundrisse* contains abundant concrete, historical material that allowed Marx to place his critique of the division of labor and the alienation theme together to demonstrate clearly how the products of workers turn to oppose them and constrain their freedom. Finally, in *Die Grundrisse,* Marx discussed Smith's conception of labor within the context of the realization of human potential through work. Although this section did not deal directly with the division of labor issue, it was the first time that Marx linked the work of Smith, and potentially the problems associated with the division of labor, to this particular dimension of the alienation theme.

Following the drafting of *Die Grundrisse,* Marx began two fragments that contain discussions of the division of labor; one is a draft manuscript, and the other is from some lecture notes he prepared. A comparison of these pieces shows clearly how the intent of Marx's work influenced the nature of his vocabulary and conceptualization process. In work intended for his own use, Marx employed a highly abstract, philosophical vocabulary. This contrasts decidedly with the language he used in work intended for public consumption and the shift in vocabulary influenced how his ideas on the division of labor could be developed and presented.

Although Marx's ideas on the division of labor developed through his work on drafts and publications throughout this period, a third factor significantly influenced his eventual presentation of his analysis of the division of labor in *Das Kapital.* During the preparation of *Zur Kritik der politischen Ökonomie,* Marx contacted Ferdinand Lassalle concerning a publisher. The publisher Lassalle suggested, Franz Duncker, imposed page limits on Marx's work; to meet those limits Marx would have had to present his material in a highly abstract style. This level of abstraction, however, created a number of problems that he and Engels discussed in 1858 just before the submission of *Zur Kritik* to Duncker. Marx's presentation of the division of labor was significantly altered through a series of events that revolved around the length and number of pamphlets he would publish in his critique of political economy.

The Division of Labor in the Paris Manuscripts

Marx made fairly extensive use of his Paris study notebooks when drafting the first, of the three, Paris draft manuscripts. In the so-called third manuscript of the draft text, he used the Smith study notebooks, but this time in connection with the division of labor issue.

Following his discussion of Hegel in the third manuscript, Marx began a section on society in which he argued political economists see humanity reduced to individuals—capitalists and workers.[6] Within this analysis, Marx commented on the division of labor insofar as political economists wrote about it. He introduced the discussion with a critical assessment of how political economists essentially treat the division of labor phenomenon. "The *division of labor* is the political economic expression of the *socialization* [*Geselleschaftlichkeit*] of labor within alienation [*Entfremdung*]. Or, since labor is only an expression of life as estrangement of life [*Lebensäusserung als Lebensentäusserung*], so too the *division of labor* is nothing other than the *alienated estranged* positing of human activity as a *real species-activity* or as *activity of men as species beings.*"[7]

With the following paragraph, in part descriptive of the development of political economy and in part critically analytical at the same time, Marx introduced his presentation of four political economists' analyses of the division of labor. "On the nature [*Wesen*] of the division of labor—which naturally had to be grasped as a prime mover of the production of wealth, as soon as *labor* was recognized as the *essence* [*Wesen*] of *private property*—i.e. as for this *alienated* and *estranged* character [*Gestalt*] of *human activity as species-activity*, the political economists are very unclear and self-contradictory."[8]

Marx began his overview of political economists' analyses of the division of labor with *The Wealth of Nations*. He first presented Smith's position in a lengthy quotation characterized by several elisions, although only a few are marked. In addition, without indication, Marx paraphrased parts of the excerpt. The quotation covers almost all of the material that he excerpted from chapters 2, 3, and 4 of *La richesse des nations*. The section includes six of the nine excerpts Marx made from chapter 2, the lead paragraph to chapter 3—Marx's only excerpt from the chapter—and the concluding sentence to the opening paragraph of chapter 4, one of two Marx excerpts from the chapter.[9]

The use of the study notebook material suggests that, at least for his commentary on Smith and the division of labor issue, Marx saw the notebooks as his primary, and almost exclusive, source. The predominance of the study notebook material in the Paris draft manuscript, the close identity of quoted material in both places including identical points of emphasis by Marx even though Smith made no such emphases, as well as the fact that Marx excerpted virtually the same material and left out the same material from *La richesse des nations* on both occasions makes this conclusion hard to deny.[10] At the same time, however, there is evidence that Marx did return to the original source while writing the Paris draft manuscript because he included one quotation from Smith not found in the study notebooks.[11] Nevertheless, as an unnecessarily inserted set of ellipsis points in the final lengthy quotation from Smith's text suggests, he did not use the original text to check all of his quotations. If he did, he was quite careless or paid little attention to detail.[12]

Marx followed the Smith quotations with excerpts from Say, Skarbek, and James Mill, all political economists represented in the Paris study notebooks.[13] This technique of listing and juxtaposing commentaries from several political economists was one that he would use several more times with the division of labor topic and others.[14] By juxtaposing commentaries, Marx could create the format of a classical dialog, and this enabled him to draw out the full dialectical nature of the phenomenon under examination.

Following the juxtaposition of quotations, Marx presented a summary of the points relevant to each economist's position. His fullest presentation centered on Smith.

> *Adam Smith's* development can be summarized as follows: The division of labor gives labor infinite productive capacity. It is rooted in the *propensity* to *exchange* and *barter,* a specifically human propensity, which is apparently not accidental, rather is conditioned by the use of reason and speech. The motive of those making exchanges is not *humanity,* rather *egoism.* The diversity of human talents is more the effect than the cause of the division of labor, i.e. exchange. Also, it is only the latter which makes the diversity useful. The different attributes of different breeds of animal species are by nature sharper than the diversity of human ability and activity. But because the animals do not have the capacity *to exchange,* no individual animal benefits from the different attributes of their species; they are incapable of contributing to the common advantage and convenience of their species. It is otherwise with *men,* where the most disparate talents and forms of activity are turned to reciprocal advantages because they can bring together their *different* products to a common mass, from which each can buy. As the division of labor springs from the propensity to *exchange,* so it grows and is limited by the *extent* of the *exchange* of the *market.* In advanced conditions every man [becomes a] *merchant,* the society a *market society.*[15]

In this summary, which accurately portrays the fundamentals of

Smith's position, Marx presented the largely descriptive account of the division of labor that tended to dominate most thinking on the subject. His summaries of Say, Skarbek, and Mill were not penetrating critiques, but merely indications of some of the basic ways in which they differed from Smith. Say regarded exchange as accidental and not fundamental to human society; Skarbek argued that exchange arose from the ownership of private property and not egoism; and Mill presented trade as the result of the division of labor and not its cause.[16]

Marx's next task was to develop his critique more fully, which he tried to do by linking his critical analysis to the estrangement theme already present in the draft manuscript. He noted, for example, that the "examination of the *division of labor* and *exchange* is of greatest interest because they are the *manifestly alienated* expressions of human *activity* and *essential power*, as a species-limiting [*Gattungsmässigen*] activity and essential power." A paragraph later he argued, "*[d]ivision of labor* and *exchange* are the two *appearances* with which the political economist boasts about the sociability of his science and expresses unconsciously in the same breath the contradictions of his science, the motivation of society through unsociable particular interests."[17] But Marx added little to his analysis. Basically, he re-presented the same contradictions among Smith, Mill, Skarbek, and Say and then left the section unfinished.[18] Perhaps at this point Marx exhausted the general critique that he could make of political economists' discussions of the division of labor.

Aside from the limited material Marx used in this analysis, there are three further points to note about his treatment of the topic. First, Marx's knowledge interests on the subject—the general framework he drew from political economy—were strongly influenced by Smith's discussion in the second chapter of *La richesse des nations*. This is understandable given Smith's importance on this topic, but in developing his knowledge interests in this manner, Marx, virtually by default, had to accept Smith's discussion of the division of labor as a comprehensive treatment, not perfect to be sure, but inclusive and largely exhaustive nonetheless. This contrasts markedly with the treatment of the division of labor in 1861 and 1862 or in *Das Kapital*, for example, where Smith's analysis is regarded as appropriate only for the period of manufacture ("which extends, roughly speaking, from the middle of the sixteenth century to the last third of the eighteenth century").[19] Even then, Marx did not rely solely on the work of Smith, nor did he treat Smith's views uncritically. In the 1861–63 manuscripts and *Das Kapital*, Marx also examined the division of labor in the period of large-scale industry, with Andrew Ure as the theoretician of prime importance and James Lauderdale and Charles Babbage playing supporting roles. Thus, the division of labor question takes on a greater theoretically informed, historical specificity as Marx studied political economy more fully. Indeed, he began to broaden his understanding of the question shortly after the Paris draft manuscript.

Second, because Marx accepted Smith as the major authority on the division of labor, and *La richesse des nations* was the major focal point of Marx's knowledge interest in the Paris draft, he did not approach the issue from a genuine empirically informed historical discussion of the work process. Nor did Marx present a concrete history of the rise of market society. As I will show in the following discussion of *Die Deutsche Ideologie,* the reliance upon Smith in 1844 significantly limited the nature of Marx's analysis and critique of the division of labor in the Paris draft manuscript.

Finally, Marx's discussion of the division of labor in the Paris draft revolved almost exclusively around the material found in the 1844 study notebooks. He may have consulted *La richesse des nations* again—the book was in his personal library—but by and large the only ideas he dealt with in the Paris draft manuscript were found in the study notebooks. This raises two minor issues.

First, Marx's discussion in *Das Kapital* of the division of labor in the manufacturing period is highly influenced by Smith's first three chapters, but material omitted from the 1844 study notebooks is included in the 1867 analysis (chapter 5). Marx had reread *The Wealth of Nations,* and on the basis of a broader, more precise set of knowledge interests had seen significance in the detail of the pin-making process, for example, which in 1844 had held little importance for him.

Second, although the 1844 draft manuscript stayed close to the study notebook material, Marx's next treatment of the theme differed considerably. While trying to address political economy in general, and the division of labor issue in particular, within the Paris draft manuscript, Marx was led beyond his conceptions of 1844 to develop his ideas more fully in his critique of *Die Deutsche Ideologie.*

The Division of Labor in *Die Deutsche Ideologie*

Within a year of the Paris draft manuscript, Marx and Engels began to write *Die Deutsche Ideologie,* which was intended to set out, in a preliminary form at least, the premises of a materialist view of history while simultaneously criticizing the views of the Left-Hegelians. Within the long first chapter in which they established the premises of their position, Marx and Engels dealt with the division of labor at several points.

In terms of my treatment of the question and the development of

Marx's views, *Die Deutsche Ideologie* has three significant dimensions. First, the division of labor question is approached far more from the perspective of concrete historical analysis than by way of political economic theorizing. Second, Adam Smith's commentary on the division of labor is not addressed explicitly, although some of the concrete analysis could be viewed as an implicit response to his alleged historical examples. Finally, because Smith plays such a minor role in the text, none of the Paris study notebook material appears in *Die Deutsche Ideologie*, a marked contrast with the Paris manuscripts of 1844.

Early in the first chapter of *Die Deutsche Ideologie*, Marx and Engels established the premises of their new materialist position: "One can distinguish men from animals by consciousness,[20] by religion, or as one wants. They themselves begin to distinguish themselves from animals as soon as they begin to *produce* their means of life, a step which is conditioned by their physical organization. Insofar as men produce their means of life, they are indirectly producing their material life."[21] Phrased more succinctly, they argued that "What they [individuals] are, therefore, coincides with their production, not only with *what* they are producing but also with *how* they are producing. Thus, what individuals are depends on the material conditions of their production."[22]

The bulk of the first chapter follows through on these premises and makes a number of points. One, of course, is that because men and women produce their lives, it is only through practical action that people can change the conditions under which they live. Humans can only understand their present conditions by examining their concrete material past, especially those aspects pertinent to the production process as a whole. Marx and Engels present several such analyses that explore various aspects of production; one theme that they could not avoid was the division of labor.

Although Marx and Engels never mention Smith explicitly, in the majority of their commentary on the division of labor he certainly appears to be present implicitly. Whereas Smith, for example, saw the division of labor as a fundamental, natural relation of the human species found throughout history and a relation that necessarily improved the human condition, Marx and Engels differed on both points. They argued that one had to grasp the division of labor's historical specificity. "After all, the division of labor and private property are identical expressions—in the one the same thing is being stated in relation [*Beziehung*] to activity as is stated in the other with respect to the product of the activity."[23] Furthermore, this historically specific means of producing goods is not the cohesive force Smith had suggested. According to Marx and Engels, the division of labor is "at the same time the

41

contradiction between the interest of the single individual or the single family and the common [*Gemeinschaftlichen*] interest of all individuals who interact with one another."[24] They went further to indicate that the idea of common interest "does not exist merely in the imagination, as the 'Universal' [*Allgemeines*], but first of all in actuality as the interdependence of the individuals among whom labor is divided."[25] This idea was developed within the alienation framework—that is, the practical pursuit of individual interests through the division of labor creates conditions that run counter to the real general interest of the majority. Furthermore, this leads to the practical intervention and control of individuals by the state in the name of some illusory general interest.

They next argued that the evolution of society led to the division of labor, creating a division "between the particular and the general interests" and because "activity is not voluntarily, but spontaneously divided, man's own act becomes an estranged power standing opposed to him, which enslaves him rather than him dominating it. For as soon as the division of labor comes into being, each man has a determinate, exclusive sphere of activity, which is forced upon him and from which he cannot escape."[26] With these statements, Marx and Engels went much further toward linking the division of labor issue to the problems associated with alienated labor than Marx had in the 1844 draft manuscript.

Next, the analysis moved from theory to history. "This settling of social activity, this consolidation of our own products into a material power [*sachlichen Gewalt*] above us, which outgrows our control, thwarting our expectations, bringing nothing to our calculations, is one of the main moments in historical development up to now."[27] The historical analysis that follows contrasts markedly to Smith's account of how the division of labor emerged, whose interests it served, and the presence or absence of conflict it generated. On manuscript page 30, the division of labor is identified as one of the chief forces of history and its role documented in the development of ideologies by specialized personnel in the ruling class. More important to this analysis, however, is the fact that most likely on manuscript page 36, although it could be anywhere on the missing pages between 36 and 39 inclusive, Marx and Engels began a fairly detailed historical analysis of the rise of the division of labor and its determination by the growth of exchange.[28] Throughout the section, they provided a concrete history of the emergence of the division of labor that presented a marked contrast to Smith, on the one hand, and Marx's analysis of the division of labor in the 1844 draft manuscript on the other.

Marx and Engels argued in *Die Deutsche Ideologie* that the most important early division of labor centered on the division of town and country, a point Marx would reiterate in *Die Grundrisse* and *Das Kapital*. They enumerated several conflicts associated with the division, including conflicts surrounding serfs leaving the countryside and entering the towns, the establishment of market halls and struggles over their control, the attempt by some groups to protect their monopoly control over particular types of labor, conflicting interests among crafts, and the eventual formation of guilds. Towns and guilds, Marx and Engels argued, provided for the "protection of property, and to multiply the means of production and means of defense of the single members."[29]

> The division of labor between the individual guilds was still quite natural and, in the guilds themselves, it had not taken place between the individual workers. Every worker had to be versed in a whole range of labors, and know how to make everything that was to be made with his tools. The limited traffic and the weak ties between the individual towns, the lack of population, and the narrow realm of wants did not allow a further division of labor to take place, and therefore every one who wanted to become a master, had to conduct his whole craft. Medieval craftsmen therefore had an interest in their special work and proficiency in it, which was capable of rising to a limited artistic sense. For this very reason, however, every medieval craftsman was completely absorbed in his work, had a complacent servile relation to it, and was much more than the modern worker, who is indifferent to his work, subsumed under it.[30]

There are two points of note in this statement. First, Marx and Engels agreed with Smith that the size of the market affects the extent to which the division of labor will develop. However they also suggested—and later developed—the idea that the guilds' craft workers themselves had a vested interest in resisting the fragmentation of tasks. This resistance to the division of labor is totally absent in Smith. In fact, it contradicts his presentation of the virtually inevitable, natural, lawlike tendency toward the division of labor as a means for developing human talents. Marx's and Engels's example suggested that talent— almost artistic talent—is developed in the absence of the division of labor, not through it. They argue that the development of talent is more likely to occur in the guilds than in modern manufacture because of a worker's commitment to his or her trade.

Marx and Engels next noted that a growth in trade fostered an increase in the division of labor at the level of towns initially and later within the towns themselves. The intensive development of the division of labor took place because some forms of manufacture grew alongside the guild system. Weaving was the first such manufacture of consequence because it could be mechanized and broken down into a sequence of semiskilled tasks.

Manufacture led to competition and conflict at several levels. Unskilled serfs entering the towns competed for jobs; guilds competed with manufacture for market share; towns competed for trade; and countries competed over markets, duties, and balances of trade. Finally, as the money supply grew in response to the growth of trade, large-scale industry began to emerge from within manufacture at the end of the eighteenth century, and competition between manufacture and large-scale industry ensued. The impact of large-scale industry on a number of social relations was, according to Marx and Engels, decisive.

> Large scale industry universalized, despite preventive measures, competition . . . established means of communication and the modern world market, subordinated trade to itself, transformed all capital into industrial capital, and thus produced the rapid circulation . . . and centralization of capital. It compelled, through universal competition, all individuals to strain their energy to the utmost. It destroyed, as much as possible, ideology, religion, morality, etc. . . . It produced world history for the first time, insofar as it made all civilized nations and every individual member of them dependent for the satisfaction of their wants on the whole world. . . . It subordinated natural science under capital and took the last semblance of natural growth [*Naturwüchsigkeit*] from the division of labor. It altogether destroyed the naturalness [*Naturwüsigkeit*], as far as this is possible with regard to labor, and resolved all natural [*naturwüchsigen*] relations into money relations.[31]

On the basis of the last two quotations, it is important to emphasize the nature of the insights that this more empirically informed historical analysis permitted. Marx and Engels introduced in 1845 and 1846 not only the major set of distinctions between guild production, manufacture, and large-scale industry that Marx would subsequently employ in *Die Grundrisse* and *Das Kapital,* but they also indicated some of the practical dynamics favoring and opposing the development and transformation of the division of labor. Had Marx acted solely as the gadfly of Smith, he would not have developed his analysis in this direction.

What had taken place was a deepening of Marx's ability to use his Hegelian background, which sensitized him theoretically to contradictions and changes through opposition, to grasp the division of labor more fully as he incorporated more historical material into his knowledge interests of 1845 and 1846. The positive, mutual relation of abstract and concrete is apparent in the draft text for *Die Deutsche Ideologie.*

44

Marx and Engels pursued their analysis of production and noted that a greater division of labor exists between the owners of tools, materials, and capital on the one hand, and those who have only labor to offer on the other. In developing this point, they related the division of labor to a major topic within the alienation problematic, although their language is devoid of any philosophical terminology. This is noteworthy for three reasons. First, Marx and Engels successfully advanced, although they did not finish at this point, the task Marx had tried to undertake in the Paris draft manuscript before breaking off the analysis —developing part of their critique of the division of labor within the alienation framework.

Second, as would be the case in the future, when writing material for publication Marx tried to work as concretely as possible even though major philosophical issues and terminology lay behind his analysis. This approach was particularly pronounced and deliberate here where, in opposition to an idealist opposition—the Left-Hegelians—Marx and Engels were consciously setting out a materialist position that would necessarily take into account the concrete processes of human production and break all links to their erstwhile philosophical past.

Finally, Marx and Engels indicated only one of the major themes within the alienation problematic—that is, humans creating a product that becomes independent of them and subsequently opposes them— while the other major theme—the failure of humans to realize their species' potential—was not addressed. Both themes, however, are brought to play in later discussions of the division of labor in *Das Kapital*.

As a summary statement of the tendency for the growth of the market and the division of labor, Marx and Engels wrote the following, which clearly yet implicitly draws in the alienation framework.

> Thus two facts are here revealed. First the productive powers appear as totally independent of and divorced from the individuals, as a world of their own beside the individuals and the basis for this is that the individuals, whose powers they are, exist split up and in opposition to one another, while, these powers, on the other hand, are the only actual powers in the interaction and association of these individuals. Thus, on the one hand, a totality of productive powers, which have, as it were, taken on a thing-like character [*sachliche Gestalt*] and are for the individuals themselves no longer the powers of the individuals but of private property, and therefore of the individuals only insofar as they are owners of private property. In no earlier period have the productive powers taken on this indifferent character to the interaction of individuals as individuals, because their interaction itself was still a restricted one.[32]

Before leaving the division of labor discussion in *Die Deutsche Ideologie,* one more point requires emphasis. Although Marx's treatment of the division of labor in 1845 and 1846 differs considerably from that of the 1844 commentary, and in fact improves upon it, the two analyses share something in common. Neither really examines the division of labor phenomenon at the shopfloor level; the bulk of the critique is macro in nature or else it only implies micro themes without examining them empirically. In addition, no analysis of the work process or valorization process precedes the analysis of the division of labor to contextualize the analysis in a set of micro issues. This did not change when Marx drafted his critique of Proudhon in 1847, although the introduction of a lengthy quotation from Ure's *Philosophie des manufactures* represents an initial step toward the micro level of analysis.

The Division of Labor in *Misère de la philosophie*

In *Misère de la philosophie,* Marx devoted the second section of chapter 2 to an analysis of Proudhon's discussion of the division of labor and machinery.[33] While the bulk of the discussion contains essentially the same historical analysis of the division of labor found in *Die Deutsche Ideologie,* the first part of the section at least echoes the mode of analysis found in 1844.

In the initial part of section 2, of chapter 2, Marx critically dissected Proudhon's theoretical understanding of the division of labor. Freshly armed for this critique in view of his work on *Die Deutsche Ideologie,* he argued that Proudhon treated the division of labor like an eternal law, a simple, abstract category, and overlooked "the numerous influences which give to the division of labor a determinate character in each epoch."[34] Marx noted that history does not proceed categorically and illustrated his point with examples. His next comments were directed toward Proudhon's use of Smith. Proudhon had argued that Smith had seen both the advantages and inconveniences of the division of labor but emphasized the former and neglected the latter. Furthermore, Proudhon added, "[n]ot one economist, not before nor since Smith, has even perceived that there was a problem to elucidate."[35] Marx's response was to argue first, quite unpersuasively, that Smith was more aware of the problems inherent to the division of labor than Proudhon admitted.[36] He then followed that position with two examples from political economists who wrote before Smith, Lemontey, and Ferguson to show that scholars before Proudhon had studied the negative side of the division of labor.[37]

Marx then criticized Proudhon's analysis of the problems inherent to the division of labor and subsequently rejected Proudhon's attempt to present machinery as a means for reconstituting the community lost through the division of labor.[38] This critique led him into a historical analysis similar to that found in *Die Deutsche Ideologie.* "Let us now examine from the viewpoint of history and economics," he wrote in his critique of Proudhon, "whether the workshop or the machine really introduced the *principle of authority* into society after the division of labor; whether on the one hand, it rehabilitated the worker while submitting him to authority on the other; whether the machine is the recomposition of divided labor, the *synthesis* of labor as opposed to its *analysis.*"[39]

In the historical overview that follows this statement, Marx telescoped much of his discussion in *Die Deutsche Ideologie,* although he added a lengthy quotation from Ure's *Philosophie des manufactures* showing how machinery eliminates human dexterity and skill so that no human discretionary judgment is permitted in the production of goods.[40] Rather than machinery alleviating the problems created by the division of labor as Proudhon had suggested, Marx maintained that it increases them.

In the future, Proudhon would not play a role in Marx's discussion of the division of labor, but the Proudhon critique did result in two developments. First, the presentation allowed Marx to combine the two techniques of criticism developed in 1844–45 and 1846—that is, a dialectical critique of theoretical concepts and the use of concrete historical material to refute Proudhon's position. Furthermore, Marx's critique of Proudhon's theorizing both established weaknesses in his opponent's position and also advanced Marx's grasp of the division of labor. At the same time, his use of empirically informed historical material also aided the further development of his position.

Second, Proudhon's ideas on machinery spurred Marx to include Ure. Ure's inclusion, on the one hand, represents Marx's first treatment of the division of labor issue at the micro level; on the other hand, it represents the inclusion of historical specificity that Marx would employ in later discussions of the division of labor. From this point on, he would begin to develop his understanding of the division of labor within two separate periods, manufacture and large-scale industry.

The Division of Labor in *Die Grundrisse*

Although one might expect a lengthy discussion of the division of labor within *Grundrisse der Kritik der politischen Ökonomie (Rohentwurf),* this is not the case. There are, to be sure, detailed analyses of the labor process, the valorization process, and historical analyses of various modes and means of production, but little space is devoted to the division of labor issue itself. In fact, even though Marx set up a heading "B) Division of Labor," when establishing an index to the contents of *Die Grundrisse* so that he could write the third chapter to *Zur Kritik der politischen Ökonomie,* he made only one entry under the heading.[41] The entry referred to a couple of quotations taken from Wakefield's notes to his edition of the *Wealth of Nations.*[42] Nevertheless, there are a few sections of *Die Grundrisse* where Marx does discuss the division of labor question itself and although they are not extensive, they do indicate some further developments of his ideas.

In notebook 3, within a section on value and surplus value, Marx showed how Smith's conception of surplus value has a striking similarity to that of the physiocrats even though the *The Wealth of Nations* contains, among other things, a critique of physiocracy. For the physiocrats, agricultural labor created social surplus because of the natural productivity of the soil. According to the physiocrats, surplus value "does not arise from labor as such but from the natural power which is being used and conducted by labor—agriculture."[43] Marx argued that despite his differences with the physiocrats, Smith also saw surplus value as a natural occurrence. With Smith, "labor [is] generally [the] source of value, likewise wealth, but it [labor] actually posits surplus value only insofar as in the division of labor, the surplus appears likewise as a natural gift, natural power of society. Therefore the importance that Smith lays on the division of labor."[44] In other words, Smith and the physiocrats both saw surplus as the bounty of nature, but in Smith's analysis surplus was the naturally created increase in productivity afforded by the division of labor. Marx did not agree with Smith's position on the source of surplus value and centered his criticisms on Smith's failure to understand labor and the division of labor as historically determined. He showed how this omission led to several contradictions in Smith's theory of value and surplus value.

This short section marks the first time Marx explicitly linked the division of labor question to issues of value and surplus value. His later statements on the division of labor all confront the issue within this context, thereby providing Marx with more analytic power than previously possible, as well as providing him with additional critical power by linking others' discussions of the division of labor to faulty conceptions of value and surplus value.

In notebook 4, in a clearly marked digression found within the general topic of the "Original Accumulation of Capital" and just before the lengthy section on precapitalist economic formations, Marx addressed the division of labor question again.[45] Marx identifies the digression as an attempt to explain the relations between wage labor and capital as "relations of property or laws." He argued that one could do this by considering each side involved in the valorization process as sides in the process of appropriation, and he showed that essentially an "inverted" law of appropriation took place.

Because surplus labor is posited as the surplus value of capital, Marx maintained that the product of labor does not belong to the worker; it appears to him or her as *"foreign property."* Not only that, but the foreign product of the worker, his or her foreign labor, "appears as the *property of capital.*"[46] Thus, it is not just any form of estranged property that confronts the worker, but property apparently belonging to capital. The valorization process has been inverted in the process of who appropriates the results of labor.

Marx then pushed the argument further by looking at the consequences this has when labor becomes collective under capital; that is, Marx examined the division of labor within the alienation problematic. Although the prose of Marx's digression is hurried and uneven, I cite his argument at length to show how he expressed the connection.

> In fact, in the production process of capital, as will be shown more fully with further development of it, labor is a totality—a combination of labors—of which the single components are foreign to one another, so that the total labor [*Gesamtarbeit*] as totality [*Totalität*] is *not* the *work* of the single worker and is thus the work of different workers together insofar as they are combined, [but] not conducting themselves as combining together [voluntarily]. In their combination this labor appears likewise as serving a foreign will and a foreign intelligence and is led by them—having its *animating unity* outside itself just as its material unity is subordinated under the *objective unity of machinery,* fixed capital, which, as *animate monster* objectifies scientific thought and is in fact the summing up, does not in any way relate to the single worker as his instrument, rather he exists as an animate individual punctuation mark, as its living isolated accessory. The labor is, along these lines, combination *in itself* in a double way; not combination as relationship of individuals working upon one another, nor as overarching them whether over their particular or isolated function or whether it is over the instrument of labor. Therefore just as the worker relates to the product of his labor as something foreign, then similarly he relates to combined labor as something foreign, as belonging to his own labor and thus to him, but foreign to him, forced expression of life, which is grasped as a *burden, sacrifice* etc. therefore A. Smith etc. The labor itself, like its product, *is negated as that of the particular, individuated worker.* The negated individuated labor is now in fact the assumed communal or combined labor. The thus posited *communal or combined labor*—transformed not only as activity but in the static form

of the object [*Objekts*]—is at the same time posited immediately as foreign to the actual, existing, individual worker—as *foreign objectivity* [*Objektivität*] (foreign property), as *foreign subjectivity* (that of capital). Capital thus represents not only labor but its product as negative, individuated labor and therefore the [negated] property of individuated workers. . . . Capital for its part appears therefore as the overarching subject and owner of *foreign labor* and its relation itself is as completely contradictory as that of wage labor.[47]

In notebook 6, in a discussion about the nature of capital based on the work of John Wade, Marx wrote another section linking the division of labor to the alienation theme. He noted that in Wade's *History of the Middle and Working Classes*, "the association of workers—cooperation and division of labor as the basic conditions of the productivity of labor—appear . . . as the *productive power of capital*."[48] Marx continued to outline Wade's position, but the outline was progressively formulated in Marx's own terms. "All social powers [*Potenzen*] of production are productive powers of capital and it [capital] itself appears therefore as their subject. The association of workers, as it appears in the factory, is therefore not posited by itself but by capital. Its combination is not *its* being-there, rather the *being-there* of capital." At this point, Marx's perspective took over fully. "[The individual worker] relates to his own association with the other workers and cooperation with them as estranged [association/cooperation], as capital's means of operation."[49] He then directed the analysis of associated workers to historical terrain.

Marx expressed the view that "productive capital, or the means of production corresponding to capital can only be one of two: manufacture or large-scale industry. In the first the division of labor predominates, in the 2nd combination of powers of labor (with proportionate means of production) and the employment of scientific power, where the combination and, so to speak, social spirit of labor is located in the machine etc."[50] He also noted that both cases presuppose the concentration of capital, raw material, and means of labor in an objective form on one side, and "on the other side, in subjective form, accumulation of labor powers and concentration of them in one point under the command of capital."[51] This led to some specific points about the division of labor, which Marx saw as "the specific development of manufacture . . . . But this presupposes the assembly (preliminary) of many workers under one command, just as the *change from money to capital presupposes the previous making free of a given amount of means of life, raw materials, instruments of labor.*"[52] Marx followed this comment with a historical discussion of the early preconditions for the division of labor. This discussion is noteworthy in two respects. The first is the obvious continuation of an analysis linking the division of labor to the alienation theme. Second, and more important at this point, for the first time Marx introduced the determinate historical distinction between manufacture and large-scale industry. He would later use this distinction to set Smith's analysis of the division of labor into the period of manufacture. In fact, he would argue that the division of labor itself falls within the period of manufacture, whereas large-scale industry involved a different means of production and thus different organizational framework.

The last section from *Die Grundrisse* I will examine does not deal with the division of labor specifically, although it does deal with Smith's conception of labor and also treats an aspect of the labor process that Marx would later analyze within the division of labor theme. On manuscript page 17 of notebook 6, Marx critically examined Smith's conception of labor as sacrifice. "You must work by the sweat of your brow! was Jehovah's curse on Adam. And thus A. Smith terms labor a curse. 'Peace' appears [to Smith] as the adequate condition, as identical with 'freedom' and 'happiness'."[53] But, Marx argued, he fails to recognize that people need a normal portion of work to maintain a peaceful life. He fails to recognize that overcoming obstacles through work is itself a condition of freedom because in the process of confronting external goals, the individual transforms his or her "external, natural necessity" into "goals that the individual himself posits—thus as self-actualization, objectification of the subject, therefore real freedom whose action, even the labor, Adam Smith knows so little."[54] To be sure, Marx noted, Smith's view of labor was correct for the historical forms of slave labor, serf labor, and wage labor, but these forms are merely the results of determinate subjective and objective conditions; they are not necessarily inherent to the nature of labor itself.

I have chosen this section—although there are several like it in *Die Grundrisse*—to show that in 1857 and 1858 Marx still wrote of the potential of labor to permit human self-actualization through objectification and mediation.[55] This is the second major theme of the alienation framework, and although Marx did not link it to the division of labor theme at this time, it was linked to Smith's ideas about labor. In *Das Kapital*, Marx would incorporate this dimension of the alienation theme to the division of labor issue.

The Division of Labor in Two Fragmentary Texts of 1859

Before examining Marx's discussion of the division of labor in the August 1861-March 1862 manuscripts, there are two more phases of development to note. The first concerns the short analyses of the division of labor that Marx developed in some lecture notes and in the draft text to *Zur Kritik der politischen Ökonomie.* The second concerns the development of Marx's overall outline for his critique of political economy within *Die Grundrisse* and in correspondence with Lassalle and Engels over the form and content of the critique.

In the original text to *Zur Kritik,* Marx included a section entitled "Appearances of the Law of Appropriation in Simple Circulation," which he placed after his analysis of "The Precious Metals as Bearers of the Money Relation."[56] In the "Appearances" section, subsequently omitted from *Zur Kritik,* Marx examined "[t]he economic relationships [*Beziehungen*] of individuals who are the subjects [*Subjekte*] of exchange . . . as they appear [*erscheinen*] in the exchange process thus far described, without reference to more developed relations of production [*Produktionsverhältnisse*]. The economic determinations of form [*Formbestimmungen*] constitute even the determinateness [*Bestimmtheit*] wherein they interact with one another in trade (face themselves)."[57]

As I have indicated with the inclusion of German terms in this quotation, there is more of interest in this analysis than the content alone. Marx's vocabulary takes advantage of many Hegelian-rooted terms and contrasts. Concrete relationships between individuals are contrasted to abstract relations of production, the realm of exchange is one of apparent social relations, and the economically determinate form of exchange relations constitute the determinateness within which individuals face one another. Thus, even though Marx is describing what most would think of as a fairly straightforward set of concrete relationships, he has employed a rather abstract, theoretical vocabulary that by itself implies that considerable empirical detail would be needed to make the discussion concrete. His vocabulary presents the logic of the relations under study, which is one of its strengths. Marx could use this vocabulary to think through and represent, with great economy, some very complex relations. At the same time, however, the vocabulary cannot indicate any of the historical specificity from which this logic has been deduced, a limitation that researchers confront when trying to interpret the actuality Marx saw represented by the logical analysis.

A little later in the analysis presented in the draft to *Zur Kritik,* Marx commented on the social division of labor.

> One other presupposition of exchange, which concerns the whole [*Ganze*] of the movement, is that the producing subjects [*Subjekte*] are included within the division of labor. The commodities exchanging against one another are thus in fact nothing other than labor objectified [*vergegen-*

ständlicht] in different use values, they are in fact only the objective being-there [*gegenständliche Dasein*] of the division of labor, objectification [*Vergegenständlichung*] of qualitatively different, corresponding labors—different systems of wants. In that I produce *commodities,* the presupposition is that indeed my product has use value but not for me, it is not immediately means of life for me (in the widest sense), rather for me [it is] mediately exchange value; means of life becomes first, when it has taken on in money the form of general social product and can now be realized in every form of estranged, qualitatively different labor. I produce therefore only for myself, insofar as I produce for the society, of which every member [*Glied*] works for me again in another circuit.⁵⁸

This quotation employs a number of abstract terms: subjects and objectified labor, mediate and immediate, estranged labor, as well as an expression of determinate being, *Dasein*. With this latter term Marx has captured, in one phrase, a complex, concrete process; labor objectified in different use values is in fact the objective, determinate being of the division of labor. The commodity has a mediate, not immediate, being that is, in this context, given precise determinations in a tremendously economical use of vocabulary. The idea presented is rich although, again, Marx does not fill in the actual concrete content.

Both of these quotations contrast to the lecture notes that Marx prepared on the division of labor. When directing his ideas to a popular audience, he was often far more concrete, although some of his theoretical vocabulary was still evident. Compare the following to the quotations cited previously.

Considering the division of labor, which produces itself thus in the exchange of different useful labor, two things are to be distinguished.
First: What labors relate here to one another is their *distinctiveness* not their *similarity,* their *manifoldness* not their *unity.* The division of social labor is a manifold whole [*Ganzes*] and through its difference, its distinctiveness, of labors complementing one another.
The shoemaker wants to exchange the cobbler work contained in boots, with bread, tea, sugar, cabbages, meat, garments, hats, etc., thus with the baker's labor, labor of the tea grower, labor of the sugar refiner, labor of the butcher, labor of the tailor, labor of the hat maker, etc.. He exchanges his own labor against that of the others because the labors of the others are different and therefore satisfy wants which his own labor does not satisfy. . . . The labors are thus exchanged against one another insofar as they are useful labors because they are *different from one another,* insofar as they are different from one another and belong to different systems of human wants.⁵⁹

After pointing out, second, that the opposite held true—that is, if

53

one did their own cobbling, baking, brewing, weaving, and growing then there was no need for exchange—Marx concluded the fragment of lecture notes. "My labor is *one-sided*; but it satisfies a *social* want, the want of another member of society. I cannot carry out this one-sided labor exclusively if I do not know that other members of society carry out other necessary labors and thereby complement my labor. Labor towards satisfying a social want is thus exclusively labor of single, determinate individuals, who make their professions from it."[60]

The contrast between the two analyses in terms of vocabulary is obvious, as is the pace at which ideas are presented and developed. When writing for himself, Marx used a highly abstract, economical vocabulary that captured the logic of capitalist relations and suggested a broad sweep of concrete detail and many ramifications. However, when writing for a popular audience, he often filled in the concrete detail and dropped much of the philosophically based vocabulary. The problem, however, is that concrete analysis develops much more slowly and cannot imply as easily relations beyond the relationships under analysis. Thus, Marx's popular presentations often expand in size while reducing the scope of analysis. This fact, coupled with the developments I will present in the next section, constitute part of the reason why Marx's eventual critique of political economy grew to such a lengthy treatment of the subject.

The second point of importance in development relates to the debates about Marx's use of the alienation conception following the 1846 period. Although *Die Grundrisse* clearly shows that both the conception and the term remained in Marx's work well after 1846, the quotations I have cited demonstrate one of the main reasons why the term *alienation* is absent from *Das Kapital* whereas the conception is not. *Die Grundrisse* was written for Marx's own reference, and *Das Kapital* was published for general consumption. Following Marx's practice, the concept and conception remain in *Die Grundrisse*, while the word is dropped from *Das Kapital* as Marx employs a more concrete form of presentation and vocabulary. The conception remains within the text itself.[61]

Problems over the Form of Marx's Critique

From mid-September 1857 to the publication of *Zur Kritik der politischen Ökonomie* in June 1859, Marx made at least ten statements about how he would develop his text. He began with the idea that he would first present the abstract categories of political economy common to all societies and follow that with a development of categories peculiar to bourgeois society. His last plan was to begin with the central categories unique to bourgeois society and have a separate project that would contain a historical sketch of economic categories.[62] Between these extremes were many changes and developments.[63]

Without tracing through all of the changes, it is important to note that by working through the *Grundrisse der Kritik der politischen Ökonomie*, where numerous proposals for change occur, Marx slowly conceptualized how he could ultimately develop his critique. This exercise of conceptual ordering and clarification did not, however, finally determine the form, content, and length of his final project. A series of events involving demands by the eventual publisher of *Zur Kritik*, Franz Duncker, and consultation with Engels significantly influenced the fate of the book.

On February 22, 1858, Marx wrote to Lassalle to outline how the critique of political economy was progressing.[64] A central motivation behind the letter was Marx's request for Lassalle to find, if possible, a Berlin publisher for the "Economy." But the letter now has more significance as evidence of several of Marx's decisions concerning the presentation of his critique. First, he noted that because he was "not the master of my own time but rather [its] slave" it would be best if "I could edit the work in 'informal pamphlets' [*zwanglosen Heften*]."[65]

> The presentation is, in my opinion, completely scholarly [*Wissenschaftlich*] thus not contrary to police regulations in the usual sense. The whole thing divides into 6 books. 1. On capital (contains a few *Vorchapter*). 2. On landed property. 3. On wage labor. 4. On the state. 5. International trade. 6. World market. I cannot help, naturally, now and then taking a critical view of other economists, namely polemics against Ricardo, insofar as he, as a bourgeois, is constrained to commit blunders *even from a strictly economic viewpoint*. But on the whole, the critique and history of political economy, the socialist object should constitute another work. Finally, the short *historical sketch* of the development of economic categories and relations a third.[66]

Lassalle's response to the proposal was positive, but he needed more information.[67] "How many such serial pamphlets [*Lieferungshefte*]—this is a very good idea—should it become? . . . How many printer's sheets should each pamphlet [*Hefte*] amount to and approximately how many in total?" Lassalle also suggested that each pamphlet should be four to five printer's sheets, "6 at most, otherwise make more installments [*Lieferungen*]." Eight days after Lassalle's letter, Marx responded that "[t]he first part [*Lieferung*] must, under all conditions, be a relative whole and, because it contains the groundwork for the whole development, it could be, only with difficulty, under 5–6 [printer's] sheets

55

[that is, eighty to ninety-six pages]. Still, I will see that with the final elaboration. It contains 1. value, 2. money, 3. capital in general [*allgemein*] (production process of capital, circulation process of capital, unity of the two or capital and profit, rent). This constitutes an independent brochure."[68]

Several points emerge from this communication. First, the introductory chapters mentioned in Marx's previous letter to Lassalle are now indicated. Moreover, it is apparent that even before Marx had finished *Die Grundrisse,* well before he wrote the section on value "to be brought forward" at the end of notebook 7,[69] and before the index to his seven notebooks, he decided to begin the analysis of his critique with a discussion of value. Second, Marx's movement into capital in general as the main theme of the text centers the analysis upon production at a determinate stage of social history: capitalist production. His description of capital in general within *Die Grundrisse* provides some idea of the level of abstraction he would employ for this brochure.

> Capital, insofar as we consider it here, as a relation distinguished from value and money, is *capital in general.* i.e. the quintessence of the determinations which distinguish value as capital from it [value] as pure value or money. Value, money, circulation, etc., price, etc., are presupposed, likewise labor etc.. But we have to deal with neither a *particular* form of capital nor with *individual* capital as distinct from other individual capitals etc.. We are witnessing its developmental process [*Entstehungsprozess*]. This dialectical developmental process is only the ideal expression of the actual movement wherein capital becomes. The later relationships are to be observed as developments coming from this germ. But it is necessary to fix the determinate form from which it [capital] is posited at a *given* point. Otherwise confusion arises.[70]

This leads to the third point. Marx was essentially proposing a brochure that would be about the length of *Zur Kritik* (170 pages plus a forward of 8 pages when it was published in 1859),[71] but it would deal with topics that constituted most of the eventual three volumes, almost 2,300 printed pages, of *Das Kapital.* This would mean a highly condensed style, so it is obvious that Marx intended to proceed with a highly abstract form of analysis in the book he proposed.

> Concerning the total number of [printer's] sheets, I am in fact very unclear about that because the material of the book is in my notebooks [*Heften*] only in the form of monographs which often *go into considerable detail which disappears in the summary presentation.* It is also in no way my intention to work out uniformly all 6 books into which I divide the whole, rather, in the last 3 to give merely sketches while the first 3, which contain the actual basic economic development, elaborations cannot be

avoided everywhere. I believe that the whole can be made scarcely under 30–40 sheets [that is, 480–640 pages].[72]

Three weeks later, on April 2, 1858, Marx wrote a long letter to Engels that included a "short outline of the first part. . . . All this shit should divide into 6 books, 1. on capital, 2. landed property, 3. wage labor, 4. state, 5. international trade, 6. world market." The letter provides a more detailed plan than Marx's earlier correspondence with Lassalle. The book on capital would contain four sections (*Abschnitte*): "a) capital *en general* (*This is the subject matter of the first pamphlet* [Hefte], b) *competition* or the action of many capitals on one another, c) *credit*, where capital appears as the general element opposite the individual capitals, d) *share capital* as the most complete form (transcending towards communism), together with all its contradictions." In the remainder of the letter Marx outlined "the first section [*Abschnitt*] '*Capital in General* [*allgemein*],'" but all he covered was value, money as measure, money as means of exchange or simple circulation, and money as money. He wrote at the end of the letter, "3. *Capital*. This is, actually, the most important part of this first pamphlet where I need your viewpoint most. But today I cannot write any longer."[73]

There are no contradictions concerning Marx's plans between the earlier letter to Lassalle and the subsequent one to Engels. The letters indicate that the book on capital would likely consist of two pamphlets. The first definitely would deal with the single section on capital in general with some introductory chapters; that is, it would cover value, money, and capital in general (production process of capital, circulation process of capital, and the unity of the two) requiring just over 150 pages. The second *Heft* would, as outlined to Engels, likely contain the remaining three sections of the book on capital; that is, competition, credit, and share capital.[74]

Marx's inability to complete his letter to Engels was due to recurring liver and gallbladder problems that had affected his ability to work since early February.[76] The illness is noteworthy for what it did not allow as well as for what it caused which might not have taken place otherwise. Unable to sketch out the remainder of his plan, the historical record does not contain an outline of how Marx planned to treat capital in general within the compressed framework indicated to Lassalle and Engels. It was not until January 1859, at the earliest, that Marx set out a rough plan of how he would select from the material related to capital in general in *Die Grundrisse*, and by then important changes in plans had already been introduced. Nevertheless, the letter to Engels, abbreviated though it was, and the illness were enough to establish a set of conditions that dramatically altered Marx's plans.

Engels, in response to Marx's April 2, 1858 letter, noted that the "study of your abstract of the first half of the pamphlet has occupied me considerably, it is very abstract indeed, but with conciseness it could not be avoided and I must often seek with effort the dialectical transitions because all abstract reasoning has become foreign to me." But, he added, the "abstract dialectical tone of this *epitome* will, of course, disappear in the elaboration."[76] This appraisal must have created some anxiety in Marx because even though he favored a condensed presentation of his critique, it was apparent that even Engels would have difficulty with the compressed style Marx must have had in mind.[77]

It is at this juncture that Marx's illness played a major role in the future development of his critique. On doctor's orders, he went to Manchester and stayed with Engels from May 6 to 24, and the two must have discussed the pamphlet on "Capital in General" at length.[78] Seven days after returning from Manchester, Marx wrote both Engels and Lassalle on May 31 and informed them he had returned to work on his "Economics."[79] This referred, in fact, to work on the last few pages of notebook 7 of *Die Grundrisse.*[80] Marx also informed Lassalle that his liver ailments had prevented preparation of the manuscript for Duncker by the end of May as previously anticipated.[81]

Five and a half months later, Marx instructed Lassalle about how he was to explain the further delay of the manuscript to Duncker.[82] Marx maintained that because *Zur Kritik* would be the first scholarly (*wissenschaftlich*) treatment of social relations he did not want it marred by a "dull and wooden style." There was also a major change in the manuscript which, despite Marx's claim, cannot be attributed solely, or even largely, to his working through the material. Engels's letter of April 4, 1858, and their discussions in May were the major reasons for the manuscript's changed size. "It is probable" Marx wrote to Lassalle, "that the first part [*Abteilung*] '*Capital in general*' will take up 2 pamphlets since I find with elaboration that here, where the most abstract part of political economy is to be presented, too much conciseness will make the thing indigestible to the public. But, on the other hand, this second part must appear *at the same time*. The internal interconnection requires that and the whole effect depends on it."[83]

In many ways, the eight-month period between mid-March and mid-November represents a watershed in a major transition in the developmental history of *Das Kapital,* one not discussed at all by Henryk Grossman, Maximilien Rubel, Roman Rosdolsky, Vladimir Adoratsky, or David Ryazanov.[84] First, Marx rejected the compressed abstract style he initially considered when thinking of a six-book project consisting of several pamphlets. Second, he committed himself to a project—two pamphlets to be published simultaneously by Duncker—that Marx did not, and probably could not, deliver on time. The ensuing failure of *Zur Kritik* to arouse any significant response frustrated Marx and became a major, although not exclusive, factor that led him to expand *Das Kapital* significantly.[85] Due to this expansion Marx was, to use his own 1851 description, "mired in the economic shit" for yet another eight years.[86]

By January 13, 1859, Marx had finished the manuscript to *Zur Kritik*'s first pamphlet. He wrote to Engels that the "manuscript is about 12 printer's sheets . . . and—brace yourself—although its title [is] 'Capital in General', this pamphlet still contains nothing about capital, rather only two chapters: 1. *Commodity*, 2. *Money or simple circulation*. Thus you see that the part elaborated in detail (in May when I came to you) still does not appear at all."[87] Marx sent *Zur Kritik,* part 1, to Duncker on January 26, 1859, although for a number of reasons, it was not published until June 1859.[88] The decision to expand and clarify the first part meant that Marx did not write the chapter on capital at all. Part of the reason lay in the "Vogt Affair," part in the strained relationship between Marx and Duncker, and part in the poor reception his work received in Germany.[89]

When Marx did begin to write the second pamphlet in December 1861, he informed Engels that his writing was proceeding slowly. "It is much more popular in this part and the method is much more concealed than in part 1."[90] Notebook 5, of the 1861–63 notebooks was completed in March 1862, and Marx wrote to Ludwig Kugelmann about his work at the end of that year. "The second part [of *Zur Kritik*] is now finally ready, that is up to writing out cleanly and polishing for publication" Marx indicated. "It is the continuation of pamphlet I but appears independently under the title '*Das Kapital*' and '*Toward the Critique of Political Economy*' appears only as a sub-title. It only contains, in fact, what should constitute the third chapter of the first part, namely, 'Capital in General.'"[91] This draft was never polished and prepared for publication. Instead, between March 1862 and January 1863, Marx began his lengthy draft manuscript on the theories of surplus value. In January 1863, he returned to the question of machinery and large-scale industry—where he had left off in March 1862—and examined the mechanization of industry from a concrete, historical viewpoint. Consequently, it is to the draft of the third chapter and Marx's draft on machinery, notebooks 1 to 5, 19 and 20, that I will turn in the next two chapters because they play central roles in the development of his conception of the division of labor.

Marx cast his work on "Capital in General" within the 1861–63 manuscripts in a totally different fashion than had he completed the project outlined in April 1858, or even had he met his November 12, 1858 objective and published the first part of *Zur Kritik* in two simultaneous pamphlets. A number of concrete events and conceptual considerations resulted in the significant expansion of his critique, a change in form that allowed inclusion of more concrete historical content and greater conceptual clarification and elaboration. These changes, of course, are evident in Marx's ensuing discussions of the division of labor.

NOTES

1. Karl Marx and Friedrich Engels, *Gesamtausgabe: Werke, Artikel, Entwürfe* [hereafter cited as *MEGA*] (Berlin: Dietz Verlag, 1975ff), II, 2.1, pp. 99:24–26, 100:17–23.

2. Karl Marx and Friedrich Engels, *Werke* [hereafter cited as *MEW*] (Berlin: Dietz Verlag, 1956–90), 1:499–524.

3. Apparently Engels was equally convinced that Marx had mastered the intricacies of political economy and was ready to publish the results of his work. Writing in early October 1844, he implored Marx to "take care that the material you have collected [on economics] shall soon be flung out to the world. It is high time [!]." *MEGA* III, 1, p. 245:26–27. Four months later, Engels was even more insistent. "[W]hat above all is needed by us now are a pair of large works in order to give the many half-educated, who would like to become ready themselves but cannot, a reference point of their own. See that you become ready with your work on political economy. . . . Do as I do, set yourself a time by which you positively *want to be finished* and ensure an early printing." Ibid., pp. 260:33–36, 261:6–7.

4. See the correspondence from Engels to Marx in October 1844, January 22, and March 7, 1845 concerning the proposed volumes; *MEW* 27:8, 16, 23. Engels also published advance notices of the work in *The New Moral World; MEW* 2:514–19.

5. See, for example, Joachim Israel, *Der Begriff Entfremdung: Zur Verdinglichung des Menschen in der bürokratischen Gesellschaft* (Hamburg: Rowohlt Taschenbuch Verlag, 1985); John Maguire, *Marx's Paris Writings: An Analysis* (Dublin: Gill and Macmillan, 1972); Istvan Meszaros, *Marx's Theory of Alienation* (London: Merlin Press, 1970); Bertell Ollman, *Alienation: Marx's Conception of Man in Capitalist Society* (Cambridge: Cambridge University Press, 1971).

6. *MEGA* I, 2, pp. 292:17–306:17.

7. Ibid., p. 309:5–18.

8. Ibid., p. 309:19–23.

9. In the Paris draft manuscript, Marx used the following material from his study notebooks; ibid., pp. 309:25–311:10. He began with *MEGA* IV, 2,

pp. 335:41–336:8, although the material presented is a fuller quotation of Smith than actually found in the study notebook, he followed it directly with material from the study notebook (p. 336:8–16) plus an additional sentence not found in the study notebook; cf. *MEGA* I, 2, p. 309:37–40. Marx omitted *MEGA* IV, 2, p. 336:17–20; used p. 336:21–23; omitted his study notebook commentary and a quotation from Smith, pp. 336:28–32, 336:33–38; and then used quotations from pp. 336:39–40, 336:41–337:5, 337:6–8, 337:9–32, and 337:33–40; omitted his comments on 337:41–338:3; and used 338:3–5, where the discussion of Smith ends.

10. Concerning Marx's use of emphases not found in Smith, see *MEGA* I, 2, 310:37–40 and 311:5–6, and compare it to his study notebook in *MEGA* IV, 2, pp. 337:33–36 and 338:3–5.

11. *MEGA* I, 2, p. 309:37–40 and 309:19–23.

12. Ibid., p. 310:28; cf. Adam Smith, *An Inquiry into the Nature and Causes of the Wealth of Nations,* vol. 2 of the Glasgow Edition of *The Works and Correspondence of Adam Smith,* ed. Roy Hutcheson and Andrew S. Skinner (Indianapolis: Liberty Press, 1976), p. 30.

13. *MEGA* I, 2, pp. 311:11–312:12.

14. See, for example, *MEGA* II, 3.1, pp. 248:4–252:7, 254:32–261:42, Karl Marx, *Misère de la philosophie* (Paris: Alfred Costes, 1950), pp. 150–57.

15. *MEGA* I, 2, p. 312:18–39. This accurate and astute summary puts into a brief compass Smith's key ideas. For other summaries of Smith's position, see Joseph Schumpeter, *History of Economic Analyses,* ed. from the manuscript by Elizabeth Schumpeter (New York: Oxford University Press, 1954), pp. 187–88, and Charles Gide and Charles Rist, *A History of Economic Doctrines,* 2d English ed., trans. Robert Richards (Toronto: George Harrap, 1948), pp. 73–81.

16. *MEGA* I, 2, pp. 312:40–313:21.

17. Ibid., p. 313:21–4, 33–37.

18. Ibid., p. 314:17. Marx did not finish filling the page with written text. Instead, he moved to the next manuscript page and began the intended preface to the work.

19. Karl Marx, *Das Kapital,* 1st ed. (Hamburg: Otto Meissner, 1867), p. 318.

20. The most obvious referent here is Hegel, who argued that "it cannot be emphasized often enough that what distinguishes men from animals is thought." Georg Wilhelm Fiedrich Hegel, *Wissenschaft der Logik* (Frankfurt/M: Suhrkamp, 1969), 1:20; see also Hegel, *Enzyklopadie der philosophen Wissenschaften* (Frankfurt/M: Suhrkamp, 1970), 1:70. Marx could also be referring implicitly to Smith, who argued that men could take advantage of the division of labor while animals could not because the latter had no means of establishing exchange; the propensity to exchange, according to Smith, was most probably rooted in the capacity of reason and language. Thus, for Smith too, thought distinguished men from animals.

21. Karl Marx and Friedrich Engels, *Historisch-kritische Gesamtausgabe* [here-

after cited as *MEGA*[1]], I, 5, ed. David Ryazanov and Vladimir Adoratsky (Berlin: Marx-Engels Verlag, 1927–32, Moscow-Leningrad: Verlagsgenossenschaft Ausländischer Arbeiter in der UdSSR, 1935), p. 10:30–36.

22. *MEGA*[1] I, 5, p. 11:5–8.

23. Ibid., p. 22:13–16.

24. Ibid., p. 22:16–20.

25. Ibid., p. 22:20–23.

26. Ibid., p. 22:25–30.

27. Ibid., pp. 22:42–23:2.

28. Concerning the missing pages, see ibid., p. 55:39–41.

29. Ibid., p. 41:7–9.

30. Ibid., pp. 41:30–42:3. The argument that a craftsman had a "complacent, servile relationship" to his work may seem to be an incongruous statement for Marx and Engels to make, but it is not. The worker is servile to his or her own concrete work in which she or he has a strong interest. The worker is not, as under the conditions of capitalism, servile to the labor process, nor is she or he servile to abstract labor (that is, value). For Marx, the distinction between these two particular historical relations is of critical importance.

Marx and Engels were not totally pessimistic about the conditions in which capitalist workers carried out their labor. They continued their summary statement about work done under capitalism with the following scenario: "On the other hand, standing against these productive forces, we have the majority of the individuals from whom these forces have been wrested away, and who, robbed thus of all real life-content, have become abstract individuals, who are, however, by this very fact put into a position to enter into relation with one another *as individuals.*" Ibid., p. 42:3–5.

31. Ibid., pp. 49:28–50:5.

32. Ibid., pp. 56:39–57:11. In the right-hand margin, at the beginning of this paragraph, Engels had written in Jean-Charles Simonde de Sisimondi's last name (p. 56:42–43).

33. Marx, *Misère de la philosophie*, pp. 150–74.

34. Ibid., p. 151.

35. Ibid., pp. 152–53.

36. Marx argued (ibid., p. 153), "[Smith] saw clearly that 'in reality the difference of natural talents between individuals is much less than we realize. These aptitudes, so different, which seem to distinguish men of diverse professions, when they have become mature, are not the cause but the effect of the division of labor.' In principle a porter differs less from a philosopher than a mastiff from a greyhound. It is the division of labor which has set the gulf between them." Proudhon noted in the margin to his own personal copy of *Misère de la philosophie*, "Fine. But has Smith clarified the problem? No!" Proudhon is correct here; Marx was only using this very weak point to try and polemically discredit Proudhon's ability to understand his sources. When he went on to discuss Lemontey and Ferguson as political economists who fully understood the problems inherent to the division of labor, then Marx

was on firmer ground. Because Marx had not excerpted from Book 5 of *La richesse des nations,* where Smith shows some of the problems inherent in the division of labor, Marx did not use the material in Smith's work that could have best supported his position.

37. Ibid., p. 153. Marx also added Sismondi's name, but without elaboration. It was Engels who inserted Sismondi's name in the margin beside the summary statements made on the division of labor in *Die Deutsche Ideologie* cited in note 32, so he is the most likely source for the input.

38. Ibid., pp. 155–60. Marx summarized the substance of Proudhon's position as follows. "The division of labor reduces the worker to a degrading function; to this degrading function corresponds a depraved soul; to the deprivation of the soul is added an ever increasing reduction of wages. And to prove that this reduction of wages is fitting to a depraved soul, M. Proudhon says, to relieve his conscience, that the conscience wills it thus. Is the soul of M. Proudhon to be included in the Universal soul?" (p. 157).

39. Ibid., p. 160.

40. Ibid., pp. 170–72. Urc's book, in French translation, was owned by Marx; see Bruno Kaiser, *Ex Libris Karl Marx: Schicksal und Verzeichnis einer Bibliothek* (Berlin: Dietz Verlag, 1967), p. 216.

41. Marx drew up several indexes to *Die Grundrisse.* His "Index to the 7 Notebooks" (the first draft is *MEGA* II, 2, pp. 3–7, the second on pp. 8–14) was compiled in the spring of 1858. It places material in *Die Grundrisse* under such specific headings as "Value," "Money," and "Capital in General," with subheadings for the latter two categories. A second "index" is Marx's "Excerpts for the Chapter on Capital," *MEGA* II, 2, pp. 256–63. In this index he included the heading for the division of labor (p. 258:23). There are three possible dates when Marx might have organized this set of excerpts. It could have been as early as January 22, 1859, following a letter to Engels in which he reported the completion of *Zur Kritik's* first part and said he would work on the second part for the next eight days; see Marx to Engels, January 21, 1859, *MEW* 29:385. He might have drafted the plan and excerpts in early October 1859; see Marx to Lassalle, October 2, 1859, ibid., p. 613. Finally, he could have made the draft just before the first of the 1861–63 notebooks, although the outline differs so much from the August 1861-March 1862 notebooks that this is unlikely.

Marx constructed an extensive index to *Die Grundrisse,* "Abstracts to my own notebooks," which was drafted no earlier than January or February 1860. If my dating is correct, then it would mean that the editors to the first edition of *Die Grundrisse* were off by at least a year with their indication of February 1859 as the date for this index. See Karl Marx, *Die Grundrisse der politischen Ökonomie (Rohentwurf) 1857–58* (Berlin: Dietz Verlag, 1953), p. 950. The editors to the new *MEGA* date the "Abstracts" as June and July 1861, following Marx's break to write *Herr Vogt.* To avoid confusion in references to follow, it is important to note that the seven notebooks of *Die Grundrisse* are published as *MEGA* II, 1.1 and 1.2, and the indexes, written after the text, are published in *MEGA* II, 2.

42. *MEGA* II, 1.2, pp. 502:38–503:3. "Volume III of his edition of Smith, *Wakefield* remarks: 'the labor of slaves being combined, is more productive than the much divided labor of freemen. The labor of freemen is more productive than that of slaves, only when it comes to be combined *by means of greater dearness of land* and *the system of hiring wages* . . . . In countries where land remains very cheap, either all the people are in a state of barbarism, or some of them are in a state of slavery [quotation in English, Marx's emphases]."

43. *MEGA* II, 1.1, p. 244:13–15.

44. Ibid., p. 245:16–20.

45. *MEGA* II, 1.2, pp. 371:18–378:27, 378:28–415:41. When Marx prepared an index to his 1857–58 notebooks, he designated the digression as follows. "Inversion [*Umschlag*] of the law of appropriation. 50. Actual foreigness [*Fremd-heit*] of the worker to his product. Division of Labor. Machinery etc. 50." *MEGA* II, 2, p. 279:8–9. In the first edition of *Die Grundrisse* and its subsequent reprints the first section is entitled "Inversion of the law of property [*Eigen-tumsgesetzes*]" rather than "Inversion of the law of appropriation [*Aneignungs-gesetzes*]"; cf. Marx, *Die Grundrisse*, p. 958:8, although the heading is correct when placed within the text (p. 363:5). The heading is noted correctly in the *MEW* index to Marx and Engels's works, writings, and articles; see Karl Marx and Friedrich Engels, *Verzeichnis Werke, Schriften, Artikel* (Berlin: Dietz Verlag, 1968), p. 245.

46. *MEGA* II, 1.2, p. 377:22–25.

47. Ibid., pp. 377:31–378:27.

48. Ibid., p. 476:26–29.

49. See ibid., p. 476:32–40 for the two quotations.

50. Ibid., p. 477:10–15.

51. Ibid., p. 477:5–7.

52. Ibid., p. 477:21–26.

53. Ibid., p. 499:3–6.

54. Ibid., p. 499:13–17.

55. Ibid., pp. 270:13–276:3, 389:27–401:36, 580:38–583:3, 583:39–585:41, and 589:1–590:2 for other parts of *Die Grundrisse* concerned with self-actualization through labor.

56. *MEGA* II, 2, pp. 47:16–62:45 and 39:14–47:15.

57. Ibid., p. 47:18–32.

58. Ibid., p. 50:15–30.

59. Ibid., p. 287:7–27. 9.

60. Ibid., pp. 287:28–288:13.

61. My explanation for the absence of the term *alienation* in Marx's later work is, of course, only partial. For more detailed accounts, see Israel, *Der Begriff Entfremdung: Zur Verdinglichung des Menschen in der bürokratischen Gesellschaft*, pp. 60–105, 31–33, Ollman, *Alienation: Marx's Conception of Man in Capitalist Society*, or Isaac Rubin's excellent discussion of alienation within the context of commodity fetishism, "Marx's Theory of Commodity Fetishism," in *Essays on Marx's Theory of Value*, trans. Milos Samardzija and Fredy Perlman (Montreal: Black Rose Books, 1973), pp. 5–60.

62. Compare *MEGA* II, 1.1, p. 43:1–13 to Marx's outline in correspondence with Lassalle on March 11, 1858, *MEW* 29:554.

63. See, for example, *MEGA* II, 1.1, pp. 43:1–13, 151:26–152:3, 187:10–33, 199:16–39, and 237:7–29.

64. *MEW* 29:549–52.

65. Marx noted that "by 'Heften' I mean something like the way [Friedrich] Vischer's *Aesthetic* appeared piece by piece." Ibid., p. 550.

66. Ibid., pp. 550–51.

67. Lassalle to Marx, March 3, 1858. Ferdinand Lassalle, *Der Briefwechsel zwischen Lassalle und Marx* [hereafter cited as *BZLM*], vol. 3 of *Nachgelassene Briefe und Schriften,* ed. Gustav Mayer (Berlin: Springer Verlag, 1922), pp. 118–19.

68. See either *MEW* 29:554, or *BZLM,* pp. 119–20.

69. *MEGA* II, 1.2, p. 740:2.

70. *MEGA* II, 1.1, p. 229:4–15. For a detailed discussion of the importance and nature of *capital in general,* see Roman Rosdolsky, *The Making of Marx's Capital,* trans. Peter Burgess (1968, repr. London: Pluto Press, 1977), pp. 41–50, 67–70.

71. *MEGA* II, 2, pp. 102:37, 224:8.

72. *MEW* 29:554, emphasis added. For comparative interest, the material contained in the seven notebooks of *Die Grundrisse* amounted to approximately 750 pages: 747 pages in the new *MEGA* edition (see *MEGA* II 1.1 and 1.2) and 764 in the Dietz Verlag edition of 1953 (Marx, *Die Grundrisse*). Julian Borchardt condensed the three volumes of *Das Kapital* into 322 printed pages, but this represents only one-sixth of the entire project Marx outlined. Karl Marx, *Das Kapital: Kritik der politischen Ökonomie,* comp. Julian Borchardt (Berlin-Schöneberg: Neuzeitlicher Buchverlag, 1919).

73. *MEW* 29:312–18.

74. It is possible that Marx would have published pamphlets for each of these sections, but they would have been short. An additional hundred pages for each would have reached his minimum estimate for the whole project. The three sections would likely have required fewer than a hundred pages in a single pamphlet had Marx kept to the projection indicated to Lassalle. That would have left him with between three hundred and four hundred and fifty pages for five more books.

75. Marx to Lassalle, May 31, 1858, Jenny Marx to Engels, April 9, 1858, and Jenny Marx to Lassalle, April 9, 1858, *MEW* 29:560, 648, 649; or Vladimir Adoratsky, ed., *Karl Marx: Chronik seines Lebens in Einzeldaten* (Moscow: Marx-Engels Institute, 1934), pp. 170–71.

76. Engels to Marx, April 9, 1858, *MEW* 29:319, emphasis added. Engels's comment further underscores my point regarding the character of Marx's critique. An *epitome* is a condensed account that contains only the most important points related to the subject matter treated in the text.

77. Marx to Lassalle, February 22, 1858, ibid., p. 551.

78. Marx to Lassalle, May 31, 1858, ibid., p. 580. Concerning Marx's visit with Engels, see ibid., p. 696 n292, or *MEGA* II, 1, p. 1112. With respect to

Marx's discussion with Engels about the section on capital in general, see Marx to Engels, January 13, 1859, *MEW* 29:383. Curiously, regarding Marx's visit, *Karl Marx: Chronik seines Lebens in Einzeldaten* notes only "Marx with Engels in Manchester; played sport, rode, convalesced" (p. 171).

79. Ibid., pp. 329, 560–61.

80. *MEGA* II, 1.2, pp. 738–47; *MEGA* II, 1, p. 790.

81. Concerning Marx's first estimate of when *Zur Kritik* would be completed see Marx to Lassalle, March 11, 1858; *MEW* 29, p. 554.

82. Marx to Lassalle, November 12, 1858, ibid., p. 566.

83. Ibid., p. 567. There is no existing published record of this elaboration, and Marx's comments to Lassalle (October 2, 1859, ibid., p. 613) that the manuscript for the second part would have to be reworked because it is "already a year old" suggests that no written elaboration other than that found in *Die Grundrisse* was ever developed. The only material available on the chapter on capital following *Die Grundrisse* is that found in the first five notebooks of 1861–63.

84. Henryk Grossman, "Die Änderung des ursprünglichen Aufbauplans des Marxschen 'Kapital,'" *Archiv für die Geschichte des Sozialismus und der Arbeiterbewegung* 14 (1929):305–38; Maximilien Rubel, "A History of Marx's 'Economics,'" in *Rubel on Marx*, ed. Joseph O'Malley and Keith Algozin (Cambridge: Cambridge University Press, 1981), pp. 82–189; Rosdolsky, *The Making of Marx's 'Capital'*, pp. 10–56; David Ryazanov, "Siebzig Jahre 'Zur Kritik der politischen Ökonomie,'" *Archiv für die Geschichte des Sozialismus und der Arbeiterbewegung* 15 (1930):1–32; or Adoratsky, ed., *Karl Marx*, pp. 170–75. Rubel published "Une échange des lettres entre Lassalle et Marx," *La revue socialiste*, December, 1949, pp. 434–47, from the April 26, 1857 to February 27, 1858 period, but the letters only cover Lassalle's offer to look for a publisher and Marx's outline of the plan of his *Kritik*. They do not cover the material I have emphasized in this section.

85. Marx's frustration regarding the scant attentionn accorded *Zur Kritik* can be seen in correspondence with Lassalle, October 2, 1859, November 6, 1859, *MEW* 29:613, 618; and Ludwig Kugelmann, December 28, 1862, *MEW* 30:640; and October 11, 1867, *MEW* 31:562. The expansion of *Das Kapital* is noted in Marx to Engels, June 18, 1862, *MEW* 30:248.

86. Marx to Engels, April 2, 1851, *MEW* 27:228. It would be a mistake to think that Marx dealt only with economic matters over the next eight years. To get a sense of his varied activities from 1858 to 1867, see Adoratsky, ed., *Karl Marx*, pp. 162–254; David McLellan, *Karl Marx: His Life and Thought* (London: Macmillan Press, 1973), pp. 286–341; Maximilien Rubel, "Chronologie," *Oeuvres de Karl Marx: Économie* (Paris: Éditions Gallimard, 1965), 3:xcvi-cxxxi; or Marx and Engels, *Verzeichnis: Werke, Schriften, Artikel*, pp. 94–127.

87. *MEW* 29:383. Marx rationalized that in some respects the separate appearance of the chapter "Capital in General" might be a good thing. First, if the chapters on commodity and money sold well, it would hasten the appearance of the third chapter on capital. Second, because of the nature of the first part, "the dogs" (that is, the critics) could not "simply abuse it." Marx felt

that he could then get the better of the "Canaille" because they would have to take his views on capital "rather seriously." Marx to Lassalle, March 29, 1859, ibid., p. 586. Finally, Marx argued, "the chapter on money will [also] be interesting to experts."

88. Marx to Engels, January 26, 1859, ibid., p. 387. The history behind the publication of *Zur Kritik* constitutes a study in itself. On the one hand, it shows how suspicious Marx had become of publishers and illustrates his strained relationships with them. See, for example, Marx to Lassalle, March 28, 1859, June 10, 1859, October 2, 1859; and Marx to Engels, May 24, 1859, *MEW* 29:586, 606, 613, and 440; see also Marx to Duncker, May 28, 1859, June 2, 1859, and June 22, 1859, *The Letters of Karl Marx*, trans. Saul Padover (Englewood Cliffs: Prentice-Hall, 1979), pp. 135–36, 136, 136–37.

Padover (p. 135 n3) claims that Duncker paid Marx the remainder of his due honorarium on June 25, 1859 and informed Marx he would have nothing more to do with him. Nevertheless, Lassalle (*BZLM*, p. 226)—in a letter to Marx dated July 11, 1859—said that Duncker would publish the second *Hefte* of *Zur Kritik*.

Part of Marx's anger and frustration centered on an English translation of *Zur Kritik*. He informed both Engels (January 21, 1859, *MEW* 29:386) and Lassalle (February 2, 1859, ibid., p. 586) that he was negotiating with an English publisher for an English edition of *Zur Kritik*. On October 2, 1859, Marx told Lassalle that the English edition was lost because of the delayed publication of the German edition (ibid., p. 613). In the same letter he noted "I am occupied with an *English* edition of the first pamphlet which likewise is interrupted by bourgeois thunderstorms. In any case, I am sure of a better reception in England than in Germany where, so far as I know, no cock has crowed in support of or against the thing. I only wish that the *first part* at least was totally available to the German public. If it should continue to take no further notice of the work then I similarly intend to write all subsequent parts in English and have nothing further to do with the German philistines."

89. For a full description of the so-called "Vogt Affair," see McLellan, *Karl Marx: His Life and Thought*, pp. 310–15; the result was a volume pubished by Marx entitled *Herr Vogt* (*MEW* 14).

90. Marx to Engels, December 9, 1861, *MEW* 29:207.

91. Marx to Kugelmann, December 28, 1862, *MEW* 30:639.

THREE

THE 1861–62 MANUSCRIPTS

Because the draft manuscript for the intended third chapter to *Zur Kritik* represents Marx's first attempt to incorporate the division of labor into his full critique of political economy, its relatively recent publication date, and the absence of an English translation or extensive English-language commentary on the text, I will examine the division of labor section of the 1861–62 manuscript in this chapter. My first intent is to present the content of Marx's arguments concerning the division of labor in 1861–62. As will become apparent, the number of ideas he dealt with was not large, although his treatment of the division of labor was his most comprehensive to date. Nevertheless, in terms of the development of Marx's ideas and an understanding of how he conceived them, it is important to know which ideas he had originated in 1861 and 1862 and how he expressed them.

My second intent is to convey, as much as possible, the chronology and context of Marx's ideas as he wrote them out in 1861–62. Even though he only dealt with three broad groupings of ideas, he did not present them, let alone the dozen or more associated subthemes, in a systematic, wholly logical manner. Marx's discussion of the division of labor is replete with repetition, jumps from one topic to another, contains several excurses, and presents isolated ideas that either are never developed or not elaborated upon until much later in the analysis. The text is, in short, very much a rough draft. For this analysis, however, the draft nature of the text is a strength rather than a liability. As a result, I have not imposed my own order upon the draft and presented its content within some externally constructed thematic framework for two reasons.

First, by adhering closely to the chronology of the text, one can almost look over Marx's shoulder and observe how he selected, organized, interpreted, grouped, and reacted to various materials and ideas. It is almost possible in some places to induce how Marx connected certain themes as he tried to assemble a variety of ideas into a coherent logic. Thus, for example, my discussion will show that Marx began with at least part of a plan in mind, but after setting out some of his ideas, he appears to have moved into some excurses purely as a reaction to the material he had written down. In other parts of the manuscript Marx wrote out quotations with minimal comment to stand more or less as reminders of ideas he did not want to forget but chose not to develop at that time.

Thus, the way Marx externalized his ideas influenced how these ideas were developed in his mind as he wrote out the draft manuscript, as well as their further development in a subsequent encounter with this material. His method at the site of concrete production, and the form in which he set out his ideas, ultimately influenced the content of his ideas. Although he had a framework in mind as he wrote, in the concrete process of externalizing his ideas Marx's abstractions were engaged dialectically with the resulting product of the externalization process—the notebook manuscript. The resulting product became a significant component for the subsequent development of his ideas on the division of labor.

Because the 1861–62 draft manuscript shows exactly what ideas Marx placed on paper, as well as their sequence and development through association, I have chosen to examine that process quite closely to help grasp the development of Marx's position on the division of labor and gain insight into dimensions of his method concerning inquiry to some extent, but predominantly intellectual reconstruction and exposition.

The second reason for following Marx's externalization process so closely is related to the particular status of the 1861–62 draft manuscript itself. The division of labor analysis presented in these notebooks is worked up (*verarbeitete*) or developed further than Marx's study notebooks of the 1840s or 1850s, his presentation in 1844, *Die Deutsche Ideologie*, the text of *Die Grundrisse*, or even *Die Grundrisse* in conjunction with its various indexes. But at the same time, the 1861–62 draft was not a work submitted for publication. It stands at a level of completion comparable to some of Marx's drafts for volumes 2 and 3 of *Das Kapital* or the original draft text to chapters 1 and 2 of *Zur Kritik*. As a result, the 1861–62 draft manuscript provides a unique opportunity to see how Marx moved from a rough setting out of ideas to a finalized form with few intermediary stages.

In terms of development, the 1861–62 draft manuscript represents a return to Marx's earlier emphasis on political economic theory rather than the more concrete, historical approach found in *Die Deutsche Ideologie* and *Die Grundrisse*. Marx spent much of his time in 1861 and 1862 drawing together the commentaries and analyses of a large number of political economists concerning the division of labor. Large parts of the manuscript are reminiscent of the 1844 treatment of the division of labor issue as Marx again juxtaposed political economists' ideas to draw out contradictions, tensions, and a more synthetic conception of the division of labor.

In 1861 and 1862, Marx also followed a pattern similar to that of 1844 insofar as he described the division of labor—although now it began with a lengthy discussion distinguishing the social division of labor from the division of labor in the factory. He then presented a variety of criticisms based on the work of other political economists, followed finally by an analysis of the alienation theme. The major difference between the 1861–62 treatment and that of 1844 is the more extensive concrete historical background that Marx drew upon in 1861 and 1862 and the success with which he demonstrated how the division of labor, as a product of the capitalist mode of production, created conditions of objective alienation for workers. When Marx addressed the alienation theme in 1861 and 1862, he did so within the context of commodity production, value, and an emergent theme of the fetishism of commodities.

Within this study of the 1861–62 draft manuscript, it is also possible to document how Marx located and incorporated ideas into his critique. For example, one can trace back to the original source that introduced Marx to the ancients' work on the division of labor and see how that work influenced his critical understanding of the division of labor.

Finally, although my analysis of the 1861–62 draft manuscript continually points beyond an internal study of the draft to an external comparison with the same section of *Das Kapital* and the themes of earlier texts discussed in the last chapter, I have kept the comparisons with *Das Kapital* to a minimum because that is the substance of chapter 5. I have, however, made linkages between the 1861–62 draft manuscript and the texts before 1860 wherever I feel that they are helpful.

The 1861–62 Draft Manuscript

The manuscript begins on page 149 under the heading "b) division of labor," the second subsection under the general topic "Relative Surplus Value."[1] The discussion runs to the end of manuscript page 189 and thus comprises about a fifth of the total draft manuscript. The first three broad themes Marx dealt with concern the distinctions between the social division of labor, or the division of social labor on the one hand and the division of labor in the workshop on the other. Closely associated with this is an attempt to link the historical development of the former to the emergence of the latter.

Marx's second theme concerns an elaboration of the specifically capitalist character of the division of labor in the workshop, the most complex theme in the manuscript. He distinguished between the division of labor in manufacture and that of large-scale industry. He examined how the division of labor in the capitalist workshop affected the labor process—as a unique form of cooperation, simplifying work tasks, reducing production time, increasing the productive burden of fewer workers, and expanding capital—and how it affected the workers themselves. Concerning the latter topic, Marx used the alienation problematic in a far more sophisticated manner than he had in earlier attempts to use alienation to examine the division of labor.

The third theme relates to both of the preceding ones but is also separate from them. Marx contrasted and compared the writings of the ancient Greeks (mainly Plato and Xenophon) to modern economists. The analysis shows how much some political economists relied on the ideas of the ancients, but it also shows how some, because of their location in changed historical conditions, accentuated the capitalist economy's real interest in the division of labor—that is, producing goods in less time—which the ancients necessarily ignored. Conversely, Marx emphasized that the ancients stressed how the division of labor improved the quality of products, whereas modern political economists had no concern for the use value side of the question except insofar as production related to profit.

The Social and Technical Division of Labor: A Differentiation

Marx's first task in the division of labor section of the 1861–62 notebooks was to establish the exact meaning of the division of labor. Thus, at the top of manuscript page 149, he opened his discussion with the following commentary.

> The division of labor is a particular, specific, highly developed form of cooperation, a powerful means to increase the productive power of labor, to perform the same work in less labor time, thus to reduce the labor time necessary for the reproduction of labor capacity and increase the surplus labor time.

In simple cooperation it is the joint action of many performing the *same labor*. In the division of labor it is the cooperation of many workers under the command of capital who are producing *different* parts of the *same commodity*, of which each particular operation and each worker, or a determinate multiple of workers, performs only a particular operation, the other performs another and so forth; but the totality of these operations produces *one commodity*, a determinate, particular, commodity.[2]

Rather than developing this dimension of the division of labor further and presenting an illustration like Smith's pin-making example or William Petty's discussion of watch production, Marx decided to pursue one of the major themes in his analysis: distinguishing the division of labor in the workshop from the social division of labor at large. Why he made this decision becomes clear, in part, toward the end of manuscript page 150.

Marx noted that different production processes are needed to produce a use value such as cotton. But, Marx continued, these different processes do not represent "the division of labor in the presently observed sense"; they represent a social division of labor. "The labor necessary for the production of pressed cotton is divided into spinning, weaving, and pressing and each of these branches represents the employment of a particular division of workers in which each carried out only the particular operation of spinning, or weaving, or pressing."[3] Thus, although cotton represents "a totality of particular labor," the workers are not working concurrently to produce the same commodity. They produce "commodities independently from one another."[4]

Following a paragraph excursus describing the nature of a commodity,[5] Marx spent manuscript page 150 re-presenting some of the points I have outlined thus far, although in a slightly different sequence with varying emphases. "We have seen," he wrote, "that the product becomes overall a commodity and commodity exchange as the condition of production takes place overall if a social division of labor, or a division of social labor takes place. . . . This social division of labor, which is presupposed in the being-there of products as commodities and exchange of commodities, is essentially different from the division of labor that we are examining here."[6]

Marx followed these points with the new observation that although the latter division of labor arose from the first, it is quite different from it. Rather than relating to each other as independent commodity producers, as is the case in the social division of labor, workers appear as "non-independent [workers] because they provide the whole commodity only through their cooperation."[7] As a result, workers in the latter form of the division of labor do not stand opposite each other as commodity producers in the market; they stand as "non-independent workers" opposite their capitalist counterparts.

Following this point, Marx finally noted one of the major reasons— which must have been at the back of his mind as he began the discussion—for stressing his conception of the division of labor and why he distinguished the social division of labor from the division of labor in the workshop. "A. Smith" Marx argued, "constantly confuses the division of labor in these very different, though complementary, but also in this particular regard, opposing conditions."[8]

This theme, which recurs a few times in the manuscript, held some importance for Marx in 1861 and 1862 as compared to his pre-1859 writings. There are probably two reasons for this. First, in *Zur Kritik der politischen Ökonomie* and in the 1861-62 draft manuscript, Marx dealt explicitly and critically with a number of political economists' errors in conceptualization. In the case of the division of labor, he was particularly concerned with Smith, the bourgeoisie's major exponent of the division of labor. Second, as Marx moved from his earlier works to *Zur Kritik,* his project expanded. In this chapter of *Zur Kritik,* he was concerned with how his labor theory of value and his particular theory of valorization and the extraction of relative surplus value influenced the production process. By 1861-62, as a result, he had to specify not only how the division of labor affected the increased extraction of relative surplus value but, on the basis of his own particular theory of value, valorization, and extraction of surplus value, he could clearly distinguish between the social division of labor and the division of labor in the workshop.

Marx followed his comments on Smith with another concrete example distinguishing the social division of labor from the division of labor in the production process.[9] More important, however, are his concluding comments to the example because they show how Marx, at this point of the manuscript at least, planned to focus his discussion. "Also this form of the division of labor, which we are considering here, in no way exhausts the division of labor. Ultimately [the division of labor] is, in a certain relationship, the category of all categories in political economy. But we have to consider it here only as a particular productive power of capital."[10] This intent, however, was virtually impossible to maintain because Marx continually had to contrast the division of labor found under capitalism—that is, manufacture—with other determinate forms of divided labor. Using Hegel's logical development of categories while writing *Das Kapital* helped him over this difficult strategic hurdle (chapter 5).

Nevertheless, the specifically capitalist character of the division of labor is the second of Marx's major themes, and he dealt with it in many ways, from several points of analysis, and at various points throughout the division of labor section. Following his statement of intent, he set out exactly what he meant within the concept "division of labor in the workshop" and also linked that assessment to such issues as the impact of the capitalist division of labor on increasing productivity, simplifying tasks, the changing organic composition of capital, alienation, and others. Marx accomplished this analysis in some places by presenting and linking a number of direct quotations from political economists, while in other places he set out his own ideas at some length.

The Capitalist Character of the Division of Labor

Marx initiated his study of the specifically capitalist character of the division of labor by noting halfway down manuscript page 152 that the division of labor, as he was examining it, assumes that a highly developed social division of labor exists already.[11] Second, many workers are thus under the command of capital and put to work at different tasks producing a single commodity in a particular manner under determinate conditions. "Their work is forced because it, insofar as they [the workers] enter the labor process, belongs not to them but already to capital, is incorporated in it [capital] already."[12] But Smith, Marx argued at the top of page 154, "has not comprehended the division of labor as a property of the capitalist means of production; whereby the labor is not only formally but in its actuality changed through subsumption under capital. He grasps it [the division of labor] in the same way as Petty, and after Petty other predecessors (see the East India essay)."[13]

Marx maintained that Smith and his predecessors saw the division of labor as the ancients did—as a social division of labor—although unlike the ancients, Smith noted that the division of labor increased the productive power of capital and lowered a commodity's value.[14] On the bottom of page 154 and on most of page 155, Marx organized nine quotations, each between twenty and ninety words in length, from *La richesse des nations* to illustrate these aspects of Smith's position on the division of labor.[15] These quotations and a series of summary statements led into a comparison of Smith and Ferguson that dominates page 156.[16] "In the whole section on the division of labor" Marx argued, "Smith essentially follows, often copies, his teacher Adam Ferguson (*Essai sur l'histoire de la sociét é civile*, translated by M. Beriger, Paris, 1783)."[17] Marx presented a few quotations from Ferguson—some paired with excerpts from Smith—to support his claim. He then noted that what "distinguishes him [Ferguson] from Smith is that he develops more sharply and more emphatically the negative side of the division of labor."[19] As an example, Marx cited the following from Ferguson.

There is reason to doubt whether the general capacity of a nation grows in proportion to the progress of skill. Many mechanical skills do not require any talent; they succeed perfectly at times when they are totally destitute of the need of reason and feeling; and ignorance is the mother of industry as well as of superstition. Reflection and fancy are subject to err; but a habit of moving the foot or hand depends on neither the one nor the other. As a result, one can say that perfection, with regard to manufacture, consists of being able to by-pass the mind (and especially important with regard to the workshop) in such a manner that without the effort of the head, the workshop can be *considered like a machine of which the parts are men.*[20]

Marx noted further that Ferguson was more aware than Smith of the changed relations between the worker and the capitalist within the division of labor in manufacture.[21] In addition, with Ferguson still in mind, Marx wrote that with respect to the whole nation, industry "brings nations to the point of being composed of members who, excepting their trade, are extremely ignorant about everything in life." Ferguson substantiated this claim by making a comparative reference to the Greeks.[22]

Leaving Ferguson, but before beginning his own extended commentary on the division of labor, on manuscript page 157 Marx listed some quotations from Alonzo Potter, George Scrope, and Dugald Stewart on the division of labor. From Scrope and Potter, he made the following excerpt, not contained in *Das Kapital* later.

"The first essential towards production is labour. To play its part efficiently in this great business, the labour of individuals must be *combined;* or, in other words, the labor required for producing certain results must be *distributed* [Marx's emphasis] among several individuals, and those individuals thus be enabled to cooperate" (p. 76 Scrope) To this Potter remarks note l.c. "The principle here referred to is usually called the *division of labour.* This phrase is objectionable since the fundamental idea is that of *concert* and *cooperation,* not of *division.* The term of division applies only to the *process;* this being *subdivided into several operations,* and these being *distributed or parcelled out among a number of operatives.* It is thus a *combination* of *labourers* effected through a *subdivision of processes.*"[23]

From Stewart's *Lectures on Political Economy,* Marx excerpted the following almost immediately after the Scrope and Potter material.

"The effects of the division of labor, and of the use of machines . . . both derive their value from the same circumstances, their tendency, to *enable one man to perform the work of many.*" (p. 317) "It produces also an *economy of time,* all of *which may be carried into execution at the same moment . . . by carrying on all the different processes at once,* which an individual must have executed separately, it becomes possible to produce a multitude of pins f.i. *completely* finished in the same time as a single pin might have been either cut or pointed." (319)[24]

With all of these quotations in place, Marx formulated on manuscript pages 158 and 159 his first extensive account of the division of labor that did more than merely describe its structure. He began by indicating that labor is divided into "independent operations or processes separated, isolated, from one another and the workers are subsumed under these isolated functions. . . . [I]ncreased productivity and complication of the total production process, its enrichment, is thus being purchased through the reduction of the capacity of labor, in each particular function, to a purely barren abstraction." Production becomes multifaceted and is carried out simultaneously thus "*reducing the labor time* . . . so that not only in a given time more *complete commodities,* more commodities become *ready* but [also] *more* ready commodities are being supplied. . . . Through this combination the workshop turns into a mechanism, in which the individual workers constitute the different parts."[25]

Through this combination, Marx continued, the "total mechanism as such" stands opposed to the workers as "an external power, ruling over them and surrounding them, in fact as the power and a form of existence of capital itself." For the workers themselves, however, there is "no combination of activities," their function is one-sided and abstract. "The combination is not a relation that belongs to them [the workers] themselves, and is subsumed under them as united." To this, Marx added, so much for "the beautiful phrases of Herrn Potter on combination and concert, in opposition to division."[26]

Marx had noted earlier in the section at the top of manuscript page 154 that Smith failed to see that labor was changed "not only formally but in its actuality through subsumption under capital." At this point in the manuscript—midway down page 159—he expanded upon this particular point within his extended commentary on the division of labor.

The capitalist mode of production has here already affected and changed labor in substance. It is no longer purely the *formal* subsumption of labor under capital; it [labor] works for another, under foreign command and foreign supervision. It is also no longer purely as with simple cooperation, with many, with which it carries out simultaneously *the same* labor, which leaves it [labor] as such unchanged and produces an inter-relation only temporarily, which according to the nature [*Natur*] of the thing [is] easily dissolvable, and in most cases of simple cooperation takes place only for a particular passing period, by way of exceptional want.[27]

Instead, Marx continued, under the capitalist division of labor in the workshop, labor is one-sided; it is "a living component of the workshop and through this means one's labor itself becomes an appendage of capital." This transmutation is all due to the fact that the worker has only his or her labor capacity to sell. In summary, Marx wrote the following at the bottom of manuscript page 159.

The increase of productive power, which proceeds from the division of labor, this social mode of being-there of capital, is thus not only the productive power of capital but the productive power of the worker. The *social form* of these combined labors is the being-there of capital against the worker; the combination stands up to him as an overwhelming fate which hits him through the reduction of his labor capacity to a wholly one-sided function which is nothing separated from the total mechanism and therefore totally dependent on it. It [labor] has turned itself into a pure detail.[28]

What is important to note about Marx's argument thus far is that its organizational structure has moved from description to criticism. He began by describing aspects of the division of labor as a "particular, specific, highly developed form of cooperation" that was a "powerful means to increase the productive power of the workers." He proceeded to distinguish the social division of labor from that of the workshop, his real interest. When he began to discuss the capitalist character of the division of labor in the workshop, Marx finally began to move beyond description to evaluation, although even here he relied primarily on the citations of others to imply some of the problems inherent to the division of labor for the worker. With the use of Ferguson, Marx formally moved into critique; in his lengthy commentary, he linked his critical assessment of the division of labor to the alienation framework.

In many ways, this organizational approach replicated Marx's earlier treatments of the topic. He basically dealt with the whole of the division of labor in a descriptive fashion and then proceeded into a critique that ultimately centered on the alienation theme. The strength of this approach in the 1840s and 1850s is that it allowed Marx to draw upon the literature of left-wing German idealism, a body of thought that no previous political economist—including Ferguson—had considered. In 1861 and 1862, Marx presented his most extensive assessment of the division of labor within that framework. The problem with the approach was that it showed few areas of dynamism and change, tendencies that would suggest why the division of labor came into being, how it would mature, and what would ensue. Nor did the approach allow Marx to focus upon which moments of the division of labor represented antagonisms. In *Das Kapital,* through a changed format of presentation, he would attempt to overcome the limitations of his 1861–62 mode of presentation.

The Ancients and the Division of Labor

Immediately after the summary paragraph from the bottom of manuscript page 159, Marx noted at the top of the next manuscript page that Stewart calls the workers "subordinated to the division of labor 'living automatons . . . employed in the details of work' while the 'employer will always be on the stretch to economize time and labour'."[29] Marx continued by referring to material seven pages earlier in Stewart's *Lectures.* "D. Stewart quotes relative to the division of labor within society the maxims of the ancients. 'We are everything and nothing.' 'In all we are capable of something; in total nothing.' 'He understands many works, nevertheless he understands them all poorly.' (From *Margites,* cited in the second Alcibiades, one of the spurious dialogues of Plato)."[30]

The significance of these quotations is not so much their content, but the insight that they, and the ensuing manuscript material, provide into how Marx's intellectual labor process led him to new information on the division of labor question. The Stewart material was excerpted between 1859 and 1861 and included on manuscript page 148 of study notebook 7.[31] On page 172, Marx had excerpted some ideas from Thucydides' *De bello Peloponnesiaco libri octo* beside which he wrote "belongs to the *division of labor.*"[32] In 1861 and 1862, Marx placed this latter material almost immediately after the Stewart citations, an impetus that moved him into his presentation of material concerning the ancients on the division of labor.

Drawing from Thucydides, Marx noted that he let Pericles term "the agriculturally based Spartans, where no mediation of consumption takes place through exchange, thus also no division of labor takes place, as self-managed [*Selbstwirtschaftende*] (working not for profit, rather subsistence) in contrast to the Athenians."[33] He then cited from Thucydides a quotation from Pericles, subsequently incorporated into a footnote in *Das Kapital,* that maintained seafaring was an art that had to be one's sole occupation.[34] All of this material is almost meaningless as it is arranged in the 1861–62 manuscript. In fact, it only allowed Marx to transfer some ideas to paper so that they could be worked with and developed at a later time.

Immediately following the excerpt from Thucydides, Marx began a discussion of Xenophon, a section that provides additional insight into how he worked. He first encountered the use of Xenophon in Stewart's *Lectures on Political Economy* in a lengthy quotation from *Cyropaedia* that Marx also excerpted in his 1861-62 manuscripts.[35] It is clear, however, that because Marx cited the excerpt in the original Greek, rather than in Stewart's English, and because the excerpt comes from a later segment of the seventh 1859-62 study notebook than the Stewart excerpts in the same notebook, that Marx returned to the original after encountering it in Stewart.[36]

Tracing the source of Marx's introduction to the Xenophon material is instructive in three ways. First, it is further proof that when given a lead on some issue or idea, he frequently pursued it to the original source. Second, it was apparently while reading Stewart's commentary on Xenophon that Marx was introduced to the Greek material on the division of labor, which he incorporated into his analysis for the first time in 1861-62 and carried over into *Das Kapital*.[37] Stewart had argued that "It is very observable ... in the foregoing quotation, that what Xenophon lays chief stress on, is the effect of this division in improving the *quality* of the articles produced, whereas the circumstance which has chiefly attracted the attention of Mr. Smith and other modern writers, is its astonishing effect in increasing their *quantity*."[38]

Marx, however, was not a mere copier of ideas, although he did not always cite where his ideas were first stimulated, and his discussion of Xenophon in 1861 and 1862 shows how much more he saw in the writings of the Greek thinker than had Stewart. This contrast is the third benefit to tracing this question to its source.

In contrast to Stewart, Marx noted that Xenophon "has many bourgeois instincts and therefore often points not only to bourgeois morals but also bourgeois economy." Xenophon, Marx argued, "goes further than Plato into the division of labor insofar as it performs not only as a whole but also in the workshop. His following disputation, because of this, is interesting since he 1) notes the dependency of the division of labor on the *size of the market*. 2) ... [H]e stresses the reduction of labor to simple labor and the easier skill contained in the simple labor brought about by the division of labor."[39] None of these ideas were discussed by Stewart. Like Stewart, however, Marx noted that although Xenophon had many modern conceptions, his main concern was "the *use value*, the improvement of *quality*. The reduction of labor time does not interest him just as little with Plato, even in the one place where

79

this, by way of exception in passing, shows that *more* use values can be created. Even here it deals only with the increase of *use values;* not with the effect of the division of labor on the product as commodity."[40]

Following the lengthy citation from Xenophon, corresponding to Stewart's citation, Marx began a discussion of Plato, and this too was not a wholly fortuitous addition to his analysis of the division of labor in 1861 and 1862 over previous treatments. Stewart had argued that Smith's ideas about the increase in the "powers of labor" through the division of labor "had, before Smith's time, been adopted by various modern writers; particularly by Mr. Harris in his *Dialogue Concerning Happiness,* 1741; and by Dr. Ferguson in his *Essay on Civil Society.* The fact, too, has been very strongly stated by different writers of a much more early date; particularly by Sir William Petty and Dr. Mandeville."[41]

Marx, possibly unfamiliar with James Harris's work, turned to it and placed excerpts from it as well into study notebook 7 of the 1859–62 period.[42] As a result, he introduced the discussion of Plato in the 1861–62 manuscript with the following statement: "*Plato's* dispute in the Republic [*sic*] shapes the direct basis and departure point for a group of English writers who wrote after Petty and before Smith on the division of labor. See e.g. *James Harris* (later Earl of Malmesbury) *Three Treatises* etc. 3rd ed. Lond. 1772, the 3rd Treatise wherein the Division of employments is presented as the natural basis of society, p. 148-55, [and] about which he himself says in a note, that he got the whole argument from Plato."[43]

The bulk of the Plato selection consists of a long paraphrasing, interspersed with some commentary, of a lengthy quotation from the *Republic.* Marx argued that in the *Republic,* Plato began with the rise of the polis, which arises because individuals cannot exist independently. Socrates notes that needs are best met when each individual attends to one particular occupation. This is true, Socrates argued, because innate differences fit different people to particular occupations. In addition, "work cannot wait for the leisure of he who has to perform it, rather the one performing the work must govern himself according to the condition of his production, etc., it therefore cannot be managed as a secondary task. . . . The main point of view is the *better:* the quality," Marx noted. "Only in the situation to be cited does more appear; otherwise always better."[44] Marx followed this paraphrased discussion of Plato's arguments about the division of labor in the *Republic* with an extensive excerpt of that part of Plato's dialog taken from the Greek original. Only a very small segment of the Plato citation, however, was eventually incorporated in to *Das Kapital.*[45]

Shortly after the excerpt, Marx formulated a relatively comprehensive summary of both Plato's and Xenophon's positions. Concerning Plato, Marx argued that he believed that (1) men have different abilities and some are more suited to certain types of work than others; (2) the division of labor also develops to meet a multitude of wants; (3) by specializing in a work task, one performs the work better and the quality of the work is improved; and finally (4) the division of labor frees some men for more important work in the community. Concerning Xenophon, Marx noted that "Xenophon goes further: in that he accentuates first the reduction of labor to the simplest possible activity, second, the degree to which the division of labor can be carried out is dependent on the expansion of the market."[46]

Although this ended Marx's formal discussion of the ancients, it did not end his interest in them for comparative purposes with modern writers. Immediately below the summary of Xenophon, Marx wrote "*Vgl.* [compare]."[47] The remainder of manuscript page 164 and most of 165 is filled with excerpts from Jérôme-Adolphe Blanqui, Cesare Beccaria, and William Petty to show some contemporary replications of the ancients' position on the division of labor.[48] Marx pointed out that Petty and the authors of "The advantages of the East India Trade to England considered etc. . . . 1720" differed from the ancients, however, insofar as they emphasized how the division of labor reduces the value of a commodity rather than improving the quality of the product, an idea partially taken from Stewart.[49] Marx closed the section with the following summary: "Later authors like Harris . . . only explained Plato's development further. Then Ferguson. What makes A. Smith stand out—is that he employs the phrase '*increasing the productive powers of labor.*' Since Smith found himself still in the infancy of large-scale industry, it seems to him that the machinery appears only as a corollary to the division of labor and the worker makes mechanical discoveries for it in order to lighten and shorten his labor."[50]

Fragments on the Character of the Division of Labor

From manuscript pages 166 to 174, Marx developed no lengthy, sustained arguments. Instead, he more or less recorded various quotations, made comments on themes that were only loosely related or connected, and he paraphrased summaries about particular aspects of the division of labor. The section appears a bit like a jigsaw puzzle, where one places certain pieces in proximity because it is obvious that they will eventually fit that area once more of the puzzle has been fully assembled.

Thus, for example, Marx noted that the division of labor creates a hierarchy of skill and a hierarchy of wages, but no matter how complex the division of labor becomes, the basic principle of the division of labor remains the presence of workers. This contrasts with the automatic workshop, Marx suggested, where the machine is the basic principle carrying out the various operations, and the machine operator brings little skill to the job and adds none to the final product.[51] The division of labor in the workshop creates a few organizational problems. First, workers with appropriate skills must be organized in the correct proportions to ensure smooth, efficient production. Second, proportionately more capital is consumed in the purchase of raw material because productive power has markedly increased.[52]

On manuscript page 168, Marx cited material from Francis Wayland concerning those who benefitted most from the division of labor: "the middling and lower classes" according to Wayland (which Marx refuted). He also cited the following comment from James Mill's *Élémens d'économie politique,* which is found on page 167 of Marx's draft manuscript: "For the division of labor and the distribution of human power and machines in the most advantageous manner, it is necessary that a large group of them operate on a large scale, or in other words, the production of wealth by the great masses."[53]

Predictably, Marx disagreed strongly. "The division of labor—or furthermore the workshop based on the division of labor—increases only the surplus value which falls to the capitalist . . . —or this increase of the productive power of labor proves itself to be only the productive power of capital insofar as it is employed for use values which enter into the consumption of the worker, therefore to reduce the necessary labor time for the reproduction of labor capacity."[54]

At the end of manuscript page 168, Marx drew together, to some extent, some of the loosely related material contained in this section of the manuscript.

> The ready commodity is the product of the workshop which itself is a means of the being-there [*Daseinsweise*] of capital. The exchange value of labor itself—and the labor, not its product—becomes through the means of production itself, but not only the contract between capital and labor, the only [commodity] the worker has to sell. Labor becomes in fact his only commodity and the commodity above all general category under which production [is] subsumed. We begin with the commodity as the most general category of bourgeois society. Such a general category is first changed as the means of production itself is subordinated by capital. "there [*sic*] is no longer any thing which we can call the natural reward of labor. Each laborer produces only some part of the whole, and

each part, having no value or utility itself, there is nothing on which the laborer can seize, and say: it is my product, this I will keep for myself." (p. 25 *Labour defended against the claims of Capital etc.* London. 1825.)[55]

From the top of page 169 to the middle of page 171, Marx presented a number of quotations from Henri Storch, Smith, Pierre Lemontey, Thomas Hodgskin, and his own *Misère de la philosophie* to show how the division of labor was influenced by the natural division of labor in the family, geography, improved transport, population concentration, coordination of workers with raw materials and machinery, influences of science and inventions, and authority structures both in the workshop and outside.[56] From mid-manuscript page 171 to the end of page 172 Marx argued that, concerning the division of labor, "it is thus assumed" that there will be a conglomeration of workers, a concentration of the instruments of labor, and an increase in raw materials. He elaborated on each of these points with a two- or three-paragraph summary.[57]

Concerning the conglomeration of workers, Marx noted that communication could make up for the absence of a dense population, but more important than large numbers of people was the concentration "of the purely industrial population. . . . The separation of labors, connected with agriculture, from agriculture and the restriction of agriculture—progressively—to fewer hands is the main condition for the division of labor and manufacture over all, with that it [division of labor] [is] not [found] in single spots, in scattered points, rather dominating."[58] Marx quickly traced how this led the variable capital exchanged for wage laborers to be concentrated into fewer hands. Thus, what is crucial is not only the growth of capital, but also its concentration.[59]

On the concentration of the instruments of labor, Marx argued at the outset: "*The division of labor leads to differentiation and therewith simplification of the instruments which serve as the means of labor;* therefore also to the perfection of these instruments." But insofar as the division of labor in manufacture is concerned, things remain much the same because the employment of the "means of labor, instruments of labor, instrument [*Arbeitsmittel, Arbeitswerkzeug, Instrument*] . . . depends on the personal skill [*Virtuosität*] of the individual workers." There is a differentiation of tools, but not an increase in the number; "this part of the constant capital [that is, tools] grows only in the relation to which variable capital is expended in wages, or the numbers of workers employed simultaneously by the same capital." He pointed out that just as the new concentration of instruments of labor takes place, so, too, does the development of the workshop.[60]

"The part of capital expended on raw material" Marx wrote in the section entitled "Increase of Raw Material," "grows *absolutely* against that set out in the wages of labor, in that the same quantity of raw material absorbs a smaller quantity of labor time or the same quantity of labor time realizes itself in a greater quantity of raw material."[61] This means that capitalists control more raw material within a country as well as larger quantities of raw material overall. He followed these summary statements with three points of reminder. First, Marx again noted that "*manufacture* (in distinction from the mechanical workshop or factory) is the means of production or form of industry corresponding specifically with the division of labor."[62] Second, Marx commented on the emphasis Petty and "the apologists of East India trade" put upon the division of labor cheapening commodities. This emphasis, he continued, relates to the expansion of world trade, and this point, it seems, could have been related to his points on raw material. Finally, he quoted Smith concerning how, in a civilized country, even the day laborer's coat is the product of a multitude of workers. Marx might have related this point to the section on the concentration of workers, but it also had a polemical purpose. "The whole passage [in Smith] and means of examination is copied from *Mandeville* 'Fable of the Bees'" he argued and then produced two lengthy quotations from Bernard de Mandeville to document his claim.[63]

A Return to the Alienation Theme

Following the points of reminder, Marx began an assessment of the division of labor that was once again structured within the language of the alienation problematic. This time, it is strikingly close to the perspective he adopted in the fetishism of commodities theme. "As soon as the *commodity* becomes the general form of the product, or production takes place on the basis of exchange value and therefore the exchange of commodities, first, the production of each individual becomes one-sided while his wants become many sided." Consequently, a concourse of workers is required for the production of goods to meet even the simplest of wants. More important, however, the whole circuit of materials needed for production becomes a circuit of commodities, and shortly thereafter, production "ceases to be the immediate production of the means of subsistence for individuals—[it] has become trade."[64]

This section draws on themes related to the fetishism of commodities and contains all of the elements Marx attributed to the phenomenon.

He argued in 1872, in the second German edition where the fetishism theme was presented in detail within the discussion of the commodity, that fetishism arises from the commodity form of production. In the section of the 1861–62 draft manuscript cited previously, Marx wrote about the existence of commodity production: "as soon as the *commodity* becomes the general form of the product, ... or production takes place *on the basis of exchange value* [my emphasis]." The addition indicates Marx's second point about fetishism, the role of value in production as the major concern. In 1872 he argued that "[t]he equality of the kinds of human labor takes on a physical form in the equal objectivity of the products of labor as values."[65]

In the fetishism analysis of 1872, Marx continued by pointing out that "finally, the relationship between the producers, within which the social characteristics of their labors are manifested, take on the form of a social relation between the products of labor." Although there is no equivalent general statement of this sort in the 1861–62 discussion, there is a statement of the particular relationship between producers and products. Marx argued in 1861–62 that "the production of each individual becomes one-sided while his wants become many sided," thus indicating a particular manifestation of what happens to workers once "the definite social relation between men themselves ... assumes, for them, the fantastic form of a relation between things."[66] Once an abstract, humanly created form, the value form of the commodity, dominates production, then the relations of workers become the relation of things and they are conglomerated into a division of labor that simplifies work tasks and turns out products more quickly and inexpensively. The workers become cogs in a machinelike process. I raise this connection with the fetishism theme at this point not because I believe Marx had worked through his position so fully that his 1861–62 analysis of the division of labor was couched in fetishism's analytic terms, but only to indicate that as he consciously or subconsciously replaced the general alienation theme with the particular fetishism framework, it is possible to see other areas of his analysis slowly move into the new problematic as well.

Marx essentially ended this analysis of the relationship between commodity production and the division of labor by arguing that the viewpoint of Mandeville and others shows nothing more than the fact that "the *commodity* is the general form of bourgeois wealth." He continued the paragraph with a lengthy set of statements that again pointed out that commodity production assumes a "universal [*allseitige*] division of labor" but did not complete his analysis. He wrote, "the general opposition of the products as commodities presupposes the opposition of the activities producing them. Such an examination [is] thus historically important" and left the remainder of manuscript page 174 blank.[67]

The Division of Labor within the History of Bourgeois Society

Manuscript page 175 marks the beginning of notebook 5. The first material presented in the *MEGA* publication of the 1861–62 manuscript, however, comes from manuscript page 179, which contains a number of quotations from various authors. Marx had written "to p. 175, beginning"[68] beside a quotation taken from Stewart that claimed that even in the 1850s some peasants in the Scottish highlands were virtually self-sufficient.[69] The theme Marx examined on page 179 concerned various stages in the development of society. His decision to move this quotation ahead seems to indicate somewhat of a chronological order to stages of social development. Below the intended insert, Marx admonished Smith for not "comprehending sharply and determinately the division of labor as a specific capitalist means of production," although Smith had seen the division of labor as part of manufacture and thus shown that "in his time the modern factory [*Fabrikwesen*] was conceived in origin [*Entstehen*],"[70] but this was all Smith had grasped— manufacture and not large-scale industry. Marx supported his assessment with the following quotation from Andrew Ure.

> "At the time Smith wrote his immortal work on the elements of political economy, the automatic system of industry was scarcely thought of. The division of labor seemed to him with good reason the great principle of improvement in manufacture. . . . But what was able to serve as a useful example in the time of Dr. Smith will not be so today: it leads the public to err relative to the real principle of modern industry. . . . The scholastic dogma of the division of labor according different degrees of skill has been well exploited by our enlightened manufacturers" (*Andrew Ure* Philosophie des manufactures etc. V. I, ch. I) (1853 first to appear).[71]

On the rest of page 175, Marx elaborated on this comment and on another by Ure to show that labor capacity, in the division of labor, is "appropriate for a particular operation" and that "the basis of the operation itself remains human bodies. . . . The operations themselves are being accommodated to the natural and acquired competencies in their separation. It is not the dissolution of the process to its mechanical inciples, rather a dissolution with respect to it that these single processes must be carried out as functions of human labor capacity."[72]

The importance of this distinction is that Marx himself accepted it as the objective basis with which to distinguish the division of labor and manufacture from the machine-based production of large-scale industry.

Below the comments on Ure, Marx drew a line to signify a definite break in his analysis. In the section below the line, he turned to the notes Germain Garnier had compiled to his translation of Smith's work. The Garnier comments are in part a minor excursus within this loosely unified section on the relationship between the division of labor and the developmental stages of bourgeois society, although Marx's citations quickly bring the analysis back to some historical and developmental material.

Marx began the section on Garnier by noting that Garnier had declared himself in opposition to Smith's recommendations for a national system of instruction for all people and went on to note that "a few of his remarks are good to note here."[73] The remarks Marx excerpted on the one hand showed a negative side to the division of labor that Garnier had written about but not commented upon or viewed negatively. On the other hand, they fit into the developmental theme that Marx was establishing in this section of his 1861–62 draft manuscript. "'The work which nourishes, dresses and lodges the totality of the population of a country is a charge imposed on the society *en masse* but which it naturally *casts upon* only a portion of its members.' (p. 2 l.c.) And the greater the industrial development of the society" Marx interpolated between quotations from Garnier, "the more its material demands grow."[74] Citing Garnier again, Marx wrote:

> and as a result there is work producing for them [the demands], preparing for them (the means of life on the whole) and drawing the consumers closer. *At the same time*, however, and *as a result of the same progress*, the *class* of people freed from these manual labors, grows in its proportion with the other class. Thus the one has consequently at the same time, more people to provide for a more abundant, and more elaborate provision to furnish to each of them. . . . [T]he man devoted to a mechanical profession has *less time to save*. The more the society enriches itself, the more time the worker creates value. . . . Consequently, the more society advances toward a state of splendor and power, *the less time the working class has to give to study and intellectual and speculative labors.*[75]

Marx also cited Garnier's favorable comments that as the work shifted increasingly to productive workers, the opportunity existed for others to develop such components of a civilized society as philosophy, literature, sales, and transport of commodities, and this led Garnier directly into the development theme. "Like all of the other divisions of labor, the one between mechanical work and intellectual work pronounces most strongly and trenchantly an indication of how advanced a society is toward wealth. This division, like all others, is a result of a past progress and the cause of progress to come."[76]

Marx made no further commentary to the Garnier excerpts although it is quite clear from the entire context of the division of labor section in the 1861–62 manuscript that he had selected these observations for critical commentary at a later date. Again, these excerpts show how Marx used this draft to draw together into a partially organized structure a variety of materials on the division of labor theme. In *Das Kapital,* despite the wealth of material cited here, only one quotation was used as Marx criticized Garnier's position on education and the consequences of the division of labor.

Contradictions and Antagonism within the Division of Labor

Marx's next paragraph begins a summary of the development and impact of the division of labor. As the mass of production increases and the number of workers remains constant, the extension and intensity of labor time increases. Handwork and crafts soon fall under the control of capital, and workers and children are employed as cheaper sources of labor. "The development of productive powers under the regime of capital increases the mass of the annually produced means of life and cheapens it so that the *average wage* can be calculated on a greater scale of the reproduction of workers, although it sinks in value, represents smaller quantity of materialized labor."[77] Although this seems to portray development, things are not what they appear.

> [T]he conglomeration and separation from all other enjoyments of life, the complete hopelessness to reach a higher social position and a certain trustworthy decorum, the emptiness of his whole life, the inter-breeding of the sexes in the workshop, the isolation of the worker himself, all contribute to early marriage. The shortening and almost abolition of necessary time to learn, the early age at which children themselves can appear as producers, the reduction of the time thus in which they must be supported increases the stimulus to accelerate human production. If the average age of the generation of workers decreases then there is always an overflowing and constantly rising mass of short living generations on the market and that is all that capitalist production wants.[78]

The next long paragraph points out further contradictions in the growth of wealth through capital. As wealth grows, so does poverty; as the mass of workers grows, so does the stratification of workers; as mass of commodities grows, so does the mass of value and surplus labor; and as the mass of workers grows absolutely, it decreases relative to constant capital.[79] All of page 179, plus a segment from 178 later marked as pertinent to page 179, either presents quotations elaborating upon these points or repeats the same arguments.[80]

Manuscript pages 180 and 181 contain quotations from Smith and Thomas Hodgskin on the same theme, none subsequently used in *Das Kapital,* and Marx questioned how Smith could believe that as the division of labor increased productivity, so would the number of workers employed. If productivity increased, Marx argued, then fewer workers would be needed to produce the same number of goods.

What is more important than the content of either the Smith quotations or Marx's criticisms is what they indicate about how Marx worked. All three of the quotations had been excerpted in Marx's study notebooks of 1844.[81] In addition, he used these quotations in his Paris draft manuscript[82] and placed the first one into his citation notebook.[83] Thus, Marx's study notebooks were enduring sources of reference; when preparing some of his later works, he was not afraid to rely on them for information to develop his arguments. The use of the Smith quotations in several places also suggests that Marx used drafts as an opportunity to assemble material into an ordered framework without necessarily polishing it at that moment. The 1861–62 draft manuscript analysis of the division of labor, when compared to earlier notebooks and drafts as well as *Das Kapital,* shows quite clearly how much material Marx had to work with and how he set it out in different orders of progression to polish it for subsequent publication. All of these mechanical aspects to his methodology influenced how the critique finally took shape.

Following the Smith excerpts, Marx again excerpted from Ferguson. He did not use the citation in *Das Kapital,* but it clearly captures many of the ideas discussed in this section and shows a continuity of perception about work under capitalist conditions, which Marx first began to express in 1844 and continued to work on in his analysis of *Das Kapital.*

> In the progress which makes *the division of labor,* the occupation of the most important portion of those who live through work, that is to say, the mass of the people, is restricted to a very small number of simple operations, very often to one or two. Well, the intelligence of the greater part of men is necessarily formed by their daily occupation. A man who spends all of his life filling a small number of simple operations experiences effects that are also possibly always the same or about the same as not developing his intelligence nor training his imagination to seek

the right circumstances to avoid difficulties, who has never encountered it; he therefore naturally loses his aptitude to deploy or train his capacities and he becomes in general so stupid and ignorant that it is not possible for him to become human; the numbness of his moral capacities, . . . the uniformity of his sedentary life naturally corrupts, . . . it degrades at the same time the activity of his body and renders it incapable of deploying his power with vigor and steadfastness in all other employment to which he was raised. Thus his dexterity in his particular occupation is a quality 'that seems to have been acquired at the expense of his intellectual qualities, his social virtues and his warrior disposition. This condition is that of the poor worker that is to say [the condition to which] the mass of the people must necessarily fall in all civilized societies that are advanced industrially.[84]

Marx's Concluding Comments on the Division of Labor

On the remainder of manuscript page 183 through almost the end of page 188, Marx wrote a closing section to his study of the division of labor. "What strikes us about the division of labor," he began, "as with all forms of capitalist production, is the character of the antagonism." Marx had three particular antagonisms or contradictions in mind. First, in the workshop, workers are "quantitatively distributed according to certain proportional numbers," but in terms of the social division of labor, workers are distributed according to the law of supply and demand.[85] "Without entering further into this point" Marx noted, "the difference of this anarchic division within the society compared to the fixed, enduring [division] within the workshop is obvious."[86]

Second, "within the society are different lines of business which themselves represent purely different phases of production through which a product must pass in order to obtain its finished form."[87] But within the workshop itself, the product progresses without the mediation of exchange. Thus, parts of the production process proceed immediately from one phase to the next, while other parts and phases are mediated by exchange on the market.

The third antagonism Marx indicated relates to the appearance of freedom and constraint in the division of labor within the workshop and in society as a whole. "Within the workshop, the different operations [are] systematically divided according to a plan and different workers are divided according to a rule which stands opposite them like a coercive, estranged law imposed on them from the outside." But "within the society, on the other hand, the division of labor appears free, i.e. fortuitous, thus combined through an inner inter-relation but which likewise presents itself as the product of conditions like the discretion of the commodity producers independently of one another."[88] Both, however, condition each other and develop one another, thus they only appear as antagonistic.

After outlining these three points, Marx went back to the opening theme of *Zur Kritik*—"the commodity, as the most elementary form of wealth was our departure point"—and drafted a cursory summary of some of the main points of development leading from the commodity to the division of labor issue. He pointed out, among other things, that commodities and money are "both the elementary means of the being-there [*Daseinsweise*], means of existence of capital."[89] Capital formation takes place on the basis of commodity production and circulation, and once the commodity becomes the general form of all products, even those goods needed for subsistence and for production assume the form of commodities. Nevertheless, Marx emphasized, "[t]he transformation of money—which itself [is] only a transformed form of the commodity—to capital only takes place as soon as labor capacity (not the worker) is transformed to a commodity."[90] He also noted within this cursory overview that the social division of labor, which eventually produces and mutually develops the capitalist division of labor in the workshop, is presupposed by all these developments.

Marx's comments on the division of labor were not all critical. He pointed out that capitalist production and the division of labor in the workshop increase the social division of labor by increasing productivity and freeing labor time for the pursuit of new wants. They also allow for an increase in the population "through the cheapening of the means of life required for the reproduction and duplication of labor capacity." Finally, the surplus value created by the division of labor is invested in the production of many diverse use values.[91]

However, Marx spent more time critically examining the impact of the division of labor on workers' lives. In the bulk of the remainder of his concluding section, he placed the division of labor within the fetishism theme. Marx argued that where the commodity becomes the dominant form of the product and individuals no longer produce only products—that is, use values or means of subsistence—but produce use values as the material carriers of exchange value, then individual relationships progressively become those of purchaser and seller. "The *social* form of their product and their production, i.e. the social relationships in which the commodity producers as such appear, are now only the representations of their product as *commodity* and *money* and the act, movement in which it [the product] assumes the alternating different determinations, sale and purchase."[92] At the bottom of manuscript page 187, he noted that "the *social* relationship in which commodity owners appear is the representation of their product as commodity and money and the movement in which they stand opposite one another [is] as carriers of the metamorphosis of commodities."[93] Marx argued that this relation of purchase and sale constrains freedom because in order for exchange to take place, the commodity must be a use value for the society and not require more than the socially necessary labor time for its production. Thus the production of products as commodities conditions the social division of labor.

> On the other hand: [where] the product assumes only generally the form of the commodity—the relation of the producers to one another as seller and purchaser become only the social interconnection controlling them,—where labor capacity itself has become a commodity for its owner, the worker has therefore become wage-labor and money has become capital. The social interconnection between the owner of money and the worker is thus only that of commodity owners. The relation modifies itself, brings forth new social relations through the specific nature of the commodity which the worker has to sell and the characteristic manner in which the purchaser consumes it. . . . Capitalist production entails with it, among other things, the division of labor within the workshop, which [is] like the other means of production employed by capital, that further develops mass production, therefore the similarity of the use value of the product for the producers, production for mere sale of the product as pure commodity.[94]

As a result, the apparently unregulated division of labor within society is linked to the systematic, rule-regulated division of labor within the workshop, and both mutually develop one another.[95]

Considerations on the 1861–62 Manuscripts

By the end of the 1861–62 draft manuscript, Marx had developed his analysis of the division of labor well beyond his previous discussions to include far more substantive material concerning the alienated conditions under which workers labored. He also had assembled a large body of documentation supporting his numerous arguments on the division of labor. Furthermore, Marx had focussed upon a few of the specific contradictions and antagonisms created by the division of labor. Finally he had established a conscious separation of the division of labor in manufacture from that of large-scale industry.

Close examination of the text reveals a number of features of Marx's intellectual labor process. First, as the inclusion of the material on the ancients indicates, he actively pursued new knowledge and material right up to the time he was drafting what was intended to be a publishable manuscript. This was a practice Engels had complained about in the early 1850s, but Marx continued to follow it throughout the 1860s and even into the 1870s as new references to *La richesse des nations* for *Le capital* indicate.

Second, the inclusion of the material on the ancients also demonstrates that Marx's knowledge interests clearly attuned him to points relevant to his rapidly expanding critique of political economy. As he read and excerpted, he had particular aspects of his critique in mind and was able to connect what others had written to his own critique. Thus, the use of Stewart's reference to the ancients was included in a section in Marx's analysis of the division of labor that might not otherwise have been developed. The material also shows Marx's thoroughness in tracing ideas to their sources and following various arguments fully through.

Third, the text shows that Marx put order into his work by constructing a loosely connected draft that contained a wide range of completeness. Parts of the manuscript contained well-developed arguments, but other parts were more or less collections of quotations or commentary that required much more work. Based on the state of the 1861-62 manuscript, Marx either intentionally deceived Lassalle in October 1858 about how soon the second part of *Zur Kritik* would be ready, or, given his capacity for intellectual labor, he simply overestimated what he could accomplish during that difficult period in his life.[96] The latter scenario seems to be most accurate; upon completion of the fifth notebook of the 1861-62 manuscript, Marx informed Kugelmann in March 1862 that the second part of *Zur Kritik* was ready, "that is up to writing [it] out clearly and polishing for publication."[97] It is apparent that Marx did not spend a great deal of time polishing his drafts; he worked quickly and moved almost immediately from a rough draft to the finished product.

Fourth, the 1861-62 draft material shows how Marx experimented with formats of presentation in his material. Frequently in this draft, he employed a style similar to a classical dialog as he paired authors against one another and thereby dialectically (in the classical sense) developed a more comprehensive representation of the division of labor. At other times, Marx developed the critique himself, the format he eventually settled upon in 1867.

Fifth, the discussion in this chapter also demonstrates that Marx's numerous study notebooks and citation notebooks were used for more than the recording and internalizing of information as he read a text. The notebooks were sources of reference as Marx worked through his draft manuscript, and it is common to find that he set quotations together that were taken from the 1840s, 1850s, and 1860s. Likewise, as in the case of Smith's work, Marx also used one set of study notes from the 1840s and another from the 1850s as sources of information. Thus, it appears that he seriously and closely read through his study notebooks when—or before—writing, and he used them as his primary sources of information rather than the original texts themselves.

The importance of this practice cannot be stressed too strongly because it meant that Marx's reading interests while reading a text, and the state of his knowledge interests at that time, influenced the quality of the material he had at his disposal as he wrote later manuscripts. Material from the early study notebooks, to be sure, was read in the 1860s from the vantage point of a broader, more comprehensive set of knowledge interests, but except for those works that Marx either read and excerpted from again—like Smith and Ricardo—some of the material in the later works was shaped to a considerable degree in the 1840s. The question to arise from this, of course, is whether Marx kept many of the same interests throughout the twenty-year span so that his reading notes from the 1840s could suffice, or whether his reading notes restricted the development of his ideas. I think it is clear from the return to some sources in the 1850s and 1860s that the reading notes did not, in any way, restrict Marx's conceptions of capital, capitalism, or capitalist society. Instead, many early concerns such as the alienation theme remained relevant, and his later work merely deepened and sharpened his insight into those problems.

NOTES

1. Karl Marx and Friedrich Engels, *Gesamtausgabe: Werke, Artikel, Entwürfe* [hereafter cited as *MEGA*] (Berlin: Dietz Verlag, 1975ff), II, 3.1 p. 237:28.
2. *MEGA* II, 3.1, pp. 237:29–238:3.
3. Ibid., p. 238:18–19, 21–26.
4. Ibid., pp. 238:26, 238:30.
5. Marx's comments on the commodity produced by "a totality of particular labor" seem to have drawn his attention away from the central point of his argument for a moment as he made the following points about the commodity. "The being-there of a use value as commodity does not depend on the nature of this use value, thus also not on the character [*Gestalt*] it has from near or far, or whether it finally enters consumption as a means of labor or means of life. It depends only hence that a determinate quantity of labor time is represented in this product and that it is the material for the satisfaction of a certain want, whether that is the want of a later production process or the consumption process." Ibid., p. 238:32–39. Marx returned the focus to the division of labor with the following linking sentence. "If on that account," he

wrote, "the pressed cotton appears on the market as a *commodity* as soon as it has passed through the process of spinning, weaving, and pressing, then it would be produced through a *division* of labor." Ibid., p. 238:39–41.

6. Ibid., p. 241:1–4, 12–15.

7. Ibid., p. 241:39–40; see pp. 241:16–242:4 for the full development of this idea.

8. Ibid., p. 242:5–7. Marx notes on manuscript page 151, "A. Smith does not distinguish between the division of labor in both senses. The latter division of labor appears with him therefore also not as something specific to capitalist production" (p. 243:9–11).

9. Ibid., p. 242:11–23. As if the point were still not clear, Marx noted halfway through the next manuscript page: "The first is the division of social labor in different branches of labor; the other [is] the division of labor in the manufacture of a commodity, thus the division of labor not in the society rather social division of labor within one and the same workshop [*Ateliers*]. The division of labor in the latter sense corresponds to *manufacture,* as a particular *means of production*" (p. 243:3–8).

10. Ibid., p. 242:23–27. Several paragraphs later, Marx notes that Smith "does not distinguish the division of labor in the two senses" (p. 243:9). Marx presents a series of quotations from *La richesse des nations* to support this claim (p. 243:14–41) and concludes with a specific statement about Smith that makes, in a negative fashion, the point about the particular, capitalist nature of the division of labor in manufacture. "Smith comprehends the division of labor thus not as [a] particular, specifically different form characteristic of the *capitalist* means of production" (p. 244:16–18).

Before entering into the Smith excursus, however, Marx wrote the following (pp. 242:28–243:2), which began as a summation of his major point in the section. It soon developed, however, another side of the relationship between the two types of the division of labor. "It is clear that this division of labor presupposes the social division of labor. First, from the particularity of social labor developing in the exchange of commodities, the branches of labor separate themselves so far that each particular branch is to be traced back to the special labor, in which now the division within this special labor can take place in its analysis. 2) it is also clear that the second division of labor conversely must expand the first—rebounding. *First,* insofar as it is common with all other productive powers it has to reduce the labor required for a determinate use value, thus free to posit labor for a new branch of social labor. Second, and this is specific to it, insofar as it can split in its analysis a specialty, so that the different *component parts of the same use value* are now produced as different commodities independent of one another or also that the *different types of the same use value,* which earlier fell to the same spheres of production, now through the analysis of the individual spheres of production are falling to different spheres of production."

11. *MEGA* II, 3.1, p. 244:19–27.

12. Ibid., p. 245:2–4.

13. Ibid., p. 246:29–34. Marx refers to the East India essay later in the

manuscript and cites it in *Das Kapital.* Karl Marx, *Das Kapital,* 1st ed. (Hamburg: Otto Meissner, 1867), pp. 321–29, 327–37. The reference in the 1861–62 manuscripts occurs in a comparison between Petty's view of the division of labor and that of the ancient Greeks. Petty differs from the Greeks because he sees the division of labor reducing the value of a commodity. Marx continues this idea by stating, "the same viewpoint is expressed, more decidedly, about the reduction of the labor time necessary for the production of a commodity is made effectively in *The Advantages of the East India Trade to England, considered, etc London. 1720."* *MEGA* II, 3.1, p. 261:20–23.

14. Ibid., pp. 246:35–247:27.

15. The quotations are found in ibid., pp. 247:27–35, 247:35–40 (not excerpted in 1844), 248:2–6 (excerpted in German in 1844, cf. MEGA IV, 2, p. 335:3–9), 248:10–14, 248:15–17, 248:21–23 (not excerpted in 1844, cf. p. 335), 248:28–36 (not excerpted in 1844, cf. ibid., p. 336:39–40), 248:36–38, and 248:39–249:1 (cf. p. 337:33–40). This documents that Marx used his study notebook material as a lasting resource and referred either directly to the original notebook or to one of his citation notebooks that contained selections from his study notebooks. It also shows that Marx had read through Smith again between 1844 and 1861 and would do so again before *Das Kapital.*

16. Marx's summary statements basically repeat ideas he has already set out. "*Spontaneous [Naturwüchsige] division of labor* leads to exchange and this exchange of products as commodities develops itself first *between different communities [Gemeinwesen], not within the same community [Gemeinwesens]* (based in part not only on the spontaneous [*Naturwüchsigen*] differences of men themselves, but naturally [*natürlichen*], the natural [*natürlichen*] elements of production which these various communities [*Gemeinwesen*] come upon). The development of products to commodities and commodity exchange reacts upon to be sure reacting on the division of labor so that exchange and division work in relation of the effect of exchange.

"Smith's chief service with the division of labor is that he makes and stresses the point that [the division of labor works] directly as productive power of labor (i.e. capital). With his conception he is dependent on the then existing developmental stages of *manufacture* which is still very different from the modern factory. Therefore also the relative predominance that the division of labor is given over machinery which only appears in its [division of labor] appendage." *MEGA* II, 3.1, p. 249:4–19.

17. Ibid., p. 249:20–23. On the previous manuscript page, Marx made essentially the same point. "A. Smith remarks that if on the one hand the division of labor [is] the product, result of the natural differences of human abilities, in the final result [the differences] are a much higher degree the result of the development of the division of labor. Here he follows his teacher Ferguson" (p. 248:24–27). Marx supported this with two citations from *La richesse des nations,* one not excerpted in 1844 (p. 248:36–38) and the other a more complete excerpt than found in the study notebook of 1844. Cf. *MEGA* II, 3.1, p. 248:28–36 with *MEGA* IV, 2, p. 336:39–40. Throughout these manuscripts, Marx used a French translation of Ferguson's work. *Essai sur*

l'histoire de la société civile, trans. Bergier (Paris: 1783) obviously postdates *The Wealth of Nations,* but the English edition of *An Essay on the History of Civil Society* (1776, repr. New York: Garland Publishing, 1971) predates Smith's work by almost a decade.

18. *MEGA* II, 3.1, pp. 249:23–250:11.

19. Ibid., p. 250:12–13.

20. Ibid., p. 250:15–26; Ferguson, *Essay on the History of Civil Society,* p. 280. Marx uses part of this quotation in *Das Kapital* (p. 347) within his discussion of the division of labor comparing Smith and Ferguson. He also cites the following comment by Ferguson, but only in the 1861–62 manuscript: "The nations dedicated to industry are approaching the point of being composed of members who, except for their occupations, are completely ignorant of all things in life." *MEGA* II, 3.1, p. 251:3–5.

21. Ibid., p. 250:27–29. Marx also cites the following from Ferguson: "In fact, of industry itself, the manufacturer is able to cultivate his mind while that of the subordinate worker is left to lie fallow. . . . The officer is able to become very skillful in the art of war while all the worth of the soldier is restricted to a few movements of the foot and hand. *The one gains what the other loses* [Marx's emphasis]" (p. 250:29–33). This idea links directly to Weber's concept of alienation; see Hans Gerth and C. Wright Mills, eds., *From Max Weber: Essays in Sociology* (Oxford: Oxford University Press, 1949), pp. 46–54, 70–74.

22. *MEGA* II, 3.1, p. 251:3–5, 6–11.

23. Ibid., p. 251:19–30. Marx's emphases from "process" to "operations."

24. Ibid., pp. 251:37–252:4, Marx's emphases. Marx noted with particular reference to the Stewart quotation that "it is thus not only the observation 2) of Smith, that with the movement from one operation to another [by] the same worker, which the circuit of the different operations runs through, [that] costs time." Ibid., p. 252:5–7. Smith saw three advantages to the division of labor: increased dexterity of the worker, decreased time lost moving from "one species of work to another" and the invention of machines. Adam Smith, *An Inquiry into the Nature and Causes of the Wealth of Nations,* vol. 2 of the Glasgow Edition of the *Works and Correspondence of Adam Smith,* ed. Roy Hutcheson Campbell and Andrew Skinner (Indianapolis: Liberty Press, 1976), pp. 17–20.

25. MEGA II, 3.1, p. 252:12–13, 20–23, 39–253:2.

26. Ibid., pp. 253:10–11, 253:13–15, 253:18, 253:25–27, 253:27–28.

27. Ibid., pp. 246:29–33, 253:29–38.

28. Ibid., p. 254:9–10, 23–31.

29. Ibid., p. 245:32–35. The phrases are extracted from Stewart's criticisms of Smith's advocacy of the division of labor. Marx, apparently, was not impressed with Stewart's criticisms because they do not appear either explicitly or implicitly in either the 1861–62 draft or *Das Kapital,* which is somewhat surprising given some of Stewart's points. In *Lectures on Political Economy,* ed. William Hamilton, vol. 8 of *The Collected Works of Dugald Stewart* (Edinburgh: Thomas Constable, 1855), Stewart first argued that Smith made too much of the advantages gained from the division of labor. "That the rapidity of the

hand in executing a mechanical operation, may be increased with practice to a very great degree, is an acknowledged fact. But there is obviously a limit beyond which this rapidity cannot possibly be carried; and I am inclined to think, that in such very simple operations as drawing out wire, &c, it is not very long before this ultimatum in point of rapidity is reached by the workman" (p. 314). For Stewart's full critique of Smith, see pp. 314–18.

30. *MEGA* II, 3.1, p. 254:36–40. Actually, Hamilton, the editor of Stewart's works, supplied all of these maxims. Stewart had cited the commonsense maxim "A Jack of all trades is master of none," and Hamilton noted "Indeed, all languages have a corresponding proverb." He supplied three from Latin—two of which Marx cited—and one from *Margites.* To this Greek citation, Hamilton noted, "And to this line, certainly, Mr. Stewart here makes reference." See Dugald Stewart, *Lectures on Political Economy,* p. 315. Marx, also drew on his knowledge of the classics and cited Homer's Odyssey—"Different men take joy in different works"—and Sextus Empiricus' *Adversus mathematicus*—"Everyone refreshes his mind with different work"—to counter one set of maxims with another; MEGA II, 3.1, pp. 254:41–255:2.

31. *MEGA* II, 2, p. 441.

32. *MEGA* II, 3, p. 2861.

33. *MEGA* II, 3.1 p. 255:3–6.

34. Marx, *Das Kapital,* 1st ed., p. 352 n80.

35. Cf. Stewart, *Lectures on Political Economy,* pp. 311–12, to *MEGA* II, 3.1, pp. 255:30–256:31.

36. The Xenophon excerpt is from page 175 as opposed to pages 148–49 where the Stewart notes are concentrated; see *MEGA* II, 3, p. 2861 for the location of each set of excerpts.

37. Marx was certainly aware that the Greeks' contribution to political economy existed. Say, whom Marx read in 1844, for example, discussed the Greeks' contribution to political economy in the introduction to his *Traité,* although it was largely in dismissive terms; see Jean-Baptiste Say, *Treatise on Political Economy or the Production, Distribution and Consumption of Wealth,* 6th ed., trans. C. R. Princep (Philadelphia: Grigg and Elliott, 1846), pp. xxviii–xxix.

38. Stewart, *Lectures on Political Economy,* p. 312.

39. *MEGA* II, 3.1, p. 255:15–23.

40. Ibid., p. 255:25–31.

41. Stewart, *Lectures on Political Economy,* p. 311.

42. *MEGA* II, 3, p. 3132.

43. *MEGA* II, 3.1, p. 256:32–38. Marx cites this segment from Harris in *Das Kapital* (p. 351) at the end of note 77. "The whole argument, to prove society natural (namely through 'the division of employments' [Marx's insertion]) is taken from the second of Plato's republic [*sic*]." In the same note, Marx also cited Cesare Beccaria's *Elementi di Economia* edited by Custodi, vol. 11, *Parte Moderna.* The same excerpt is contained in the 1861–62 manuscripts two paragraphs after Marx's discussion of the ancients. "Everyone knows from experience that if the hands and intelligence are always applied to the same kind of work and the same products, these will be produced more easily, in

greater abundance and in higher quality than if each individual makes for himself the things he needs. . . . In this way, men are divided up into various classes and conditions, to their own advantage and to that of the community." Karl Marx, *Capital*, vol. 1, trans. Ben Fowkes (Harmondsworth: Pelican Books, 1976), p. 486 n54. The summary is almost exactly the same as the one Marx draws from Plato.

44. *MEGA* II, 3.1, p. 257:24-27, 31-32.

45. Compare *MEGA* II, 3.1, p. 258:4-8 with *Das Kapital*, p. 352 n80.

46. *MEGA* II, 3.1, pp. 259:24-37, 258:30-259:6, 38-41.

47. Ibid., p. 260:1.

48. Ibid., pp. 260:2-261:23. Marx's excerpts on Petty are contained in one of his Manchester study notebooks, dated July 1845, and his excerpts from Blanqui and Beccaria are found in study notebook 7 of the 1859-63 period; see *MEGA* II, 3, pp. 3140, 3125-26.

49. Cf. Stewart, *Lectures on Political Economy*, p. 311.

50. *MEGA* II, 3.1, p. 261:23-34, Marx's emphasis. The full title to Book 1 in *The Wealth of Nations* is "Of the Causes of Improvement in the productive Powers of Labor, and of the Order according to which its Produce is naturally distributed among the different Ranks of the People" (p. 13). Smith begins Book 1, chapter 1 with the comment that "[t]he greatest improvement in the productive powers of labor, and the greater part of the skill, dexterity, and judgement with which it is any where directed, or applied, seem to have been the effects of the division of labor" (p. 13).

51. *MEGA* II, 3.1, p. 262:4-33.

52. Ibid., pp. 262:34-263:36.

53. Ibid., pp. 264:10-15; 264:31-265:3; Marx first excerpted the Mill quotation in his 1844 study notebook; see *MEGA* IV, 2, p. 428:7-16.

54. *MEGA* II, 3.1, p. 264:16-23.

55. Ibid., p. 265:16-30; cf. Marx, *Das Kapital*, p. 339 n54. Marx followed this statement and quotation with another, not used in *Das Kapital*, taken from page 82 of Simonde Sismondi, *Études sur l'économie politique*, vol. 1 (Brussels, 1837): "The progress of wealth led to the divisions of conditions and thus professions; it is not the *excess* of each that was the object of exchange, but the *subsistence itself*. . . . [I]n that new condition, the life of everyone who works and produces depends not on the completion and the success of his work but its *sale*." *MEGA* II, 3.1, p. 265:30-35, Marx's emphases.

56. Ibid., pp. 265:40-268:27. The quotations from Storch, Smith, and Hodgskin are from Marx's Brussels study notebook of 1845, London study notebook 7 of 1851, and London study notebook 9 of 1851; *MEGA* II, 3, pp. 3132-33, 3146-47.

57. *MEGA* II, 3.1, pp. 268:29-269:23, 269:23-270:3, 270:4-23.

58. Ibid., p. 269:1, 6-10. Immediately after this comment, Marx noted, within a set of square brackets, "This all belongs in *Accumulation*."

59. Ibid., p. 269:11-23.

60. Ibid., p. 269:25-29, 34-40.

61. Ibid., p. 270:4-8.

62. Ibid., p. 270:23-25.

63. Ibid., p. 270:38–271:41. Marx was not the only person to point out this plagiarism, although he may have been the first. Cf. Smith, *The Wealth of Nations*, pp. 13–14 n1. The editors of this edition of the *The Wealth of Nations* show quite clearly how much Smith was influenced by Mandeville on a number of points in the first chapter of *The Wealth of Nations;* see notes 19, 22, 25, and 28 on pp. 20, 21, 22, and 24.

64. *MEGA* II, 3.1, p. 272:17–18.

65. Karl Marx, *Das Kapital,* 2d ed. (Hamburg: Otto Meissner, 1873), p. 48.

66. *MEGA* II, 3.1, p. 272:1–5; Marx, *Das Kapital,* 2d ed., p. 49.

67. *MEGA* II, 3.1, pp. 272:34–35, 273:4–6.

68. *MEGA* II, 3, p. 2492.

69. *MEGA* II, 3.1, p. 273:10–19.

70. Ibid., p. 273:24–28.

71. Ibid., p. 273:30–38.

72. Ibid., p. 274:18–22.

73. Ibid., p. 274:24–28.

74. Ibid., p. 274:29–33.

75. Ibid., pp. 274:33–275:5, Marx's emphases.

76. Ibid., p. 275:15–19.

77. Ibid., pp. 275:38–276:2.

78. Ibid., p. 276:5–17. Marx emphasized the final sentence of the citation with a vertical line in the margin of his notebook.

79. Ibid., pp. 276:18–277:2.

80. Ibid., pp. 277:3–278:19.

81. See *MEGA* IV, 2, p. 358:4–20, replicated in *MEGA* II, 3.1, p. 278:23–41; cf. *MEGA* IV, 2, p. 358:20–33 with *MEGA* II, 3.1, pp. 279:6–9, 279:14–21.

82. *MEGA* I, 2, pp. 223:15–225:3.

83. *MEGA* II, 3, p. 2869.

84. *MEGA* II, 3.1, pp. 279:32–280:9.

85. Ibid., p. 284:5–8.

86. Ibid., p. 284:21–24.

87. Ibid., p. 284:25–27.

88. Ibid., pp. 285:35–38, 286:3–7.

89. Ibid., p. 286:16–18.

90. Ibid., p. 287:3–5.

91. Ibid., p. 287:38–41.

92. Ibid., p. 288:15–20.

93. Ibid., p. 288:27–30.

94. Ibid., p. 289:24–39.

95. Marx reaffirms this point by indicating that in the absence of capitalist development, the social division of labor does not develop as fully as in its presence; Ibid., p. 290:5–13.

96. Karl Marx and Friedrich Engels, *Werke* [hereafter cited as *MEW*] (Berlin: Dietz Verlag, 1956–90), 29:613.

97. *MEW* 30:639.

FOUR

FROM ABSTRACT TO CONCRETE

In mid-March 1862, at the end of his lengthy section on the creation of surplus value, Marx broke off his discussion of machinery on manuscript page 211 of notebook 5 and left the remaining eight pages blank.[1] Shortly thereafter, he began what eventually became a fourteen-notebook, nine-month-long excursus on the history of political economists' views on surplus value.[2]

At the end of that period, Marx informed Ludwig Kugelmann on December 28, 1862, that he was pleased the doctor and his friends had "taken so warm an interest" in *Zur Kritik der politischen Ökonomie.* He added that the "second part [*Teil*] is now finally ready, i.e. up to making a fair copy and the final polishing for publication." After explaining the long delay between the two parts of *Zur Kritik,* he wrote that "as soon as a clean copy (which I will begin in January 1863) is ready, I will take it to Germany, since it is easier to deal with book dealers personally."[3]

It is clear that in January 1863, Marx at least read through the five notebooks drafted between August 1861 and March 1862, although it is doubtful he ever attempted to draft a "clean copy" of the manuscript. While reading through the draft chapter on capital, it appears that he had reservations about his discussion of machinery and so, in January 1863, began to add material to his 1861–63 notebooks.[4] Marx's return to the machinery question led him into the question surrounding how one distinguishes a machine from a tool. Trying to answer this question involved not only a lengthy excursus into the history of machinery and technology, but it also created the conditions within which Marx would

101

significantly rethink his presentation of the division of labor for *Das Kapital.*

The excursus into machinery actually influenced Marx's subsequent discussions in three ways. First, Marx was influenced by Johann Poppe's mechanistic approach to the history of technology. Hans-Peter Müller, on the basis of his extensive work with Marx's study notebooks on Poppe's *Geschichte der Technologie seit der Wiederherstellung der Wissenschaften bis an das Ende des achtzehnten Jahrhunderte,* has argued that "Poppe describes the function or the employment of a determinate apparatus, process, etc., always on the basis of itself, but never within the context of the organization of society, which at any given time can first explain how it came to determine new problems, new technological demands, etc., which, with the help of new innovations, can be resolved or at least improved. Marx uncritically took the viewpoint of Poppe."[5] In other words, Marx began to stress the internal logic of mechanization after 1863 more than he had done previously. The result of this mechanistic emphasis was an implicit framework to elaborate upon the movement from cooperation to manufacture to large-scale industry (chapter 5).

The second change resulting from Marx's excursus into machinery is the development of the terms *Handwerkmässig* (handicraftlike) and *Gesamtarbeiter* (collective worker) which he subsequently incorporated into his analysis of the division of labor (chapter 5). The third impact that Marx's study of machinery had upon his study of the division of labor concerns the inclusion of significant concrete detail into his post–1863 analysis of the topic, a change in approach presented in the third section of this chapter.

Distinguishing a Tool from a Machine

On page 211 of notebook 5, Marx excerpted from, and commented on, an article from *The Times* dated November 26, 1862.[6] He also excerpted from Antoine Cherubliez's *Riche ou pauvre: Exposition succincte des causes et des effects de la distribution actuelle des richesses sociale,* in which Marx concentrated on machinery-related issues. These excerpts led to discussions of the value a machine passes on in production, profit, rate and mass of surplus value, conglomeration of workers in a workshop, and machinery within production as a whole.[7] These discussions were carried directly from notebook 5 to notebook 19, which Marx dated on the covering sheet "January 1863."[8]

Readers familiar with Marx's work will notice two things of interest in notebook 19. The first is the proportion devoted to empirically based, historical accounts of technology and machinery; the second is Marx's discussion distinguishing between a machine and a tool. He presented this point in *Das Kapital,* and it is the subject of a relatively well-known letter between him and Engels dated January 28, 1863.[9] The distinction is far from a scholastic matter, because the way it is made indicates exactly where one would locate the types and sources of change that brought it about.[10] In addition, this question in particular seems to have generated the bulk of the empirical history Marx wrote in notebook 19.[11] As a result, the issue is not only intrinsically significant but, because the resulting historical work Marx undertook throughout January 1863 affected his discussion of the division of labor, it is also of particular relevance for this analysis.

On the first manuscript page of notebook 19 (manuscript page 1159), within the context of a discussion entitled "Division of Labor and Mechanical Workshop. Tools and Machinery," Marx set up the context for his ensuing discussion about how one distinguishes a machine from a tool. He argued that the differentiation, simplification, and special-ization of the instruments of labor—"their exclusive adaptation to very simple operations"—is a "technological, material presupposition for the development of machinery as an element revolutionizing the means of production and the relations of production."[12] Marx supported the idea by citing Babbage's argument that once each particular operation is reduced, through the division of labor, to the use of a simple instru-ment, then their reunion by the action of a motor constitutes a machine.[13] One should keep in mind, however, that Babbage's com-ments were not Marx's sole source of support for this idea. He excerpted statement after statement from his freshly reread study notebooks on machinery and technology to support his conclusion. Even though Marx had written in notebook 14,[14] within the context of the real subsumption of the worker under capital, about the simplification of work tasks under the division of labor, there are some real differences between the 1862 and 1863 accounts. First, in the later account, Marx linked the simplification of tasks to production based on machinery and could thereby associate the division of labor, task simplification, and machin-ery more closely than in notebook 4. Second, he included far more empirical information in notebook 19 to demonstrate the link between the division of labor and machinery. The discussion in notebook 4 is much more deductive than that of notebook 19.

Following his citation from Babbage, Marx began to discuss how one distinguishes a machine from a tool. On manuscript page 1,160, he wrote: "One can find in English mechanics as well as political economy the opinion that a machine is not essentially distinguishable from a tool or instrument; that the latter is a simple machine and the former a complicated tool, or that they are only distinguishable as simple and assembled machinery. In this sense, even the elementary mechanical forms like lever, inclined plane, cylinder [*Rolle*] [*sic*], screw, wedge, wheel, etc. are called machines."[15] Further on, he indicated that others distinguished machines from tools by noting that the latter are moved by men and the former by some foreign, external power. "According to this opinion, a common plough, for example, is a machine while a Jenny, Mule (except those moved by selfactors [in English])[16] sewing machines, etc. and the most complicated mechanical looms, so long as they are set in motion by men themselves, are not machines."[17]

Marx continued to argue that there were two historical steps in the development of machinery. The first is the analysis of labor under different workers—the breakdown of tasks characteristic of manufacture. He noted that "[h]istorically, the overturning [of manufacture] to industry proceeds from the first form."[18] The second step relates to the tools themselves.

With regard to the first point, Marx argued on the next manuscript page and a half that machinery emerged from the simplification of tasks. Simplified tools could eventually be linked so one worker could do the work of several. Gradually the worker's role was to ensure that these complex tools worked without error, thus worker input in terms of skill was eliminated. The next step that increased the productivity of these complex tools was the development of power sources that surpassed that of the human. The historical step of note was the machine production of machinery.[19]

In essence, near the outset of his return to the machinery question in notebook 19, Marx summarized one of the major points he wanted to draw out after rereading his technological study notebooks: the major thrust behind the emergence of the industrial revolution related directly to the formation of the working machine from specialized tools developed through the division of labor. Following his lengthy empirical documentation of the simplification of tools via the division of labor and their coordination under a single prime mover, Marx returned to the same point, on manuscript page 1185 of notebook 19, almost at the close of his discussion. He quoted from, and then commented upon, a section from *The Industry of Nations:*

"In all machines there are certain parts which *actually do the work for which the machine is constructed,* the *mechanism* serving only to *produce the proper relative motion of those parts to the material upon which they operate.* These working parts are the *tools with which the machine works.* " Here we have the right answer. The tools, with which man worked, appear again in the machine, but they are now the tools with which the machine works. Through their [that is, the machines'] mechanism, such movement of the tools (performed earlier by men with the tools) is generated in order to work the material in the desired way or to bring forth the desired end. It is no longer man, rather a mechanism made by men, which handles the tools. And the man oversees the action [in English], corrects the random errors [in English] etc.[20]

Marx's Survey of the History of Technology and Machinery

Marx read through considerable empirical history by rereading his study notebooks on Babbage's *Traité sur l'économie des machines et des manufactures,* Poppe's *Geschichte der technologie seit der Wiederherstellung der Wissenschaften bis an das Ende des achtzehnten Jahrhunderte,* the second volume of *The Industry of Nations: A Survey of the Existing State of Arts, Machines, and Manufacture,* as well as other works.[21] These studies provided the empirical basis on which Marx made the analytic distinction between a machine and a tool, helped him fully grasp the concept of large-scale industry, and indicated the mechanism behind the movement from manufacture to large-scale industry.

One could substantiate the degree to which Marx dealt with empirical, historical material by quoting extensively from the study notebooks in question and from large sections of notebook 19. This seems, however, a rather cumbersome way of making the point. Instead, I have borrowed a procedure employed by Müller, who provides a good, concise indication of just how much Marx's ideas concerning machines rested on empirical material contained in the Poppe study notebooks by reproducing Marx's January 28, 1863 letter to Engels and indicating the relevant sections of the Poppe study notebook for each topic outlined to Engels. The letter encapsulates, within the context of the machinery question, the most important features of Marx's position on the interconnection of human social relationships with the development of the material means of production. In addition to indicating what material Marx had in mind with respect to Poppe's *Geschichte,* I have noted the presence of the relevant material in his draft manuscript of 1863 (that is, notebook 19) and the material from *The Industry of Nations* that Marx would have in mind. The use of this material is indicated by notes throughout the letter.

I have asked you in a previous letter[22] about selfactors [in English]. The question namely that: In what way did the so-called spinner engage *before* their discovery. The selfactor [in English] is clear to me but the previous condition is not.[23] I am inserting a few things in the section on machinery. There are a few curious questions that I ignored in the first elaboration. In order to be clear about them, I have reread entirely my notebooks [*Hefte*] (extracts) about technology and also listened to a practical (only experimental) course by Professor Willis . . . for workers. It is the same for me with mechanics as with languages. The mathematical laws I understand, but the simplest technical reality, upon which observation [*Anschauung*] is based, is more difficult for me than for the biggest louts.

You may or may not know, since the thing in itself is of no consequence, that a great debate exists about how one distinguishes a *machine* from a *tool*. The English (mathematical) machinists, in their crude way, call a tool a simple machine ["tool" to "machine" in English], and a machine a complicated tool ["machine" to "tool" in English]. The English technologists, however, who pay somewhat more attention to economics, distinguish between them (and are followed by many, by most English economists), that in the one case the motive power ["motive power" in English] derives from the human being, in the other from a natural force ["natural force" in English].[24] The German jackasses who are great in such trifles, have, therefore, concluded that a *plow* is, for example, a machine, and that the most complicated Jenny etc., insofar as it is worked by hand, is not. But there is no question now that if we take the view of the machine in its *elementary form,* the industrial revolution does not proceed from the *motive power* [but] rather by the part of the machine which the English call the *working machine* [in English] thus not, for example, by the replacement of the foot, which moves the spinning wheel, with water or steam, rather by the transformation of the immediate spinning process itself and the displacement of part of the human labor which was not purely an exertion of power ["exertion" of "power" in English] (as treading the wheel) but the processing, the direct effect exerted on the material to be processed.[25] On the other hand, it is similarly a question which, insofar as it is not treated purely about the historical development of machinery, but concerning machinery as the basis of present means of production, that the *working machine* [*Arbeitsmachine*] (for example the sewing machine) is the decisive factor[26] since as soon as this process has fallen to mechanization, everyone knows that one can, according to the dimensions of the thing, move it by hand, water or steam engine.[27]

For the pure mathematicians these questions are insignificant, but they become very important where it is a question to establish the interconnection of human social relationships with the development of material means of production.

The rereading of my technological-historical excerpts has led me to the view that, apart from the discoveries of gunpowder, the compass, and the printing press—these necessary preconditions of bourgeois development—from the 16th to the middle of the 18th century, thus for the period in which manufacture was developing from handicraft to true large-scale industry, the two material bases on which the preparations for machine industry were organized within manufacture, were the *clock,*[28] and the *mill*[29] (at first the corn mill [*Kornmühle*],[30] that is a water mill), both passed on from antiquity.[31] (The water mill was brought into Rome from the Near East in the time of Julius Caesar).[32] The clock is the first automaton applied to practical purposes, and the whole theory of production of regular motion was developed on it.[33] In the nature of things, it is itself based on the connection between semi-artistic handicraft and direct theory. Cardano, for example, wrote on (and gave practical formulae for) the construction of clocks.[34] German writers of the 16th century called clock making "learned [*Gelehrtes*] (nonguild) handicraft," and from the development of the clock it would be possible to show how different on the basis of handicraft the relation between theoretical learning and practice, as, for example, large-scale industry. There is no doubt that in the 18th century the idea of applying the automatic (that is, moved by springs) devices to production was first suggested by clocks. It can be proved historically that [Jacques de] Vaucanson's experiments in this field[35] have had an extraordinary influence on the imagination of the English inventors.

In the *mill,* on the other hand, from the very beginning, as soon as the water mill was produced, the essential distinctions in the organism of a machine [exist]. Mechanical driving power. The prime motor, on which it depends. Transmission-mechanisms ["transmission" in English].[36] Finally, the working machine, which deals with the material, all confront one another in an independent means of existence. The theory *of friction* and with it the investigations into the mathematical forms of wheel work, cogs, etc., were all made at the mill[37] ditto here first the theory of measurement of the degree of motive power,[38] of the best type, how to apply it, etc.[39] Practically, all the great mathematicians since the middle of the 17th century,[40] insofar as they occupied themselves with practical mechanics and theorized about it, proceeded from the simple water-corn mill. In fact, as a result the name *Mühle* and mill [in English] stood during the manufacturing period for all mechanical motive power adapted to practical purposes.

But with the mill, as with the press machines,[41] the forge,[42] the plow,[43] etc., from the beginning the actual work of beating, crushing, grinding, pulverizing, etc., was performed *without* human labor, even though the moving force ["moving force" in English] was human or animal. Therefore this type of machinery, at least in its origins, is very old and employed earlier with their own mechanical motive force. Therefore, almost the only machinery which existed in the manufacturing period. The *industrial revolution* begins as soon as a mechanism is employed where, from ancient times on, the final result has always required human labor; thus not where, as with tools, the actual material to be worked on has *never, from the beginning* been touched by the human hand, but where, according to the nature of the thing, man has not from the very first acted as a mere *power* [in English]. If one wants to call, along with the German jackasses, the use of animal (which is just as much *voluntary movement* as human power) power as machinery, then the use of this kind of locomotive is at any rate much older than the simplest handicraft tool.[44]

Clearly, Marx's knowledge of machinery in 1863 was based on some solid, empirically historical material.

The Inclusion of Material in *Das Kapital* from Notebook 19

The final influence that Marx's excursus into machinery and technology had on his study of the division of labor involved the incorporation of material from that excursus into the analysis presented in *Das Kapital.* In what eventually became the second and third sections of his discussion of the division of labor in *Das Kapital,* that is, the sections on the detail worker and his machine and the two basic forms of manufacture, Marx included a number of points that came directly from his 1863 reexamination of the machinery issue.[45]

The first reference occurs in a paragraph-long discussion of how productivity depends on the skill of the worker as well as the specialization of his tools. Marx argued in *Das Kapital* that

> as soon as the different operations of a labor process are separated from one another and each detail operation acquires in the hands of the detail worker, as much as possible, a corresponding and therefore most exclusive form, a change of the tools previously serving the different ends becomes necessary. The direction of their [that is, the tools] formal change comes from the solution of the particular difficulties which the unchanged form found in the way. The *differentiation* of the instrument of labor, through which instruments of the same type obtain particular, fixed forms for each particular application, and their *specialization,* whereby each such particular instrument acts only in the hand of a specific detail worker in his unique circumstances, characterizes manufacture. In Birmingham alone there are about 500 variations of hammers, of which each serves not only for a particular production process, but a number of variants often serve for various operations in the same process.[46]

The importance of the specialization of instruments of labor was originally noted at the bottom of the first manuscript page of notebook 19. At that time, Marx made the point to indicate explicitly how the division of labor laid the groundwork for the eventual emergence of machinery. "The differentiation, specialization, and simplification of the instruments of labor resulting from the division of labor in manufacture [which] is based on it [that is, the division of labor]—their

108

exclusive adaptation to very simple operations ["exclusive" to "operations" in English]—is one of the technological, material presuppositions for the development of machinery as an element revolutionizing the means of production and the relations of production."[47] When noting this in 1863, within his discussion of machinery, Marx made no notations concerning its relation to the division of labor chapter. Nevertheless, by 1867, he apparently felt that the point belonged in his discussion of the division of labor to complete his earlier conception of how the division of labor makes tasks one-sided and abstract—that is, his work in notebook 4 in 1861–62—and to set the stage for his subsequent discussion of machinery and large-scale industry in *Das Kapital.*

Concerning the first point, it is worth recalling that when writing about the reduction of work to detail labor on manuscript page 158 of notebook 4, Marx did so in relatively abstract terms. He argued that "the increased productivity and complication of the total process of production, its enrichment, is thus purchased through the reduction of labor capacity in each particular function to a purely barren abstraction—as simple property which appears in unvarying monotony in the same operation and for which the total production capacity of the worker, the manifoldness of his abilities, is confiscated."[48] In addition, he included no real empirical descriptions of the work process under manufacture and did not mention tools at all. Following his review of empirical work on machinery in 1863, he was prepared to consider the division of labor in manufacture more concretely, and the importance of the specialization of tools was much more apparent.

Concerning Marx's need to set the stage for an analysis of large-scale industry, the discussion of specialized tools represents a clear instance of how his grasp of machinery, and the points he wanted to make about it, influenced what he would highlight about the division of labor in order to present a smoothly developing, logical, and empirically informed argument.

The idea about the variety of hammers arose originally in notebook 19. On manuscript page 1177, in the context of excerpts from *The Industry of Nations,* primarily on the topic of machinery, Marx created the heading: "*Example of Specialization and Differentiation of Instruments.*"[49] The only entry under it is a quotation from *The Industry of Nations:* "It has been stated that not less than *300* varieties of hammers are made in Birmingham, each adapted to some particular trade."[50]

At the end of the section on the detail worker and his tools, Marx noted in *Das Kapital* that the "manufacturing period simplifies, improves, and multiplies the tools of labor through their adaptation to the exclusive, particular functions of the detail workers," a point supported by a reference to Darwin's *Origin of the Species.*[51] The quotation is almost exactly the same that Marx used on manuscript page 1159 of notebook 19 to begin the section entitled "Division of Labor and Mechanical Workshop. Tool and Machinery."

> I understand by low organization a small *differentiation of organs* for different, *particular performances;* thus *so long as one and the same organ has to perform various work,* one can perhaps find a ground for its variability, that natural selection so carefully preserves or represses each small deviation of form as when the *same organ is alone determined for a particular purpose.* Thus knives which are determined to cut a variety of things are on the whole thus suitable in a variety of forms, *while tools determinate for a particular use* must have for each use a different form.[52]

In other words, in 1863, Marx discussed the tool-machinery relation completely within the analysis of machinery. By 1867, even though he would not explicitly address the distinction between a tool and a machine until the section on large-scale industry, Marx introduced a few points about machinery within the context of his discussion of tool developement within the division of labor in manufacture.[53] This change in 1867 was based partly upon Marx's clearer grasp of what was most significant about machinery in 1863, and largely upon his desire to begin setting the context for his analysis of machinery within his discussion of the division of labor and machinery as he developed the analysis in *Das Kapital.*

In subsection 3 of the analysis of manufacture and the division of labor, his discussion of the two fundamental forms of manufacture, Marx included five more specific references to material he had developed in 1863 within notebook 19. The first is a point drawn directly from *The Industry of Nations* and is appropriately footnoted. In manufacture, Marx argued in *Das Kapital,* an article must be transported from one process to another, a costly limitation.[54] "The isolation of the different stages of manufacture, consequent agreement upon the employment of labour, adds immensely to the cost of production, the loss mainly arising from the mere removal from one process to another."[55] This statement from *The Industry of Nations* occurs within the context of an analysis of automated envelope manufacture.[56] Thus, even though Marx presented no empirical material behind the conclusion that the authors of *The Industry of Nations* drew, he was aware of its empirical substantiation.

The second example deals with the collective worker. Marx argued that one can view production as a series of successive steps along which, for instance, rags pass en route to becoming paper, or a piece of wire becomes a pin. One can also view production by observing the workshop as *"one* total mechanism, so one finds the raw material *simultaneously* in all its phases of production at once."[57] This latter idea was suggested to Marx when reading Stewart's *Lectures on Political Economy,* which he referenced, as well as his reading of the automatic workshop section in *The Industry of Nations.*[58] On manuscript page 1180 of notebook 19, in the midst of the paper-making example and following a discussion of the automatic production of steel pens, Marx noted: "Also *continuity of production* [in English]—(i.e. uninterruptedness of phases through which the production of raw material races.) *Automatic*—(man only to remove accidental difficulties [in English]) *Rapidity of action* [in English]. The *simultaneity of the operation* also takes place too through machinery; as if by one stroke the 'blank' in steelpen [*sic*] manufacture is cut, sliced and side slitted ["by" to "in," "is" to "slitted," in English]."[59] Marx, however, transposed this feature of the machine back into the manufacture period where it was not a machine, but the "collective worker, combined from the detail workers" which performed such continuous and contiguous productive activity.

In order for this process to take place in manufacture, work has to be coordinated so the correct proportions of workers are present in each detail task. Thus the third example of Marx including material from his notebook 19 into *Das Kapital* is his analysis of coordination and proportionality, an idea examined in a number of contexts in the 1861–62 notebooks. On manuscript page 166 of notebook 4, he cited two passages from Babbage,[60] which he subsequently used in *Das Kapital,* as well as the following unused quotation from Francis Wayland.[61]

> In establishing a manufactory, it is important so to adjust the number and kind of workmen, that, when the different operations of a process have been assigned to different persons, these persons may be in such proportions *as exactly and fully to employ each other.* The more perfectly this is accomplished, the greater will be the economy and, this is having been once ascertained, it is also evident that the establishment cannot be successfully enlarged, unless it employ multiples of this number of workmen.[62]

In *Das Kapital,* Marx introduced the problem of proportions with the comment that "[d]ifferent operations, however, require *unequal lengths of time* and therefore yield in the same time period unequal quantities of detail products."[63] This point is followed by an example of type manufacture taken from manuscript page 1184 of notebook 19, where Marx noted the process in detail.[64] Thus, even though the idea of proportionality had an earlier origin than Marx's 1863 work on machinery, his concrete grasp of the reasons behind it—reasons located within the concrete, detail work process of production—was enhanced in 1863 and allowed him to present the idea concretely through the type example.

Just before his extensive discussion of the collective worker, Marx made a paragraph-long statement that parallels a section of his January 28, 1863 letter to Engels and contains many ideas drawn from notebook 19. He argued that machinery was introduced in processes requiring great force, and included many ideas drawn from his 1863 return to the machinery question and the rereading of the early study notebooks on technology and machinery.

> So, for example, early in the manufacture of paper the crushing of the rags was done by *paper mills* and in metal factories the pounding of the ores was done by so-called *stamping mills*. The Roman empire had handed down in the *water mill* the elementary form of all machinery. The handicraft period bequeathed the great discoveries of the *compass, gun powder, the printing press,* and the *automatic clock.* On the whole, however, machinery played the subordinate part which *Adam Smith* assigns to it *next to the division of labor.* Of great importance was the sporadic use of machinery in the 17th century, because it supplied the great mathematicians of that time with practical criteria and incentive towards creating modern mechanics.[65]

The last point that can be traced to Marx's work with empirical accounts of machinery and the mechanical workshop is the notion of a hierarchy of labor powers. In *Das Kapital,* he argued that "since the different functions of the collective worker can be simple or complex, low or high," then manufacture "develops a hierarchy of labor powers" and a concomitant scale of wages. This idea was not new to Marx in 1867, or even in 1863, but his return to empirical work certainly made the point more obvious.[66] Following a review of several government reports on the factories, Marx made a lengthy analysis that compared manufacture and the automatic workshop.[67] His commentary appears to lie behind this small section of the division of labor chapter in *Das Kapital.* Among other points, he noted "[i]n manufacture, the tasks [in English] are divided according to a hierarchy of capabilities and powers according to how they are required in order to *serve* the instruments and whether the performance is easier or harder to accomplish. Determinate physical and intellectual properties of the individuals are here *seized upon* ["seized upon" in English] in order to produce through their one-sided development, the total mechanism based in manufacture on men themselves."[68]

Marx's return to the study of machinery in January 1863 was, apparently, originally intended to enhance the discussion of the machinery section of his analysis as well to resolve the question of how one distinguishes a machine from a tool. His work on machinery and technology clearly increased his knowledge of the concrete history surrounding them both. More important, however, the solution to the machine-tool issue, along with the mechanistic emphasis of Poppe's *Geschichte der Technologie*, influenced how Marx subsequently thought of the division of labor in manufacture and how he would link the historical movement from the division of labor to machinery.

Marx's return to the concrete history of technology and machinery also affected his presentation of the division of labor in *Das Kapital* by providing considerable concrete, illustrative material for his arguments. One of the major contrasts between Marx's analysis of the division of labor in 1861–62 and *Das Kapital* is the degree to which the latter's analysis is empirically substantiated. This approach in 1867, which by its concrete nature is different from the majority of analyses of the division of labor in political economy, was possible solely because of Marx's return to the machinery question in 1863.

Finally, the return to machinery is followed by the development of two new terms: *handwerkmässig* and *Gesamtarbeiter*. Both stem from the more mechanistic view Marx adopted with respect to the transition from the division of labor to machinery, an emphasis that arose from how he resolved the machine-tool distinction and Poppe's mechanistic viewpoint.

Marx's excursus into machinery in 1863 had a wide-ranging impact. Not only did it provide considerable detail concerning machinery and large-scale industry, which Marx subsequently incorporated into *Das Kapital,* but it also led to a major rethinking of how to present the material related to the division of labor. Marx's 1863 excursus fundamentally altered several key parts, including the mode of presentation, of his discussion of the division of labor in 1867 compared to his 1861–62 analysis.

NOTES

1. See Karl Marx and Friedrich Engels, *Gesamtausgabe: Werke, Artikel, Entwurfe* [hereafter cited as *MEGA*] (Berlin: Dietz Verlag, 1975ff), II, 3.6 pp. 317:36–318:11, Apparatus, p. 149; Marx to Engels, March 10, 1862, and Marx to Kugelmann, December 28, 1862, in Karl Marx and Friedrich Engels, *Werke* [hereafter cited as *MEW*], (Berlin: Dietz Verlag, 1956–90), 30:226, 639–40.

2. *MEGA* II, 3.2, 3.3, 3.4, 3.5; *MEGA* II, 3, pp. 2396–399.

3. *MEW* 30:639–40.

4. The reservations could have related to any of five possibilities. (1) It could be that Marx was generally dissatisfied with the section and simply decided to expand it. (2) While reading through the notebook Marx may have remembered some material he had recently read on machinery, that is, *The Times* article I will discuss later in this chapter (*MEGA* II, 3.6, pp. 1895:7–1896:15). It was when he decided to add this new material to the notebook that he then began an ensuing, thorough reexamination of machinery. (3) It may also be that Marx remembered some material in his readings before the 1860s that led him to reread some of his earlier study notebooks. In turn, this then could have triggered the ensuing thorough analysis of machinery (see, for example, Marx to Engels, January 28, 1863, *MEW* 30:320). (4) Marx might have run into a particular question that, when he answered it, led him to review old material and thus to a more thorough analysis of the machinery question (Marx to Engels, January 28, 1863, ibid., p. 320). (5) Finally, Marx may have reworked his discussion of machinery because of a combination of two or more of these reasons. In any event, he began, most likely in January 1863, to add material to his 1861–63 notebooks.

5. See Karl Marx, *Die technologisch-historischen Exzerpte,* trans. and ed. Hans-Peter Müller (Frankfurt/M.: Ullstein Verlag, 1981), p. lxiv.

6. *MEGA* II, 3.6, pp. 1895:7–1896:15.

7. Ibid., pp. 1896:18–1910:17.

8. Ibid., p. 1910:7–37; *MEGA* II, 3, p. 2399.

9. Karl Marx, *Das Kapital,* 1st ed. (Hamburg: Otto Meissner, 1867), pp. 357–8; *MEW* 30:319–23. This letter is included in *Der Briefwechsel zwischen Friedrich Engels und Karl Marx: 1844 bis 1883,* ed. August Bebel and Eduard Bernstein (Stuttgart: J. H. W. Dietz, 1913), 3:111–15; Karl Marx and Friedrich Engels, *Ausgewählte Briefe,* ed. Vladimir Adoratsky (Moscow-Leningrad: Verlagsgenossenschaft Ausländerischer Arbeiter in der UdSSR, 1934), pp. 117–19; *Marx/Engels Selected Correspondence 1846–1895,* trans. Donna Torr (New York: International Publishers, 1934), pp. 141–44; *Marx/Engels Selected Correspondence* (Moscow: Foreign Languages Publishing House, n.d. [a translation of the Russian edition of selected correspondence, *Izbrannye pisma* (Moscow: Gospolitizdat, 1947)], pp. 168–71; *Marx/Engels Selected Correspondence* (Moscow: Progress Publishers, 1955), pp. 137–40 (a volume that differs from the previous two volumes); and *The Letters of Karl Marx,* ed. Saul K. Padover (Engelwood Cliffs: Prentice-Hall, 1979), pp. 166–69.

10. Marx to Engels, January 28, 1863, *MEW* 30:320.

11. *MEGA* II, 3.6, pp. 1914:16–1996:28, 2012:22–2039:30.

12. Ibid., pp. 1913:4–5, 1914:1–6.

13. Ibid., p. 1914:8–11. Compare with Karl Marx, *Exzerpte über Arbeitsteilung,* trans. and ed. Rainer Winkelmann (Frankfurt/M.: Verlag Ullstein, 1982), p. 59 and Charles Babbage, *Traité sur l'économie des machines et des manufactures,* trans. Edward Benoit (Paris, 1833), p. 230; see also Charles Babbage, *On the Economy of Machinery and Manufactures* (Philadelphia, 1832), p. 126, para. 167.

14. *MEGA* II, 3.1, pp. 252:5–254:35, 272:1–32.

15. *MEGA* II, 3.6, p. 1914:16–22. In addition to the implicit reference to Hutton, Marx (ibid., p. 2016:32–38) excerpted the following from the *Course:* "*Machine*, or *Engine*, is any mechanical instrument contrived to move bodies. And it is *composed* of the *mechanical powers*. *Mechanical powers* are certain *simple instruments*, commonly employed for raising greater weights, or overcoming greater resistances, than could be effected by the natural strength without them. They are usually accounted six in number, viz. the lever, the wheel and axle, the pulley, the inclined plane, the wedge, and the screw. (174, 175) (*Hutton. A Course of Mathematics.*)." The reference to Hutton is misleading. Marx either recorded the pages incorrectly or took the idea from another source that had erred in recording the information. The correct reference is Hutton's *A Course of Mathematics* (London: Blane Brothers Printers, 1841), p. 810.

16. Following *The Industry of Nations,* Marx consistently spelled self-actor as one word; see *MEGA* II, 3.6, p. 1940:13. A *self-actor* was a specific type of spinning mule that was first developed by William Kelly in 1792, although its success in replacing the hand-operated mule was limited by technical difficulties and the expense of the self-actor itself. See Julia de L. Mann, "The Textile Industry: Machines for Cotton, Flax, Wool, 1760–1850," in *A History of Technology,* ed. Charles Singer et al. (Oxford: Clarendon Press, 1958), 4:287–90; see also *MEGA* II, 3.6, p. 1947:14–41.

17. Ibid., pp. 1914:36–1915:2.

18. Ibid., p. 1915:8–35.

19. Ibid., pp. 1916:35–1918:13. Marx seems to have taken this idea from *The Industry of Nations,* an anonymously written work that he cited extensively in notebook 19; ibid., p. 1948:13–41.

20. Ibid., p. 1949:3–14, Marx's emphases; Marx wrote *tools* in English throughout.

21. The bulk of excerpts from Poppe that Marx selected from his study notebooks are found in ibid., pp. 1913:6–1951:40; those from *The Industry of Nations* are found on pp. 1979:30–1996:29. For the study notebook material itself, see *Die technologisch-historischen Exzerpte.*

22. Marx to Engels, January 24, 1863, *MEW* 30:315.

23. See *MEGA* II, 3.6, p. 1947:17–41, where Marx cites material from *The Industry of Nations* about the operation of an automatic power loom.

24. Marx makes this same argument in notebook 19 following a lengthy presentation of material on machinery and large-scale industry; ibid., pp. 1940:15–1951:41.

25. In notebook 19, Marx discusses the spinning machine at some length, particularly with reference to motive power. Toward the bottom of manuscript page 1161, he drew a vertical line in the margin beside the following sentence. "It is thus through the division of tools, which come directly in contact with the material—the transformation of this part from which the industrial revolution, which characterizes the capitalist means of production, springs, the way from 6 to 1800 spindles." Ibid., p. 1916:32–36; see pp. 1915:39–1917:2 for more comments on the spinning machine.

26. Ibid., p. 1947:17–41 contains an excerpt from *The Industry of Nations* that shows why the working machine was a decisive factor in capitalist production leading to large-scale industry.

27. See ibid., p. 1917:3–14, where Marx expresses exactly the same idea.

28. In Marx's study notes from Poppe's *Geschichte,* he excerpted considerable material on the history of clocks; see Marx, *Die technologisch-historischen Exzerpte,* pp. 84:6–98:5.

29. Marx accumulated considerable historical material on mills; see, for example, ibid., pp. 51:30–59:36. This material was incorporated into his 1863 notebook; MEGA II, 3.6, pp. 1925:29–1928:39. Marx made almost the same point in notebook 19 that he made to Engels. "The water mill, above all for the grinding of corn [*Getreides*], could be employed naturally, with modification, as the instrument of labor for all similar goals and different materials. It encompassed therefore in the time of manufacture, all manufactures, which employed, in part or in whole, this moving power. *Oil machines.* Oil-crushing mill." Ibid., p. 1928:35–9.

30. Marx excerpted a lengthy section on the corn mill from *The Industry of Nations;* ibid., pp. 1991:27–40, 1996:1–8.

31. Ibid., pp. 1928:17–1930:11. This part of notebook 19 contains the same statement, although in notebook 19 it is followed by an analysis of water mills, wind mills, and clocks. Much of the material came from Poppe's *Geschichte;* cf. Marx, *Die technologisch-historischen Exzerpte,* pp. 98:6–103:8, 61:1–18.

32. In ibid., pp. 52:14–53:10, Marx excerpts from Poppe directly on this part of the history of the mill.

33. Within the context of an analysis of clocks and mills, Marx made virtually the same statement in notebook 19. *"Clock* based on artistic handicraft operation together with learning [*Gelehrsamkeit*] represents the dawn of bourgeois society. They provide the idea of automatons and the automatic movement employed in production. With this history goes hand in hand the history of uniform movement. Without clocks how would one calculate the period for the value of commodities and therefore the labor time needed for their production." *MEGA* II, 3.6, p. 1928:26–32.

34. Marx, *Die technologisch-historischen Exzerpte,* p. 98:4–5.

35. Ibid., p. 97:28–29.

36. See *MEGA* II, 3.6, pp. 1949:1–1950:41, where Marx cites from *The Industry of Nations* concerning exactly what a transmission mechanism is and makes a distinction between the working machine, transmission mechanisms, and other parts of the machine. This section of *The Industry of Nations* is particularly important because here Marx felt that he finally had the basis of an adequate distinction between a tool and a machine.

37. Marx discussed friction in *Die technologisch-historischen Exzerpte,* pp. 53:10–59:36 and *MEGA* II, 3.6, pp. 1922:34–1923:19.

38. Marx, *Die technologisch-historischen Exzerpte,* pp. 56:9–57:24 and *MEGA* II, 3.6, pp. 1923:20–1924:22.

39. Marx, *Die technologisch-historischen Exzerpte,* pp. 56:35–57:5.

40. Poppe discussed the influence Isaac Newton, Johann and Daniel

Bernoulli, Edme Mariotte, and Jean-Baptiste d'Alembert in the *Geschichte*. See Marx's excerpts in *Die technologisch-historischen Exzerpte*, p. 157:6-20. Marx used this material in developing his arguments about machinery in 1863; see *MEGA* II, 3.6, pp. 1923:20-1927:7, esp. 1927:1-7.

41. Concerning oil presses, paper presses, and sugar presses, see Marx, *Die technologisch-historischen Exzerpte*, pp. 61:1-17, 100:31-103:9, and 136:14-137:25. See also *MEGA* II, 3.6, pp. 1940:16-1945:22 concerning his use of material from *The Industry of Nations* and Poppe's *Geschichte* on paper presses.

42. See Marx, *Die technologisch-historischen Exzerpte*, pp. 113:29-114:14 concerning Marx's excerpts on the forge. Marx included this material in his 1863 work on machinery; see *MEGA* II, 3.6, pp. 1981:20-1988:8.

43. Ibid., p. 1974:28-39.

44. Marx to Engels, January 28, 1863, *MEW* 30:319-22.

45. Marx, *Das Kapital*, pp. 321-35; see also, Karl Marx, *Das Kapital*, 2d ed. (Hamburg: Otto Meissner, 1873), pp. 348-62.

46. Marx, *Das Kapital*, 1st ed., p. 324.

47. *MEGA* II, 3.6, p. 1914:1-6.

48. *MEGA* II, 3.1, p. 252:20-26.

49. *MEGA* II, 3.6, pp. 1936:27-1938:6, 15.

50. Ibid., p. 1938:16-17, Marx's emphasis. When using this idea in *Das Kapital*, Marx noted that in Birmingham, there were five hundred types of hammers (p. 324). The editors of *MEGA* do not indicate this error in transcription, as Marx went from his study notebook to *Das Kapital;* *MEGA* II, 5, pp. 277:24, 682, 803.

51. Marx, *Das Kapital*, 1st ed., p. 324 n31.

52. MEGA II, 3.6, p. 1913:6-16, Marx's emphases; cf. Marx, *Das Kapital*, 1st. ed., p. 324 n31. In both notebook 19 and *Das Kapital* Marx presents the quotation in German, and I have supplied my own translation of that quotation. Darwin's English text is as follows: "I presume that lowness in this case means that the several parts of the organization have been but little specialized for particular functions; and as long as the same part has to perform diversified work, we can perhaps see why it should remain variable, that is, why natural selection should have preserved or rejected each little deviation of form less carefully than when the part has to serve for one special purpose alone. In the same way that a knife which has to cut all sorts of things may be of almost any shape; whilst a tool for some particular object had better be of some particular shape. Natural selection, it should never be forgotten, can act on each part of each being, solely through and for its advantage." *MEGA* II, 3, p. 3062. In *Das Kapital*, Marx removed all emphases from the Darwin quotation he had placed in his notebook version.

53. Marx, *Das Kapital*, 1st. ed., p. 355; see also Marx, *Das Kapital*, 2d ed., p. 384.

54. Marx, *Das Kapital*, 1st ed., p. 327.

55. Ibid., p. 327 n35. Marx could have also cited *MEGA* II, 3.6, p. 1941:31-41 to present exactly the same idea from within the context of a general discussion of the automatic workshop. The idea compares with Babbage's

comments on manufacture; see *On the Economy of Machinery,* pp. 157–58, and Marx, *Exzerpte über Arbeitsteilung,* p. 60:17–25.

56. See *MEGA* II, 3.6, p. 1945:29–32, for the excerpt in notebook 19 from *The Industry of Nations,* and *MEGA* II, 3.6, pp. 1941:31–1946:5 for excerpts on envelope and paper manufacture. Marx discussed the manufacture of paper later in *Das Kapital,* (1st ed., p. 332), but did not draw on any of the excerpts found in notebook 19.

57. Marx, *Das Kapital,* 1st ed., p. 327.

58. Ibid., p. 328 n38; cf. *MEGA* II, 3.1, pp. 251:37–252:4. Although Marx used the Stewart quote from notebook 4 in *Das Kapital,* it is important to recognize that the context of the quotation had changed between 1862 and 1867. In 1862, he used the quotation to emphasize the reduction of work to detail labor that sped production; he made no explicit connections to machinery. The machinelike simultaneity of the collective worker seems to have emerged following the 1863 work on machinery.

59. MEGA II, 3.6, pp. 1938:33–1940:15, 1942:9–13. On manuscript page 1178, Marx cited the process through which the blank passed from its creation to slitting (p. 1939:3–39). All of this material was taken from *The Industry of Nations.* At the top of manuscript page 1179, Marx cited the material he had explicitly in mind when making his comments about the simultaneous nature of production. "For some time the introduction of machinery in the steel pen manufacture appeared attended with insuperable difficulties, for there seemed no possibility of completing a steel pen by anything like a continuous process. This difficulty, has, however, been surmounted, and in the Great Exhibition (1851) there was shown a machine now in great use, which effects this object. It is entirely selfacting. It receives the steel as a flat ribbon, and cuts, pierces, and side-slits two pens at one stroke, performing six processes at once [all in English]" (p. 1940:7–14).

60. *MEGA* II, 3.1, pp. 262:25–33, 262:34–263:3; cf. Marx, *Exzerpte über Arbeitsteilung,* pp. 59:9–18, 59:37–60:6.

61. Marx, *Das Kapital,* 1st ed., pp. 329–30 n39, p. 333 n45. On the question of proportionality, Marx could have cited Babbage's empirical account of pin-making under conditions of manufacture and machine production, but in his study·notebook he had not cited the numerical proportions Babbage included in his account of pin production; see Babbage, *On the Economy of Machinery,* pp. 127–40, 156–57.

62. *MEGA* II, 3.1, p. 263:28–36.

63. Marx, *Das Kapital,* 1st ed., p. 329.

64. Using *The Industry of Nations* as his source of information, Marx noted that an assembler can put together four hundred to five hundred pieces of type per hour and a breaker can dismantle two to three thousand pieces per hour; *MEGA* II, 3.6, p. 1946:8–14. In the first edition of *Das Kapital,* Marx inflated the figures to two thousand pieces per hour in assembly and four thousand per hour in dismantling the type (p. 329). *MEGA* II, 5, p. 804 notes the location of the material in Marx's 1863 notebook but not the discrepancy in the numbers between the 1863 and 1867 figures.

65. Marx, *Das Kapital,* 1st ed., p. 332.
66. *MEGA* II, 3.1,, pp. 262:5-263:36.
67. *MEGA* II, 3.6, pp. 1992:1-2021:21.
68. Ibid., p. 2020:24-30.

FIVE

FINAL FORM AND CONTENT

In the development of Marx's analysis of the division of labor, six major changes emerged through the final reworking of the section from its 1861–63 form. Most apparent is the increased organization of the material into which Marx introduced an altered (and improved) thematic development as well as a sharper focus. Second, he implicitly and explicitly used Smith's ideas in ways that contrast to 1861–62. Third, he included more information and concrete examples but fewer theoretical references while, fourth, changing what authors were used for various points of support, the material cited, and where it was placed in the text and footnotes. Marx's fifth change was his use of the alienation framework to discuss the division of labor. Finally, he employed two new concepts: *handwerkmässig* (handicraftlike) and *Gesamtarbeiter* (collective worker). Using the section titles found in *Das Kapital* to organize the presentation, I will discuss each of these six points.

The Double Origin of Manufacture

To present his finished analysis of the division of labor, Marx developed a significantly revised, five-part developmental logic to his analysis. In 1867 the parts were implicit, but in the second German edition and the first French edition, he formalized them under the headings: "The Double Origin of Manufacture," "The Detail Worker [*Theilarbeiter*] and His Tools," "The Two Basic Forms of Manufacture: Heterogeneous Manufacture and Organic Manufacture," "Division of Labor within Manufacture and Division of Labor within Society," and "The Capitalist Character of Manufacture."[1]

120

The first section begins with a theme Marx had expressed several times in 1861 and 1862. "Cooperation based on the division of labor," he wrote in 1867, "assumes its classic shape in *manufacture.*"[2] In *Das Kapital,* however, he only used this as the introduction to the section and began his analysis of the division of labor with material not employed in 1861 and 1862. That is, instead of describing the division of labor as he had previously, Marx began his analysis in 1867 with a discussion of the origin of the division of labor, arguing that it began in two ways.

In the first instance, a capitalist brings together a number of different, independent crafts workers, for example, wheelwrights, harness makers, and upholsterers, to produce a single line of commodities, say, carriages. As the crafts workers become occupied exclusively with plying their trade in the production of carriages, they lose their ability to carry out the full range of their trade. The one-sided nature of the work narrows the crafts workers' sphere of effectiveness as they become specialists in a phase of carriage production. As a result, Marx argued, carriage production itself is split into "*different, particular operations,* in which each individual operation is crystallized into the exclusive function of a worker and the totality is attained by the *association of these detail workers.* . . . Manufacture also arises in the *opposite* way," Marx pointed out. A capitalist might employ a number of workers from the same handicraft to produce a single type of commodity. In times of increased demand, however, the work is divided so that a particular crafts worker concentrates on only one step in the production process. This division, Marx maintained, "gradually ossifies to a systematic *division of labor.*"[3] This discussion is followed with a summary statement about the origin of manufacture.

> The means of origin of manufacture, its evolution [*Herausbildung*] from handicraft, is thus twofold. On the one hand it arises from the *combination of various independent* handicrafts, which come to the point of *non-independence* and one-sidedness where they constitute to one another only detail operations in the production process of one and the same commodity. On the other hand it [manufacture] arises from the *cooperation of the same type of handicraftsmen,* breaking up the same individual handicraft to its different particular operations and isolating and *making them independent* to the point where each of them becomes the exclusive function of a particular worker. On the one hand, therefore, manufacture introduces the division of labor in the production process or develops it further, and on the other hand it combines previously separated handicrafts. But whichever was its particular starting point, its end result is the same— *a mechanism of production whose organs are men.*[4]

In working through this opening section Marx developed a few subtle changes from his 1861–62 discussion. On the one hand, he added more information—two sources for the origin of the division of labor rather than the one implied in 1861–62—but on the other hand, he narrowed his explanation about the origin of the division of labor. It now appears to arise from capitalist control over the production process and not, as implied in 1861–62, from certain factors also involving the sphere of circulation. Why the shift?

One reason for the shifting emphasis is that *Das Kapital,* volume 1, is a much more sharply focussed book than either part 1 or the intended part 2 of *Zur Kritik der politischen Ökonomie. Das Kapital's* first volume is concerned almost exclusively with the production process of capital. Thus, it seems that with this single side of the economic process foremost in his mind and in the text's analysis, Marx accounted for the origin of the division of labor from the narrow vantage point of production, establishing a general trend that seems to have influenced how he dealt with the issue.

A more specific trend within *Das Kapital* also influenced Marx's analysis. Under the heading "The Production of Relative Surplus Value," chapter 4 in the first edition, section 4 in the second, he presented a particular sequential development from simple cooperation through the form of cooperation unique to manufacture (that is, the division of labor) to the development and use of machinery in large-scale industry. He sequentially located the dynamic for changes in the production process, which increased the extraction of relative surplus value within the sphere of production itself. Thus it is not surprising that Marx's 1867 discussion, because of its general and particular context, tends to emphasize the production-related origin of the division of labor to the exclusion of the influences of the realm of circulation.

A third factor was time. The 1867 discussion of the origin of the division of labor contains the dimension missing from the 1861–62 draft manuscript because Marx had more occasion to reflect on the section in the wake of additional writing and reading. Between the 1861–62 analysis and that of *Das Kapital,* he had read extensively on machinery and large-scale industry (plus its historical development), consumed numerous factory reports, read more political economy, drafted the remaining eighteen notebooks of 1861–63 as well as "Die Resultate des unmittelbaren Produktionsprozesses," and redrafted the section on the labor process, the valorization process, and the working day for *Das Kapital.* Any, or all, of these could have served as sources for the more complete conceptualization of how the division of labor originated within the production process. At the same time, they could all have deflected Marx's focus from circulation's influence on the division of labor.

The significance of the change from the 1861–62 to 1867 is an improvement; Marx showed in *Das Kapital* how the division of labor could arise from workers in the same trade employed in the production of the same commodity. The discussion is deficient insofar as the role of the circulation process broached in 1861–62 is even less evident in 1867. As a result, the discussion is comprehensive only insofar as the division of labor arises from factors accounted for solely by the production process, but it is not comprehensive if one considers the total economic process. Nevertheless, the discussion sets up the ensuing examination of machinery by moving the reader into a framework that shows the internal logic within production that would lend itself to mechanization.

Marx completed his discussion of the origin of the division of labor by arguing that "it is essential to hold fast to the following points for the correct understanding of the division of labor in manufacture." First, the *"analysis of the process of production to its particular phases* coincides exactly with the *decomposition of a handicraftlike [handwerkmässigen] activity to its different operations."* Each operation must still be done by hand, and to this extent remains handicraftlike. *"This narrow technological basis* excludes actual scientific analysis of the process of production since each partial process which the product undergoes must be feasible as a handicraftlike detail labor. Because the handicraftlike ability thus remains the basic condition of the production process, every worker is *assimilated* exclusively to a partial function and his labor power is transformed into the life-long organ of this partial function." Finally, Marx argued, the division of labor in this particular sort of cooperation derives its advantages from "the general essence [of cooperation]" and not from this particular form of it.[5]

These ideas were also present in the 1861–62 notebooks, but in articulating the ideas in 1867, Marx emphasized the thrust of his argument by employing the term *handwerkmässig.* He wanted to emphasize that the division of labor in manufacture comes from a breakdown of handicraft and guild production, a point he made several times in 1861 and 1862, yet at the same time, manufacture remains rooted in human labor power and labor capacity.[6] Although he also made this point several times in 1861–62,[7] it was more clearly and concisely emphasized in 1867 through the use of *handwerkmässig.* The only time Marx used the term *handicraftlike* in 1861 and 1862 was to describe the work process before its decomposition into detail tasks in manufacture.[8] In working through his analysis for *Das Kapital,* Marx used the concrete term to emphasize a fundamental, theoretical distinction between manufacture and large-scale industry, with the foundation of the former in human labor capacity.

The Detail Worker and His Tools

In section 2 of the division of labor chapter, Marx examined some ideas about the specialization of work and the development of tools with respect to the division of labor. In doing so, he again echoed ideas expressed in 1861–62, but in *Das Kapital* the analysis is structured almost directly parallel to Smith's arguments in chapter 1 of *The Wealth of Nations* on how the division of labor increased productivity. That is, Marx, implicitly at least, dealt with the section of Smith's work that he had not formally addressed since his first reading notes of 1844. The discussion in *Das Kapital* also contains new information, including the conceptual term *Gesamtarbeiter*, not present in the 1861–62 draft manuscript.

In *The Wealth of Nations*, Smith maintained that the division of labor increased productivity through "the improvement of the dexterity of the workman" as each concentrated upon "one simple operation," the time saved "commonly lost in passing from one sort of work to another," and the machines "which were the inventions of common workmen, in order to facilitate and quicken their own particular part of the work."[9]

In *Das Kapital*, Marx made the same three points, but their presentation simultaneously incorporated a critical dimension absent from Smith's discussion. Marx wrote that "it is above all clear that a worker who performs, life long, one and the same operation, transforms his whole body into its [the operation's] automatic, one-sided organ, and therefore consumes *less time* than the craftsman who carries out alternatively a whole series of operations."[10] As a result, more commodities are produced in less time.

Two paragraphs later, Marx presented Smith's second point by noting that a crafts worker who performs all the various operations in producing a single commodity loses time as he changes his place and tools. The division of labor eliminates such loss of time. "The increased productivity is here due either to the increased expenditure of labor power in a given time period, thus *increased intensity of labor*, or a *reduction of the unproductive consumption of labor power.*" Marx added, "[t]he excess of power expenditures which each transition from rest to motion requires, is compensated for with the longer duration of the normal speed once attained." He also noted, in a critical vein, "the continuity of the same form of labor destroys the span and liveliness of the spirit of life which finds its recreation and impulse in change of the activity itself."[11]

Concerning Smith's third point, Marx argued that "[t]he productivity of labor depends not only on the skill [*Virtuosität*] of the worker but also on the perfection of his tools. . . . The *differentiation* of the instruments of labor, through which instruments of a given type acquire *fixed* forms for each particular application, and their *specialization,* through which each such particular instrument works to its full extent only in the hand of a specific detail worker, characterizes manufacture."[12]

Four points in particular should be noted about the development and presentation of ideas in this section of *Das Kapital*. First, in contrast to 1861–62, when authors were cited within the text on points of theory, Marx does this less frequently in 1867. Rather than turning over the text of his argument to some other authority on a theoretical point, Marx either relied on the reader to recognize the source of his argument, or he supplied the reference in a footnote. In this particular section, Smith was not cited anywhere, perhaps because anyone familiar with the subject would recognize the invisible hand of Smith's analysis in the argument. The footnotes are thus used, as Engels indicated, to present a historical account of when the ideas mentioned first appeared or how they were uncritically accepted by later political economists.[13]

The second point follows directly from the first. Even though Smith is not mentioned, the contrast between the two men would be clearly evident to many readers of *Das Kapital*. This would provide an added emphasis to Marx's ideas without mentioning Smith, who uncritically cataloged the productive potential of the division of labor and thus implicitly, if not explicitly, condoned its implementation and development. In Marx's discussion, the negative side of the division of labor is carefully embedded into the analysis. Through a deliberate choice of words and accentuation, he reminded his readers that workers perform "life long, one and the same operation" that transforms a worker's body into an "automatic, one-sided organ." Although this increases productivity, it also means an "increased intensity of labor," a reduction of unproductive labor time, and a destruction of the spirit of life "which finds its recreation and impulse in change of the activity itself."

What Marx did in *Das Kapital* contrasts markedly from 1861–62. In the earlier draft manuscript, he had paired Adam Ferguson's critique of the division of labor with Smith's account. In 1867, Marx relied on his own authority, which he established as the author of the entire, lengthy critique, rather than feature another authority. In addition, he developed a more persuasive critique of the division of labor by presenting its classical justification while simultaneously weaving in an

125

implicit critique. This style was enhanced by the graphic, eighty-three-page-long discussion of the working day found in section 4 of chapter 3. That account supplied numerous concrete images of how valid his critical presentation of the division of labor phenomenon was. In 1861–62, Marx did not have this concrete material in his text to assist the development of later theoretical points.

Third, the critical dimension of the section provides a good contrast between Marx's approach to political economy and that of the majority of political economists. In chapter 4, I pointed out Dugald Stewart's criticisms of Smith's arguments concerning the productivity of the division of labor. Stewart confined his criticisms to either the logic of Smith's position—the development of machines by workers could not be used as an argument in favor of the division of labor because it related to the productivity of machines rather than that of workers—or the accuracy of Smith's points—how much increased productivity could be attributed to increased dexterity in simple tasks. Stewart did not address the question of the division of labor fully in terms of human costs and suffering, although, to be fair, he did note that job rotation should not be a problem for workers performing very simple tasks. Marx, in contrast, was more critical of what the division of labor meant to the quality of working life for the worker and omitted Stewart's more technical criticisms, although he was familiar with them.

The fourth point of note about the section is that in *Das Kapital* Marx reworked information contained in the 1861–62 draft manuscript to develop his critique even further. In 1861–62, in the context of his discussion about the ancients, Marx mentioned that people in Egypt were confined to particular occupations by virtue of heredity.[14] In *Das Kapital,* he made much more effective use of the point by indicating that the specialization of fragmented work tasks in manufacture "corresponds to the tendency of earlier societies to making trades *hereditary,* to petrify them into *castes* or, where determinate historical conditions produce a variability of the individual contradicting the caste system, the separation of labor is at least ossified into *guilds.* "[15] Presented in these terms, from the perspective of the worker, the division of labor takes on a very different light than comes from Smith's equation of the division of labor and social development.

The final point of note about this section is the introduction of another conceptual term: *collective worker,* which is first used in the second sentence. "The combined *collective worker,* who constitutes the living mechanism of manufacture," Marx wrote, "consists solely of such one-sided [detail] workers."[16] This term is employed more frequently in section 3 of the chapter and will be discussed within that context. However, a few points can be made about its origin.

In 1861–62, Marx had written about how commodities produced through the division of labor represented "the totality [*Totalität*] of these [separate] operations" and the way in which workers and tools were concentrated together in one place.[17] Thus, the raw material for the term *Gesamtarbeiter* existed, but Marx did not introduce it until he wrote "Die Resultate des unmittelbaren Produktionsprozesses."[18]

"Die Resultate," written in the mid–1860s, drew together in summarylike form the main ideas Marx felt should be grasped about production before proceeding into a discussion of circulation. Consequently, the text was written after Marx had returned to the machinery question in 1863 and had reread the history of technology. It appears that this return to the empirical study of the mechanistic world of large-scale industry suggested a machinelike concept for discussing workers within manufacture because it led to large-scale industry.

In "Die Resultate" Marx indicated that in the production–valorization process, the capitalist must ensure "that the labor is carried out in an orderly, purposeful manner, the transformation of the means of production into the products proceeds appropriately, the use value held in mind as the goal actually comes out in the *successful* form as the result. . . . Finally, that the process of production is not disturbed or interrupted and actually proceeds to the product in the given space of time (time period) for the nature of the process of production and its objective [*gegenständlichen*] conditions."[19] The capitalist accomplished such control as labor was moved from formal to real subsumption [*reale Subsumption*] under capital.

In the introduction to his analysis of "Real Subsumption of Labor under Capital or the Specifically Capitalist Mode of Production" Marx argued that "it was explained earlier in ch. III, as develops with the *production of relative surplus value* . . . the entire, real character [*Gestalt*] of the mode of production changes and a specifically *capitalist mode of production* (also technological) arises, on whose basis, and simultaneously with it, first develops the *relations of production,* corresponding to the capitalist *production process,* between the various agents of production and especially between the capitalist and wage laborer." In particular, he had in mind the following changes in the social relations of production. "The *social* productive powers of labor, or the productive powers of directly *social, socialized* (collective [*gemeinsamer*]) labor, [arises] through cooperation, the division of labor within the workshop, the

employment of *machinery,* and overall the transformation of the process
of production through the *conscious* employment of natural science,
mechanics, chemistry, etc., likewise *labor on a greater scale* corresponding
to all of these."

This discussion essentially repeats ideas expressed in 1861–62 without introducing new terms. In the next four manuscript pages, however,
Marx wrote some "Additional Comments on the Formal Subsumption
of Labor under Capital" and noted that under formal subsumption the
method of production does not change. "*The labor process, technologically
speaking,* goes on as before only now as the labor process *subordinated*
under capital."[20] Nevertheless, within the formal subsumption of labor
under capital, two changes do begin to emerge. First, "an *economic*
relation of superordination, and subordination" emerges. Second,
"there develops great continuity and intensity of labor and greater
economy in the employment of the conditions of labor since everything
is exerted so that the product represents the *socially necessary* (or rather
even less) *labor time,* and this not only with regard to the living labor
which is employed in its [the product's] production, but also with regard
to the objectified labor." This latter development peaks with the real
subsumption of labor under capital, which Marx discussed for three
manuscript pages before entering into a slight excursus on productive
and unproductive labor.[21] It is within this excursus, linking it to the
real subsumption of labor theme, that he introduced the term
Gesamtarbeiter.

> With the development of the real *subsumption of labor under capital* or the
> *specific capitalist mode of production,* not the single worker, rather more and
> more a *socially combined labor capacity* becomes the *actual functionary* of the
> complete labor process [*Gesamtarbeitsprozess*] and the different labor capac-
> ities which are concurrent and make up the whole productive machine,
> take part in very different ways in the immediate process of commodity—
> or better here product creation, the one works more with the hand, the
> other more with the head, the one as manager, engineer, technologist,
> etc., the other as overseer, the third as a direct manual worker or even
> purely a helper [*Handlanger*], thus more and more *functions* of *labor capacity*
> are arranged under the immediate concept of *productive laborers,* worker[s]
> exploited directly by capital and *subordinated* to its [capital's] valorization
> and production process. If one considers the *collective worker,* of which the
> workshop consists, then it actualizes itself, materializes its combined
> *activity* immediately in a whole product [*Gesamtprodukt*] which is at the
> same time a *total mass* [*Gesamtmass*] *of commodities* in which it is quite
> inconsequential whether the function of the single worker, who is only
> a limb [*Glied*] of this collective worker, stands closer or further from the
> immediate manual labor.[22]

This quotation, and the context within which it developed, show Marx slowly working toward the single, more or less concrete, term, *Gesamtarbeiter,* to tie together conceptually the extended, labor-capacity-based, production process of manufacture. Through the development of the term, he could conceptually present a complex process economically in terms of language and also meet another unstated objective of his popular writings, the use of a fairly concrete referent for an abstract concept.

The Fundamental Forms of Manufacture

In this section Marx introduced a conceptual distinction between heterogeneous and organic forms of manufacture not present in 1861 and 1862. The introduction and development of the distinction led to the examination of micro-level facets of the production process that were not examined thoroughly and also set up a context for the representation of some 1861–62 material so that it had a different impact than in the earlier draft manuscript. A case can be made, I believe, that the major stimulus behind this conceptualization was Marx's return to the study of machinery in 1863. His study of technology at the historical and concrete level of analysis and his use of Charles Babbage suggest that the work on machinery conceptually influenced this part of the analysis.

In addition to the influence of the study of machinery, there is also the context of *Das Kapital* as a whole. Because *Das Kapital* has a stronger evolutionary and developmental thrust than the 1861–62 draft manuscript and the heterogeneous versus organic distinction emphasized a source of change within the production process itself, Marx seems to have adopted it to bring out the developmental theme more fully. This developmental theme has its main roots in Darwin but is also present in Johann Poppe's work, so Marx could draw the idea from two sources.

In *Das Kapital,* Marx argued that the two "*basic forms*" of manufacture "play quite different roles in the later transformation of manufacture to large-scale industry carried out by machines." To exemplify heterogeneous manufacture, he used William Petty's example of watchmaking, where "[f]rom the individual work of a Nurenburg craftsman, the watch [was] transformed to the social product of an immense number of detail workers."[23] The example had been used in the context of Marx's 1861–62 discussion of the ancients, but merely to contrast Petty's view of the benefits derived from the division of labor to that of the ancients.[24] This was not how Marx used the example in *Das Kapital.* In 1867, he emphasized first that watch production was broken

129

down into a vast number of detail operations that may or may not—depending upon economic conditions—be housed in one workshop.[25] He also emphasized that the social relation of the detail worker, even though he or she may work at home, is very different from the independent crafts worker who works for his or her own customers because the detail worker is employed by a capitalist. "The second type of manufacture, its perfected form, produces articles which pass through interconnecting phases of development, a series of sequential processes, like, for example, the wire in pin manufacture which passes through the hands of 72 and even 92 specific detail workers."[26]

After setting out the distinction, Marx indicated how both forms of manufacture were involved in the transformation of manufacture to large-scale industry, a theme absent from the 1861–62 manuscript but dependent on his work on machinery in 1863. By drawing different handicrafts together, Marx argued, heterogeneous manufacture "reduces the *spatial separation* between the phases of production of an article," thereby reducing the time lost as the product passes from stage to stage.[27] Both heterogeneous and organic manufacture increase productive power due to the "*general cooperative character* of manufacture." At the same time, these forms of manufacture create barriers that encourage further development of the production process through their transcendence. "The specific principle of the division of labor occasions an *isolation* of the different phases of production which are now like many handicraftlike detail labors autonomous from one another." An article must be transported from one hand to another, and from "the standpoint of large-scale industry, this stands out as a characteristic, costly, *imminent* limitation to the *principle* of manufacture."[28]

Marx then commented on the division of labor at the shopfloor level, which enabled him to examine aspects of manufacture in ways not done in 1861–62 but made possible by his 1863 work on machinery. One can observe the raw material as it moves from step to step, Marx noted, or one can view the workshop as a "complete mechanism" where the raw material is "*simultaneously* in all its phases of production at the same time. With one part of its many instrument-equipped hands the collective worker, combined from all the detail workers, pulls the wire while it simultaneously with other hands and tools straightens it, cuts with others, points, etc." Because the phases of production have become contiguous spatially, more goods are produced in less time.[29] Finally, even though manufacture finds the power of cooperation on hand, manufacture develops that power further. Nevertheless, manufacture only "attains this social organization of the labor process by forging the workers firmly to the same detail."[30]

In terms of theoretical significance, the most important feature of this presentation of ideas is the marked contrast between Marx's account of pin production and the classical account in *The Wealth of Nations.* With Smith, pin production is presented as a human-controlled process. Marx's account, written in the wake of large-scale industry, his study of both political economists' theoretical treatises on machinery (for example, Babbage and Andrew Ure), and his own reading of the empirical history of technology and machinery, shows the tendency toward complete mechanization inherent to the division of labor, although he is careful to remind his readers that manufacture itself is rooted in human labor capacity where each worker is in charge of a single detail task. To emphasize the machinelike nature of manufacture, he noted in *Das Kapital* that in the production process, as one worker finishes a task and passes it on to the other workers, the mutual interdependence of the workers compels them to produce at the same rate. "In manufacture, the provision of a given quantity of products in a given labor time becomes a *technical law of the production process itself.*"[31]

In 1861–62, Marx had noted that workers had to be incorporated into production on the basis of particular multiples determined by the production process itself although not in a well-developed sequence of argumentation.[32] In *Das Kapital,* he argued that the "division of labor based on manufacture thus simplifies and increases not only the *qualitatively* discriminate organs of the social collective worker, but also creates a mathematically firm relation for the *quantitative range* of these organs, i.e. for the relative number of workers or relative size of the *group of workers* in each particular function."[33]

While thinking through this aspect of the division of labor, Marx presented two further ideas not present in 1861–62. The first, presented through the concrete example of glass bottle manufacture, involved the analysis of how several specialized groups worked totally independently of one another although, because of the specialized nature of their detail tasks, each worker depended totally on the others in the group. Because a glass furnace had several openings, four to six production groups would work independently alongside one another producing glass bottles. In addition, within the factory, there would be several furnaces, each of which occupied a number of production groups. Thus manufacture involves simple cooperation and the unique form of cooperation found in the division of labor.

Finally, Marx argued, "just as manufacture develops in part from the combination of various handicrafts, it also develops through a combination of various manufactures." English glass manufacturers, he pointed out as one example, produce their own earthenware melting pots "because the success or failure of the process depends essentially on their quality." Nevertheless, despite the technical and economic advantages of this combination of manufactures, combined manufacture does not develop "an actual technological unity, [based] on its own foundation. This arises first with its [the combined manufacture's] transformation to machine-based industry."[34]

At this point, Marx turned to the collective worker and, because of its context in the 1867 analysis, he developed the concept somewhat differently than in "Die Resultate des unmittelbaren Produktionsprozesses." He presented the collective worker concept so that it stressed two points in particular. The first relates to the mechanization theme, and the second is one of specialization although differing in presentation from either 1861–62 or "Die Resultate."

> The *specific machinery of the manufacture* period remains the *collective worker* itself, combined from the many detail workers. The different operations, which the producer of a commodity alternately carries out and which blend together in the whole of his labor process, make various demands on him. In one he must develop more power, in the other more skill and in the third more mental attention etc., and the same individual does not possess these qualities [*Eigenschaften*] in equal degree. After the separation, independence, and isolation of the various operations, the workers are divided, classified, and grouped according to their predominant properties.... Manufacture, once introduced, develops labor powers which, by nature, are fit for only a one-sided, particular function. The *collective worker* now possesses all productive properties at the same degree of skill [*Virtuosität*] and expends them at the same time most economically insofar as it utilizes all its organs, individualized in particular workers and groups of workers, exclusively for their specific functions. The one-sidedness and even imperfection of the detail worker turns into perfection as part of the collective worker. The habit of a one-sided function transforms him [the detail worker] into an organ operating like a force of nature, while the interconnection of the total mechanism compels him to act with the regularity of a machine part.[35]

The first sentence indicates how Marx used the term *collective worker* to develop a mechanization theme in chapter 4 of *Das Kapital:* "The specific machinery of the manufacture period remains the collective worker." The term is particularly suited to this thematic development. Each detail worker, as Marx pointed out here, is just that—a part of a much larger process—and the term *collective worker* suggests that a single machine could easily replace the many human workers who perform simplified, discrete, specialized tasks in a sequential order. This emphasis differs from the 1861–62 discussion in two ways.

First, in 1861–62, Marx described the development of detail labor out of the division of labor and thus emphasized the process of development rather than the final state of being; he also emphasized the period before the transformation of detail labor to machinery.[36] Second, Marx put his 1861–62 analysis, and that of "Die Resultate," within the alienation framework. In *Das Kapital,* that theme, because of the context in which the detail worker section is placed, is left for the final section of the chapter.

In the remainder of section 3 Marx addressed how the collective worker and collective labor lead to a hierarchy of labor powers and thus a hierarchy of wages. The simplification of detail tasks in the division of labor led to a reduction in the value of labor power because progressively more labor power is supplied by unskilled workers. Capital, as a result, does not have to pay for the cost of training such workers. Both of these points were also made in 1861–62.[37]

The Division of Labor in Manufacture and in Society

Perhaps more than any other, the fourth section on the division of labor demonstrates how much Marx reorganized and restructured his 1861–62 material to present his fully developed arguments in *Das Kapital,* how that reorganization led him to alter several points of emphasis in 1867 compared to 1861–62, and, finally, Marx's decision to eliminate certain ideas in the 1867 account that informed his earlier draft. As a result, except for a short paragraph on the separation of town and country and a lengthy paragraph concerning the resistance of the Asiatic mode of production to the division of labor characteristic of manufacture, all of the material in section 4 of *Das Kapital* is contained in the 1861–62 draft but has been reworked significantly.

One of Marx's major themes in 1861–62 was the distinction between the social division of labor and the technical division of labor in the workshop, a distinction that forms the substance of section 4 of chapter 4. In 1867, however, Marx reduced the importance of this theme. I am not making this claim because the topic was relegated to the second-last section of the division of labor chapter. On the contrary, its position in the chapter helps maintain the importance of the issue. In *Das Kapital,* Marx built his entire argument, and its individual sections, just as Hegel had built his *Wissenschaft der Logik,* from immediate, abstract elements or moments to more synthetically concrete wholes. For example, Marx noted "[w]e first considered the origin of manufacture from cooperation, then its simple elements, the detail worker and his tools, finally its total mechanism. We will now briefly touch on the relation between the division of labor in manufacture and the *social* division of labor which forms the basis of all production of commodities."[38] Thus the logic of the chapter's structure builds toward more complex issues, questions, and analysis. Consequently, the placing of the material on the division of labor in manufacture and society in section 4 does not diminish the topic's importance or emphasis.

The primary reason that Marx chose to "*briefly touch* on the relation between the division of labor in manufacture and the social division of labor [my emphasis]" is that the focus of his critique had sharpened considerably by 1867 from its less precise focus of 1861–62, which meant a series of changes throughout *Das Kapital*.

From 1861 to 1863, as is confirmed to some extent by the ensuing material in notebooks 6 to 23, Marx was almost as concerned with pointing out and correcting the various theoretical errors of other political economists as he was with developing a critique of political economy. In the section under analysis here, for example, he pointed out in the 1861–62 draft how Smith, Henri Storch, the ancients, and others had failed to distinguish between the social division of labor and the technical division of labor in manufacture. As a result, many of the arguments and material Marx advanced sought to correct what he felt was a fundamental confusion by those theorists, a confusion he sought to demystify through direct refutation because it represented a significant ideological distortion.

In 1867, Marx had decided to focus far more on the capitalist mode of production. As a result, the theorists themselves became less important and either dropped out of the text altogether or appeared in the footnotes. Consequently, Marx did not have to correct numerous shades of misrepresentation that conflated the division of labor in manufacture and the social division of labor. He could focus upon the distinction only insofar as it was relevant to grasping the capitalist political economy itself. From that perspective, the issue was somewhat less important than in 1861–62 when Marx undertook an unsystematic refutation of a particular error made by a number of economic theorists.

A second extensive difference between the texts of 1861–62 and 1867 surrounds the elimination of some material from the former text. In 1861–62, Marx included considerable discussion related to the alienation theme when distinguishing between the social division of labor and the division of labor in manufacture. In 1867, he reduced the amount and nature of that material considerably and placed it in the final section of the chapter. The reason may seem paradoxical.

Parts 1 and 2 of *Zur Kritik der politischen Ökonomie* were restricted in length by the publisher Franz Duncker. As a result, Marx incorporated the alienation theme into particular sections of the text and in the process used a relatively concise, abstract mode of expression. In *Das Kapital,* by contrast, he felt no constraints about length and dealt with commodity fetishism—the theoretical basis of the alienation theme— in one section and included lengthy concrete discussions of the working day and the extraction of relative and absolute surplus value. The concrete discussions could be linked to the theoretical parts of the text. As a result, even though *Das Kapital* was a far longer text, much of the material related to alienation that Marx had placed in the context of his 1861–62 discussion of the division of labor was eliminated from that part of the analysis in 1867 because it appeared, in a different form, at some length elsewhere.

Beginning in the second paragraph of the 1867 discussion, a number of developments and changes occur in terms of an intensive comparison between the two texts. At that point, Marx wrote that if one "only looks at *labor* itself then one can designate the separation of social production into two main genera [*Gattungen*] like agriculture, industry, etc. as *division of labor in general,* the separation of the genera of production to species and sub-species as *division of labor in particular,* and the division of labor within a workshop as *division of labor in detail* [*Einzelnen*]."[39] He cited two quotations in footnote 50 to support the claim.

The first footnote, taken from Storch, was located in the 1861–62 draft on manuscript page 169.[40] At that time Marx used the same quotation to criticize Storch for viewing the division of labor and manufacture as the outcome of the social division of labor—for seeing "the one as the final sharpening of the other . . . as the *take off* point for the other, what is an advance."[41] These criticisms are absent from *Das Kapital.*

The second quotation is abridged from a very short, autonomous section located on manuscript pages 188 and 189 at the end of the division of labor analysis. The quotation, taken from Frédéric Skarbek's *Théorie des richesses sociales,* was thus transformed from an isolated fragment entitled "Different Types of the Division of Labor," which suggests Marx may have considered developing such an independent section when organizing his draft in 1861 and 1862, to support for an opening theme contrasting the social division of labor and that of manufacture. In both cases, material originally used in one way was incorporated in *Das Kapital* to serve another purpose.

In the next paragraph of *Das Kapital,* Marx began to discuss the origin of the social division of labor, and once again he drew material together from previously disparate sections of the 1861–62 manuscript.[42]

The discussion shows quite well how the context of *Das Kapital,* particularly the style of presentation, influenced how Marx reworked some of the material found in the 1861–62 draft. At the same time, of course, conceptual refinements were introduced in the reworking of this material.

In *Das Kapital,* Marx established an analysis for the origin of the social division of labor parallel to his earlier examination of the twofold origin of the division of labor in manufacture. In 1867, he attempted to show a dynamic tension between the two different influences on the social division of labor, which he had treated more or less separately or, at most, as mutually influential in 1861–62. "The division of labor *within the society* and the corresponding restriction of individuals to particular spheres of employ, develops, like the division of labor within manufacture, from opposed points of origin."[43] One of the points of origin was internal to society, and the other was external. In developing his argument, however, Marx had to subtlely rework and rearticulate ideas from 1861–62.

Concerning the internal source, Marx borrowed heavily in *Das Kapital* from an 1861–62 statement. In the early draft, he had argued that the social division of labor "exists originally in the family where it results naturally [*naturwüchsig*] from physiological differences, differences of sex and age."[44] The idea was transferred with only minor alterations to *Das Kapital.* "Within the family, and after further development, a tribe, a natural [*naturwüchsige*] division of labor arises from the differences of sex and age, thus from a purely *physiological* basis."[45]

In the 1861–62 account, however, Marx was basically presenting an argument developed by Thomas Hodgskin.[46] As a result, Marx immediately followed his statement about sex and age with additional commentary on conditions in the natural environment. That statement, however, led directly into a discussion of exchange, and no attempt was made to treat exchange as a separate influence on the division of labor. Thus Marx directly followed the sentence from the 1861–62 manuscript with the following statements: "The heterogeneity of individual organizations, physical and intellectual abilities, become new sources of the same [heterogeneity]. But then added to this through different natural conditions, differences of soil, division of water and land, mountain and plain, climate, condition and mineral content of the earth, and particularities in its characteristic, spontaneous creations, diversity in the naturally existing instruments of labor, which divide the lines of enterprise of the different tribes and in their exchange we have to seek the general transformation of [a] product to [a] commodity."[47] These ideas were taken over into *Das Kapital,* although without the same detail, however Marx linked them to other material in the 1861–62 draft.

Earlier in the 1861–62 manuscript, in a critical discussion of Smith's conception of the division of labor, Marx argued:

> *spontaneous* [*Naturwüchsige*] *division of labor exists before exchange,* and this exchange of products, as commodities, develops first between *different communities, not within the same community* (due in part not only to all spontaneous [*naturwüchsigen*] differences of men themselves, rather spontaneously [*naturlichen*], the natural [*naturlichen*] elements of production which these different communities come upon.) The development of the product to a commodity and the exchange of commodities reacts to be sure on the division of labor so that exchange and division of work in a relation of reciprocal effect.[48]

In *Das Kapital,* Marx drew these two sets of ideas together into a more coherent, and accurate, whole. Thus, after pointing out the internal source of the social division of labor based on physiological differences, he went on to note:

> On the other hand, as I remarked earlier, the *exchange of products* comes from the point where different families, tribes, communities come into contact, because it is not private people, rather families, tribes, etc. that independently face each other in the beginning of civilization. Different communities come upon different means of production and different means of life in their *natural environs* [*Naturumgebung*]. Their modes of production, modes of life and products are therefore different. It is this spontaneous [*naturwüchsige*] diversity that brings about, through the contact of the communities, the exchange of the multiplicity of products and therefore the gradual transformation of those products to commodities.[49]

He concluded the argument by showing that through the physiologically based division of labor, the divisions become greater until the branches are more or less independent, whereas trade between formerly independent communities makes them increasingly interdependent as trade grows in scale.

Following his brief statement that "[t]he foundation of all developed division of labor, mediated through commodity exchange, is the *separation of town and country,*" Marx examined the question of density of the population. "Just as a certain *number* of simultaneously employed workers constitute the material presupposition for the division of labor within manufacture, so, for the division of labor within society, the *size of the population* and its *density,* which in this case here means concentration in the workshop, are presuppositions."[50] This idea was taken from a section of the 1861–62 draft manuscript where Marx summa-

137

rized three presuppositions necessary for the division of labor,[51] but the two quotations to substantiate the claim came from earlier, and separate, portions of the 1861–62 draft.

The quotation from James Mill's *Principles of Political Economy*— "There is a certain *density of population* which is convenient, both for social intercourse, and for that combination of powers by which the produce of labour is increased"[52]—has an ambiguous status in the 1861–62 draft. It is found in a section that lists and comments critically upon statements by political economists on the division of labor,[53] and the Mill statement, in this context, appears partially to support a point Marx was making against Francis Wayland. Marx argued in the 1861–62 draft, "[j]ust like the expansion of capital, so the use of the division of labor requires as its basic presupposition cooperation, the agglomeration of workers, which only takes place overall where there is a given density of the population." But he then added in brackets, "[a]lso at the same time where the population, after its separation from the land, is collected in the center of production. Thereupon Stewart. This is to be discussed more closely in the section on accumulation."[54] Thus, when considering population density, one must consider a potentially industrial one of wage laborers. The same qualification would also apply to the Mill quotation, but Marx does not comment to that effect in *Das Kapital* although it appears to apply in the 1861–62 context.

The quotation from Thomas Hodgskin's *Popular Political Economy* was associated with the discussion of the natural condition for the social division of labor in the 1861–62 draft manuscript and remains in *Das Kapital* as the only hint of Marx's original source of information for that section. In *Das Kapital*, Marx continued his argument to point out that density was a relative phenomenon, and a country with a well-developed communication system was effectively more densely populated than one with a poorly developed communication network even though the latter country might have a larger population. Even though this idea originally arose in the 1861–62 draft on manuscript page 171, one of the quotations from Hodgskin on page 170 emphasized the point most clearly: "Improved methods of conveyance, like railways, steam vessels, canals, all means of facilitating intercourse between countries, act upon the division of labour in the same way as an actual increase in the number of people; they bring more labourers into communication etc."[55] In *Das Kapital*, however, he did not use this or any other quotation to support or illustrate the role of communication.

In assessing this segment of *Das Kapital*, it is fair to argue that Marx had not made his points as clearly and distinctly as he might have;

even though the 1861–62 draft is disjointed and discontinuous, it suggests what could have been included to clarify the argument. The population question, as Marx noted in 1861–62, involves three issues: the density of the population, the development of communication, and the nature of the population. Twice in 1861 and 1862 Marx addressed this last issue, once on manuscript page 168 and a second time at the bottom of page 171. On the second occasion, during his three summary points about the presuppositions for the division of labor, Marx wrote, "What is thus needed above all is not an increase of the population, rather an increase in the purely industrial population, or a different division of the population." This led to a discussion of how the agricultural population was separated from the land so that it represented "free hands as Stewart says" available for manufacture. Then, in a marginal comment, Marx wrote, "this all belongs in *accumulation*."[56] Although I have no argument with this conclusion insofar as a detailed discussion of the separation from the land is concerned, Marx should have made the point about the nature of the population within the fourth section of his analysis of the division of labor within a footnote referring to its full analysis in the chapter on accumulation. The three distinctions made in 1861–62 were important enough to be kept together in *Das Kapital*.

When turning to the necessity of a well-developed social division of labor for the existence of the division of labor in the workshop, Marx dealt with a theme presented several times in 1861–62.[57] In *Das Kapital*, just as in 1861–62, Marx argued that the division of labor in the workshop influences the expansion of the social division of labor. The difference between the 1861–62 analysis and that of 1867 is that Marx examined two ways this interaction takes place in the former, but only one in *Das Kapital*. The common theme is that through specialization, phases of production once carried on in connection with one another break their immediate connection and become independent branches of the social division of labor.[58]

In an argument found only in 1861–62, Marx maintained that the division of labor in the workshop "reduces the labor required for a determinate use value, thus freeing labor to be placed in a new branch of social labor."[59] The context of the analysis of *Das Kapital* does not suggest any reason why he might have consciously chosen to omit this point from the 1867 text. Furthermore, because the point is contained as a clearly enumerated part of a summary section that has a marginal line beside it and is part of the text Marx had stroked through with a diagonal line as he extracted material from the 1861–62 manuscript, it is even more difficult to determine why the idea does not appear in *Das Kapital*. Nevertheless, in 1867, Marx did not argue that the division of labor in manufacture increased the social division of labor by making a society more productive and thus creating the opportunity for workers to be employed in new divisions of the social division of labor. The only possible explanation is that by 1867 Marx was certain that areas of production were opened up only if they promised profit to a capitalist. Thus, it was the drive for profit in conjunction with the increased productivity of labor that led to the development of new divisions of social labor and not just the productivity of labor as suggested in the 1861–62 draft.

To conclude his paragraph in *Das Kapital* Marx argued that it "is not the place here to indicate how it [the division of labor] infects [*inficirt*][60] in addition to the economic, every other sphere of society, and everywhere lays the foundation to that formation of compartmentalization [*Fachwesens*], of specializations, and to a parcelization of men which already caused *A. Ferguson,* the teacher of A. Smith, to exclaim, 'we are nations of Helots and there are no free citizens.'"[61]

Marx's major point of interest in section 4 comes in the next paragraph. "In spite of numerous analogies, and the connections between the division of labor within society and the division of labor in the workshop, both are distinguished not only by *degree* but *essentially.*" The distinction between the two is at least evident if one follows a link between different branches of an industry, from cattle breeding through tanning to boot making, for example. "Now one can imagine with *A. Smith,*" Marx argued, "the social division of labor distinguishes itself from that of manufacture *only subjectively,* that is for the observer who sees here [in the workshop] the diverse detail labors at a glance; while there [in the social division of labor] their dispersion over great expanses and large numbers of occupations in every particular branch obscures the interconnection."[62] "But" he proceeded to ask, "what produces this connection between the independent labors of the cattle breeders, the tanner and the shoemaker? The being-there of their respective products as *commodities*. What characterizes, on the other hand, manufacture's division of labor? That the detail worker *produces no product.*"[63] Although this is the major distinction, Marx enumerated others as well.

The social division of labor, he argued, is mediated through the purchase and sale of products, whereas in the workshop the division of labor is mediated by many workers selling their labor power to one capitalist. The "division of labor in manufacture places the *concentration* of the means of production in the hand of a capitalist, the social division of labor has the *dispersal* of the means of production under many commodity producers independent of one another."[64] Finally, the division of labor in manufacture assumes the "undisputed authority of the capitalist over men," whereas the division of labor in society assumes "independent commodity producers who are independent of each other and subject only to the laws of competition."[65] All of these ideas were drawn together from various parts of the 1861–62 manuscript.

The assembly of information is not surprising; its presentation as a unit in *Das Kapital* represents the improved organization of *Das Kapital* over the 1861–62 draft. What is noteworthy, however, is that in 1861–62, Marx introduced some of the contrasts discussed with the following comment. "What strikes us about the division of labor, as well as all forms of capitalist production, is the character of the antagonism."[66] He could have presented all of the contrasts within this framework of antagonism in 1867, but chose not to do so. Perhaps he chose to omit this type of framework because it appears to impose an artificial theoretical framework on a concretely dynamic set of relations. The whole of the text of *Das Kapital* suggests material antagonisms, and Marx did not have to remind his reader of them in 1867. The compressed style of parts 1 and 2 of *Zur Kritik der politischen Ökonomie*, on the other hand, may have required Marx to point out more clearly what he could not convey through concrete analysis.

In the remainder of the section Marx returned to a theme he had discussed in *Misère de la philosophie:* the resistance of some modes of production to the division of labor in the workshop.[67] In *Das Kapital*, Marx provided more information on India than he had previously and also discussed how guilds hindered the transformation of a guild master "to a capitalist."[68] Once again, this required a major reorganization of material dealt with in 1861–62 although in retrospect the presentation of 1867 appears as the most logical one. The section concluded with a sentence-long paragraph: "While the division of labor in the whole of a society, whether mediated or not through commodity exchange, belongs to the most diverse economic social formations, the division of labor in *manufacture* is one quite specific creation of the *capitalist mode of production.*"[69]

Although Marx made this same point a few times in 1861 and 1862, the following most closely replicates his 1867 paragraph. At the end of an analysis critically dealing with Smith's conception of the division of labor, Marx wrote: "This shows conclusively that the division of labor, as it is treated here—and as it is actually also treated by Smith—is not a general category common to most, and most varied types of conditions of society, rather a quite determinate, historical mode of production, corresponding to a determinate, historical, developmental stage of capital."[70]

The Capitalist Character of Manufacture

In the final section of the division of labor chapter, Marx dealt with four themes: alienation (the most dominant theme), the ancients' view of the division of labor, forces of resistance found within manufacture to further development of the division of labor, and forces leading to the transformation of manufacture to large-scale industry.

The opening section begins with the comment that a "greater number of workers under the command of the *same capital* represents the natural departure point for cooperation in general and manufacture. Conversely, the division of labor in manufacture develops the increase of the number of workers employed to a *technological* necessity."[71] Thus, the requirements of manufacture, as a mode of production, dictate how human resources will and must be divided. This idea suggests the inversion of subject and object in the labor process and, as such, is a theme that dominates the alienation problematic.

Next Marx noted that the increase of the variable component of capital and its increased productivity requires a more rapid increase in constant capital. This point suggests how workers produce the structure that confronts them in a continually expanding fashion.[72] In its growth, of course, the workers have less control of the structure confronting them and become controlled by it.

As he had in 1861–62, Marx also argued that manufacture "not only subjects the previously independent worker to the command and discipline of capital but creates a hierarchical structure amongst the workers themselves."[73] This idea suggests the pitting of one worker against another in the competition for jobs, a theme first analyzed in the Paris draft manuscript of 1844.

These three ideas, which introduce the section, were present in virtually the same form in the 1861–62 draft, however in 1867, Marx combined them into one section to develop his longest analysis of alienation in the chapter on the division of labor. In the remainder of the discussion, however, Marx introduced a number of changes, ranging from some subtle shifts of emphasis to the inclusion of material not found in the 1861–62 draft manuscript.

Marx dealt with the alienation theme in many parts of the 1861–62 manuscript although he discussed it at length only twice.[74] As he worked through his ideas, he would accentuate in one place a theme that he might not accentuate in another. In one of his lengthy analyses, Marx pointed out how the particular relation of wage labor and capital created conditions that ultimately affected the nature of the product rather than keeping his focus solely on how the division of labor affected the worker.

> The product assumes only generally the form of the commodity . . . where labor capacity itself has become a commodity for its owner, the worker has therefore become wage labor and the money has become capital. The social interconnection between the money owner and the worker is thus only that of commodity owners. The relation modifies itself, brings forth new social relations, through the specific nature of the commodity which the worker has to sell and the characteristic manner in which the purchaser consumes it, just like the particular goal for which he purchases it. Capitalist production entails with it, among other things, the division of labor within the workshop, which [is] like the other means of production employed by capital that further develop mass production, therefore the similarity of the use values of the products for the producers, production for more sale of the product as pure commodity.[75]

This analysis supplied concrete information for another theme from 1844—how the worker becomes estranged from, and indifferent toward, the product he or she produces—but in 1867, Marx neglected the theme almost entirely. In *Das Kapital,* he focussed upon how the division of labor creates conditions that oppose and reduce the worker to a mere appendage in a gigantic system. This theme also dominated the 1861–62 draft manuscript, but several shifts of emphasis or changes in treatment occured between 1861–62 and 1867.

In the 1861–62 draft, following a comparison of Smith and Ferguson on the division of labor question and amid quotations regarding how the division of labor increased productivity, Marx discussed at length, in a step-by-step manner, how the division of labor created conditions of alienation that opposed the worker. In 1867, by contrast, he compressed essentially the same analysis into two lengthy paragraphs. A comparison of the two accounts shows not only a change in terms of length, but also some interesting changes of emphasis.

In the 1861–62 draft, Marx began by noting the different operations performed one after another by a single crafts worker are separated from one another in manufacture. "[E]ach such simple and brief process turns to the exclusive function of a determinate worker or a determinate number of workers." The workers become subsumed under those functions. "The increased productivity and complication of the total production process, its enrichment, is thus purchased through the reduction of labor capacity, in each particular function, to a purely barren abstraction." These simple movements can be easily coordinated to increase the productivity of the shop, and "[t]hrough this combination, the workshop is turned into a mechanism in which the individual workers constitute the different parts."[76]

In *Das Kapital,* Marx echoed the step-by-step approach of 1861–62 and made the same point through a careful selection of language and powerful imagery reminiscent of his epigrammatical passages of 1844.

> While simple cooperation leaves the mode of labor unchanged for the most part, manufacture revolutionizes it essentially and seizes the individual labor power by its roots. It [manufacture] deforms the worker to an abnormality in that it develops hothouse-like, his detail skill through the suppression of a world of drives and inclinations, just as one in the states of La Plata butchered a whole animal in order to have its hide or tallow. The particular detail labors are *divided* not only among different individuals, but the *individual* himself is divided and transformed to the automatic mechanism of a detail laborer, thus realizing the absurd fable of Menenius Agripa which presents man as a mere fragment of his body.[77]

In 1861–62, Marx next argued at length that the form of combination found in manufacture is different from cooperation. The worker is a

> living component of the workshop and through the mode of his labor itself became an appendage to capital so that his skill can only be exercised in a workshop, only as a ring of a mechanism, which is the being-there of capital opposed to him. . . . He must sell it [his labor capacity] now because his labor capacity is only labor capacity insofar as it is sold to capital. It is no longer through the want of the means of labor, rather through his labor capacity itself, the type and mode of his labor, subsumed under capitalist production, falling to capital, in whose hand one finds not only the subjective conditions but the social conditions of subjective labor, under which his labor is generally still labor.[78]

This suggestive passage was tightened and focussed more carefully in 1867:

> The worker originally sold his labor power to capital because he lacked *the conditions for the production of a commodity,* his *individual labor power* exists now only when and insofar as it is purchased by capital. It functions only in an inter-relation which exists after its sale, in the workshop of the capitalist. In accord with his natural conditions [*naturlichen Beschaffenheit*], unable to produce some independent thing [*etwas Selbständiges*], the manufacturing worker develops his productive activity only as an appendage in the workshop of the capitalist.[79]

The final two sections of the 1861–62 text present the central issue within the alienation theme. The whole workshop, Marx argued, "stands opposite them [the workers] as an external power, ruling over them and surrounding them, in fact, as the power and form of existence of capital itself, under it [the workshop] they are subsumed individually and to it belongs their social relations of production." In this way, the workers are alienated from the process of production that dominates them. At the same time, Marx noted in 1861–62 but omitted in *Das Kapital,* the workers are also opposed by "the ready product which once more is the commodity belonging to the capitalist."[80]

At the end of this particular segment the alienation theme is presented again, only here the relations confronting the workers are explained as their own creation, a theme also dropped as an explicit point in 1867.

> The increase of the productive power which proceeds from the division of labor, this social mode of being-there of labor, is thus not only the productive power of capital, but the productive power of the worker. The *social form* of these combined labors [however] is the being-there of capital against the worker; the combination stands up to him through the reduction of his labor capacity to a wholly one-sided function, which is nothing separated from the total mechanism and therefore totally dependent on it. It [labor capacity] has turned into a pure detail.[81]

In *Das Kapital,* Marx develops essentially the same points but focuses upon the intellectual aspect of production. The reason for the particular focus is the material chosen to develop the critique of the capitalist character of the division of labor further as well as the material planned for the chapter on large-scale industry. Despite this particular focus, however, the general thrust of the argument remains the same in 1867.

> The *knowledge,* the insight, and the will which the independent peasant or craftsman, if only to a small extent, develops, just as the savage practices the entire art of war as personal cunning, are required now only for the whole of the workshop. The intellectual potential of production widens its scale on the one side because it is lost on many sides. What the detail workers lose, concentrates itself opposite to them in capital. It is a product of the division of labor in manufacture that the *intellectual potentials* of the material production process can confront them as *estranged property* and *controlling power.* This *process of decomposition* begins in simple cooperation where the capitalist represents vis-à-vis the isolated workers, the unity and will of the social body of labor. It is developed in manufacture which mutilates the worker to a detail worker. It is completed in large-scale industry *which separates science* as an independent

145

potential of production from labor and presses it [science] to the service of capital.[82]

Before continuing with the discussion of how Marx developed his critique of the capitalist character of the division of labor within the alienation framework, two points should be established about the alienation theme in the 1861–62 and 1867 texts. First, Marx did, in fact, reduce the proportion of his analysis concerned with alienation by 1867. On the one hand, by tightening his analysis and organizing it more carefully, Marx eliminated much of the repetition of 1861–62 that accounted for some of the length of his treatment of alienation in that text. On the other hand, the nature of *Das Kapital* as a whole removed some of the need to outline in detail how the worker was subsumed under the detail tasks of the division of labor because many of those ideas were covered in the earlier section on the working day.

Second, despite the compression of his argument, the alienation theme remained an integral part of Marx's discussion of the division of labor in 1867. Coming in the last section of the chapter where the capitalist nature of the process was under critical discussion confirms this to some extent. In addition, even though Marx had dealt with only one or the other of the two main issues related to alienated production in earlier discussions, he showed how the worker was confronted and opposed by a structure of his or her own creation as well as how the resulting constraints prevented the full development of the worker's human potential through the work process. Thus he dealt with both aspects of the alienation problematic in 1867, something he had not done in most of his previous analyses.

To conclude his critique, Marx cited material from Ferguson, Smith, and Germain Garnier, some of which he had used in 1861–62. This material was used in 1867 to introduce some material not contained in the 1861–62 discussion. In 1867, he argued, "[t]he enrichment of the collective worker, and therefore capital, in terms of social productive power is caused through the impoverishment of the workers in terms of individual productive power." He supported this with a citation from Ferguson placed within the text, a much less frequent practice in 1867 compared to 1861–62. "Ignorance is the mother of industry as well as superstition. Reflection and fancy are subject to err; but a habit of moving the foot or hand depends on neither the one nor the other. Thus one can say that with respect to manufacture, its perfection consists in that it is able to get rid of the mind in the manner that the *workshop can be considered like a machine whose parts are men.*"[83]

What is surprising is not the use of Ferguson itself, but the selection of this particular citation from Ferguson's work when Marx had excerpted more powerful quotations in the 1861–62 draft, and that this particular quotation represents the most extensive use of Ferguson in the 1867 analysis. From the role of primary critic in the 1861–62 draft manuscript, Ferguson was "demoted" to a relatively minor figure in the 1867 analysis.

The selection of quotations seems to have been dictated by context, although what led to the changed context in 1867 is impossible to determine. In this section of the 1867 discussion, Marx uses his own assessment of the impact of the division of labor on the worker, the Ferguson quotation, and material from Smith and Garnier to focus on the educational problems associated with the division of labor in manufacture. As a result, in this context the citation from Ferguson was the most appropriate.

The reason Ferguson was used less extensively in 1867 is attributable to two reasons. First, in *Das Kapital,* Marx felt he commanded enough authority as the author of that lengthy critique that he did not need to rely on the authority of others to gain credibility for his arguments. Second, Marx replaced Ferguson as the chief critic of the division of labor by splitting the role with Adam Smith. The use of Smith is striking because Marx had noted in 1861–62 that Smith merely followed "his teacher Ferguson" and written quite clearly that what distinguished Ferguson from Smith was that the former "develop[ed] the negative side of the division of labor sharper and more emphatically."[84] But in *Das Kapital,* Marx followed his citation from Ferguson in one paragraph with the following discussion employing Smith.

> "The spirit of the greater number of men" says *A. Smith* "develops necessarily from and in their daily work. A man who spends his whole life in the performance of a few simple operations . . . has no opportunity to exercise understanding. . . . He becomes in general as stupid and ignorant as is possible for a human creature." After Smith described the stupidity of the detail worker, he goes on, "The uniformity of his stationary life naturally ruins also the *courage* of his mind. . . . It destroys even the energy of his body and disables him, his power can be expended fully and lastingly only in the detail employment to which he is raised. His skill in a particular trade appears to be gained at the cost of his intellectual, social, and martial virtues. But in every industrial and civilized society, this is the condition in which the labouring poor, that is the great mass of the people, must *necessarily* fall."[85]

Here Smith's own words graphically criticize a process presented totally without criticism, hesitation, or caveat in the opening chapters of *The Wealth of Nations.* The reason Marx used Smith and not Ferguson at this point merits some discussion. On the one hand, Smith's inclusion is puzzling whereas, on the other hand, not surprising at all. The puzzling aspect centers on why it is not until *Das Kapital* that Marx chose to present this dimension of Smith's work. Part of the reason could have been Marx's lack of familiarity with Book 5 of Smith's work. Marx's study notebooks of 1844 show that he stopped excerpting from *La richesse des nations* at the beginning of Book 5, although that does not mean he stopped reading the volume at that point. In preparing his Paris manuscripts of 1844, Marx did not cite or employ any of Smith's ideas from Book 5 even though he did prepare a critical discussion of the division of labor. As a result, it seems that in the early 1840s, the material in Book 5 of *La richesse des nations* was not included in Marx's reading interests, nor did it trigger any parts of his knowledge interests. In 1851, Marx apparently again excerpted from *La richesse des nations* and the first volume of Edward Wakefield's four-volume edition of *The Wealth of Nations,* but there are no indications that he excerpted from, or even remarked upon, article 2 of part 3 of the first chapter to Book 5.[86]

The notebooks of 1861–62 create more puzzles than they solve. In the first five notebooks, where one would expect to find a citation concerning Smith's criticisms of the division of labor, there is not one reference even though Marx excerpted from Garnier's notes to the French translation of Smith's text and had excerpted from parts of Stewart's *Lectures on Political Economy.* The Garnier notes implicitly refer to Smith's views on education—that is, the second article of part 3 of the first chapter of Book 5—and Stewart also deals with Smith's discussion of education in the first part of his *Lectures.* In the remaining notebooks of 1861–62 that deal with Smith—notebooks 6, 7, 8, and 9—there is no material confirming that Marx had read, noted, or been influenced by Smith's criticisms. There is not even a place where Marx made Smith's criticisms without acknowledging their source. When drafting "Die Resultate des unmittelbaren Produktionsprozesses," Marx did quote from chapter 2 of Book 5, but this has nothing to do with the division of labor question.[87]

What seems most probable is that when reading through his 1861–62 material on the division of labor and coming upon the Garnier material, Marx's knowledge interests jogged his memory about the material in Book 5 of *The Wealth of Nations* or whetted his interest to pursue the implicit reference to Smith that Garnier's commentary indicated. Marx perhaps turned to the material in an English edition of *The Wealth of Nations,* read through it, recognized its utility, and decided to include it in *Das Kapital.*[88]

If this scenario is correct, it also suggests another step in the construction of part 5 of the division of labor chapter. In *Das Kapital*, Marx organized the particular thrust of part of the alienation analysis around educational concerns. It was the decision to include the Smith quote in *Das Kapital* that set up that context. Smith's quote was extremely important, and Marx chose the material preceding it and following it to build around the Smith critique.

Why Marx chose to use the Smith quotation, and why he would build other material around it, is not so puzzling. Aside from the candid comment the quotation presents on a serious problem associated with the division of labor—a significant trait in itself—the quotation's inclusion almost guaranteed a payoff that Ferguson's criticisms, no matter how astute, could not. By using this critical passage from Smith, Marx was able to show that even the greatest proponent of the division of labor in classical political economy was aware of the problems it created for workers. He could effectively turn the economic bible of the bourgeoisie upon its practitioners.

Following the Smith quotation, Marx introduced some material from Garnier's notes to his translation of *La richesse des nations*. In 1867, Marx noted that Smith recommended education for the people by the state "but also in prudently homeopathic doses. . . . Consequently, his [Smith's] French translator and commentator, *G. Garnier*, who turned out to be quite naturally a senator under the first French Empire, polemizes against that." These changes—or the context established by these opening remarks—led to the inclusion of material Marx had set out in 1861–62. "National education," he wrote in *Das Kapital*, "violates the first law of the division of labor and with it 'one proscribes our whole social system.'"[89] Marx then cited the last of three excerpts made for the 1861–62 draft manuscript to demonstrate Garnier's sentiments on the education question.[90]

To complete the material I have grouped under the alienation theme, Marx argued that "a certain intellectual and physical crippling is inseparable from the division of labor of the whole society," and, he added, it is the first to supply "the material and thrust towards *industrial pathology.*" Marx supported this claim in footnote 73 with material not present in the 1861–62 draft.[91] Two paragraphs later, he drew his discussion of alienation more or less to a conclusion. The paragraph contains no new material, but it does draw together a number of key ideas and differs, in many ways, from the summary statements of the 1861–62 draft.

The division of labor in manufacture, through the analysis of handicraftlike activity, specialization of the instruments of labor, formation of detail workers, their grouping and combination in a total mechanism, creates the qualitative organization and quantitative proportionality of the social production process, thus a determinate *organization of social labor* and develops with it at the same time, a new social productive power of labor. As a specifically *capitalist* form of the social production process— and on the foundation available it could not develop other than in the *capitalist* form—it is the only method to create *relative surplus value* or the *self-valorization of capital*—what one terms *social wealth, "Wealth of Nations"*, etc.—at an increased cost to the worker. It [division of labor] develops the social productive power of labor not only for the capitalist, instead of the worker, but through the crippling of the individual worker. It produces new conditions of the domination of capital over labor. If it [division of labor] appears on the one hand as a historical advance and necessary moment of development in the economic process of the formation of society, on the other hand, it appears as *a means* of more civilized and more refined exploitation.[92]

At this point, Marx focussed, by way of contrast, upon the view of the division of labor found among the ancients. While political economists only saw the division of labor as a means for producing more and cheaper commodities, "the writers of classical antiquity, in the strongest contrast to this accentuation on *quantity* and *exchange value,* consider *quality* and *use value.*"[93]

In terms of how Marx developed his analysis of the division of labor in *Das Kapital,* six notable features relate to the organization of the material and link themselves to themes discussed previously. In this sense, the section on the ancients is almost a microcosm of the division of labor chapter as a whole.

The first point concerns the intended use of the material for Marx's argument as a whole. He originally placed the analysis of the ancients about a third of the way through his 1861–62 draft manuscript. At that point, he compared the views of various political economists on the division of labor to the views of the ancients.[94] While this is still the case in 1867, there are differences in emphasis and use between 1861–62 and 1867.

In 1861–62, Marx not only noted, on three occasions, the similarities and contrasts between Smith's and the ancients views of the division of labor, but he also discussed them at some length and quoted Smith fully to prove his assertions. Similarly, Marx spent more time discussing the positions of Petty, Harris, and the anonymous authors of *The Advantages of the East India Trade to England* in the 1861–62 draft manuscript.[95] In 1867, by contrast, all of this material and these ideas were compressed into the opening sentence quoted at the outset of this segment on the ancients, plus a short footnote: "The older authors like *Petty, 'Advantages of the East India Trade'* etc. establish the manufacturing division [of labor] as a capitalist form of production more than A. Smith."[96]

The reason for this marked compression has been discussed previously. Whereas in 1861–62, Marx was concerned with criticizing the particular views of a number of economists' theoretical formulations, he shifted his emphasis in 1867 to the political economy itself. As a result, a thorough analysis of particular theoretical elaborations was not as significant, and Marx could treat ideas in groupings and so had no need to document his criticisms at such great length.

A second dimension to the question of organization concerns how Marx actually assembled the ideas in 1867 that he carried over from 1861–62. Without detailing these changes, I will merely note that the final presentation in 1867 represents a thoroughly revised sequence of quotations and ideas from the 1861–62 draft.[97] As much as any section of the 1861–62 draft manuscript, the section on the ancients shows how Marx used early drafts to set out his ideas so he could subsequently go through that material and organize it more fully. What appears most remarkable—especially in a comparison between the original draft text of *Zur Kritik der politischen Ökonomie* and the 1859 publication but also in the comparison of the 1861–62 draft and *Das Kapital*—is how Marx made marked organizational improvements in the simple movement from one draft to another while adding new material at the same time. While there is evidence for volumes 2 and 3 of *Das Kapital* that the process was occasionally slower than the movement from *Die Grundrisse* to 1861–62 to *Das Kapital* would suggest, no evidence indicates that Marx developed any other intermediary drafts for his analyses of the labor process, the valorization process, or the division of labor than the *Die Grundrisse* to *Das Kapital* chain noted here. Given the encyclopedic nature of his reading habits, the complexity of the task he undertook, and the conditions (physical, financial, and publisher imposed) under which he worked, Marx's ability to move rapidly from a draft to a complete manuscript is remarkable.

The third organizational feature of note is the extreme compression of the actual discussion of the ancients—only one paragraph long comprised of twenty-seven lines of text—and the concomitant movement of material to extensive supporting footnotes. Perhaps surprisingly, little is lost through this compression. Marx's main point—that the ancients focussed upon quality and use value of the goods—is made, although it did not receive the same documentation in 1867 as in 1861–62. He emphasized the same aspects of Plato's position on the division of labor as he had in his 1861–62 summary statement.[98] Marx kept Plato's main point that the division of labor is the foundation upon which the division of society into estates rests in the text, and he placed the two subpoints— one on the origin of the division of labor and the other the notion that a worker should concentrate on only one occupation—in footnote 80.[99] The material Marx used to substantiate these last two points in the 1861–62 draft was omitted from *Das Kapital* despite the work it had cost him to track them down and use them originally.[100] Finally, the material on Xenophon is also carried over fully from the 1861–62 draft to 1867 with the main point in the text—Xenophon comes close to describing the division of labor in the workshop[101]—and a subpoint on the dependency of the division of labor to the extent of markets at the end of footnote 81, which also illustrates the main point.

In the final segment of the fifth section Marx presented ideas and material not included in the 1861–62 draft manuscript. He argued that even though manufacture simplified work tasks and created a hierarchy of workers, skill still remained a limiting factor to manufacture's total control of the production process. Male workers resisted manufacture, and apprenticeship laws prevented the complete de-skilling of all jobs by manufacture: "manufacture could not seize the social production process in its whole extent, nor revolutionize it to its core. It culminated as an economic machine [*Kunstwerk*] based on the broad foundation of town handicrafts and the rural domestic industries beside them. Its own narrow technological basis, at a given degree of development, came into contradiction with the wants of production produced by it [manufacture] itself."[102]

Among the contradictions Marx noted was a workshop capable of producing machines. Machines abolish the role of the handicrafts worker "as the regulating principle of social production. So, on the one hand, the technological basis of the life long annexation of the worker to a detail function is removed. On the other hand, the barriers which the same principle still imposed of the domination of capital falls." With this ominous conclusion, he moved on to discuss large-scale industry in section 4 of the fourth chapter of *Das Kapital*.

On the basis of the foregoing analysis, it is apparent that Marx's analysis of the division of labor developed and sharpened considerably from his first full elaboration in 1861–62. In 1867, the chapter was organized to build synthetically from the origin of manufacture and the detail worker and his or her tools through the fundamental forms of manufacture and the division of labor in manufacture and society to the capitalist character of manufacture as a whole.

Marx also restructured how he used his material throughout his analysis. Smith, for example, was an implicit foil for the analysis of the detail workers and their tools so Marx could present the classical justification for the division of labor while simultaneously weaving into it his own critique. In the final section of the chapter, Marx skillfully used Smith as a critic of the division of labor by citing the latter's reservations about the influence of the division of labor on the intellectual development of the working class. Marx placed that material within the context of the alienation problematic, which he had carefully framed in terms of the development of human intellectual potential. Ferguson, in contrast to Smith, plays an almost insignificant role in 1867 as a critic of the division of labor despite the major role he had played in 1861–62. Finally, Marx either eliminated much supporting documentation for his arguments or else he moved it from the text into footnotes, with the compression of the material on the ancients serving as the best example.

In addition to changes of form, there are a number of changes in content between 1861–62 and 1867. The analysis of the division of labor in 1867 contains a new unity of abstract and concrete. In 1867, Marx presents more actual concrete material on the division of labor by drawing it from histories of machinery and technology rather than from various largely theoretical treatises on political economy. At the same time, however, he employed such new conceptual terms as *handwerkmässig* and *Gesamtarbeiter* to encapsulate concrete trends leading toward the simplification of work tasks and the conglomeration of specialized tools under a single source of control. Within this theme, Marx deals with the transition from manufacture to large-scale industry, from the tool to the machine, from human-based, handicraftlike production to machine-based, industrial production, and from the collective worker in the workshop to the machine.

In association with this reconceptualization, one can see an emerging evolutionary, almost mechanistic, dimension to Marx's analysis. The reasons for the change are primarily related first to the context of *Das Kapital* itself, which focuses primarily on the objective dimensions of capitalist production and thus lends itself to an evolutionary, mechanistic emphasis. Second, the writing of Poppe and the influence of Darwin, acquired in 1863 and thus totally absent in 1861–62, are seen more fully developed in *Das Kapital*.[103] As a result of the context of the text as a whole, and his incorporation of new material acquired in 1863, Marx presents a more dynamic view of the division of labor emerging from cooperation and leading to large-scale industry even though that model of change has specific limitations.

Finally, in *Das Kapital*, Marx presents his most complete treatment of the alienation theme within the context of the division of labor question. The discussion of how workers are prevented from developing their full human potential as they become one-sided appendages to detail tasks while simultaneously producing the social relations that oppose and exploit them is presented clearly and concisely in the culminating section of the chapter.

What is most apparent about the 1867 treatment of the division of labor is how much it had grown in terms of content, form, impact, and sophistication from its first presentation in 1844. Through all of the numerous twists and turns involved in the production of Marx's conceptual grasp of the division of labor, the twenty-three-year gestation period yielded a fully formed critique that was presented firmly within his unique intellectual framework.

NOTES

1. Marx may have introduced these headings following the advice he received from Engels just before the first edition was published; see Engels to Marx June 16, 1867, in Karl Marx and Friedrich Engels, *Werke* [hereafter cited as *MEW*] (Berlin: Dietz Verlag, 1956–1990), 31:303–4. The headings are located on the following pages of the second German edition of *Das Kapital* (Hamburg: Otto Meissner, 1873), pp. 345, 348, 352, 362, and 372; cf. Karl Marx, *Das Kapital*, 1st ed. (Hamburg: Otto Meissner, 1867), pp. 318, 321, 324, 335, 344. Virtually the same headings from the second German edition are found in the first French edition; see Karl Marx, *Le capital*, trans. Joseph Roy (Paris: Maurice Lachâtre, 1875), pp. 146, 147, 149, 152, 156. The only exception is the third heading, "General Mechanism of Manufacture. Its Two Fundamental Forms: Heterogeneous Manufacture and Serial Manufacture" in the French edition.

2. Marx, *Das Kapital*, 1st ed., p. 318. In 1861–62, Marx wrote, "*Manufacture* (in distinction from the mechanical workshop or the factory) is the means of production or form of industry corresponding specifically to the division of labor." Karl Marx and Friedrich Engels, *Gesamtausgabe: Werke, Artikel, Entwurfe* [hereafter cited as *MEGA*], (Berlin: Dietz Verlag, 1975ff), II, 3.1 p. 270: 23–25.

3. Marx, *Das Kapital*, 1st ed., pp. 319–20.

4. Ibid., pp. 320–21. The concluding idea of this paragraph is actually taken from Ferguson; see Marx's excerpts from Ferguson, *MEGA* II, 3.1, p. 250:24–26.

5. Marx, *Das Kapital*, 1st ed., p. 321.

6. For statements concerning the rise of manufacture from the breakdown of handicraft and the guilds, see *MEGA* II, 3.1, pp. 252:5–254:31, 273:39–274:23, and 275:24–276:17.

7. Ibid., pp. 270:23–28, 285:35–286:15.

8. Ibid., p. 252:8-11.

9. Adam Smith, *An Inquiry into the Nature and Causes of the Wealth of Nations,* vol. 2 of the Glasgow Edition of the *Works and Correspondence of Adam Smith,* ed. Roy Hutcheson Campbell and Andrew Skinner (Indianapolis: Liberty Press, 1976), pp. 17-20.

10. Marx, *Das Kapital,* 1st ed., p. 321. Marx did not cite Smith here, but he did reference the idea to the 1702 text *The Advantages of the East India Trade,* which he had mentioned on this same point in his 1861-62 analysis; see *MEGA* II, 3.1, p. 261:20-23, also p. 270:29-37.

11. Marx, *Das Kapital,* 1st ed., p. 323.

12. Ibid., pp. 323-24.

13. Engels made this comment in his afterward to the third German edition of *Das Kapital; MEW* 23:34-35. Marx cites Stewart concerning how the division of labor results in the simultaneous completion of a variety of operations in the production of a particular commodity, in his example, pin production. The idea of how the division of labor saves time is not new with Stewart, but the conceptualization of production as a simultaneous act was. Marx, *Das Kapital,* 1st ed., p. 328 n36.

14. *MEGA* II, 3.1, p. 259:10-23.

15. Marx, *Das Kapital,* 1st ed., p. 322. The footnote supporting this point is taken directly from the 1861-62 draft manuscript; see *MEGA* II, 3.6, p. 259:10-23.

16. Marx, *Das Kapital,* 1st ed., p. 321. In the French edition, Marx used the term *travailleur collectif;* see Marx, *Le capital,* p. 147.

17. *MEGA* II, 3.1, pp. 238:2, 232:34-238:41, 268:29-270:22, and 285:35-286:15.

18. Karl Marx, "Die Resultate des unmittelbaren Produktionsprozesses," *Arkhiv Marxsa i Engel'sa* 2(1933):128-30, 152-60.

19. Marx, "Die Resultate," p. 126, 96-98.

20. Ibid., pp. 100-118.

21. Ibid., pp. 102, 120, 126-46.

22. Ibid., pp. 128, 130.

23. Marx, *Das Kapital,* 1st ed., p. 325.

24. *MEGA* II, 3.1, p. 261:1-19.

25. Marx, *Das Kapital,* 1st ed., p. 326.

26. Ibid., p. 327.

27. Ibid.

28. Ibid.

29. Ibid., p. 328. Marx references Dugald Stewart's *Lectures on Political Economy,* ed. William Hamilton (Edinburgh: Thomas Constable, 1855), p. 319, for support of this point. *Das Kapital,* 1st ed., p. 328 n36. The full quotation is included in the 1861-62 draft. "The effects of the division of labor," he quoted from Stewart's *Lectures* "and of the use of machines . . . both derive their value from the same circumstance, their tendency to *enable one man to perform the work of many* (p. 317) It produces also an *economy of time,* by separating the work into its different branches, all *of which may be carried into execution at the*

155

same moment . . . by *carrying on all the different processes at once,* which an individual must have executed separately, it becomes possible to produce a multitude of pins f.i. *completely* finished in the same time as a single pin might have been either cut or pointed. (319.)" *MEGA* II, 3.1, pp. 251:37–252:4.

30. Marx, *Das Kapital,* 1st ed., p. 328.

31. Ibid., p. 329.

32. *MEGA* II, 3.1, pp. 262:4–263:36, especially 263:3–10.

33. Marx, *Das Kapital,* p. 329; cf. *MEGA* II, 3.1, pp. 262:13–263:36.

34. Marx, *Das Kapital,* 1st ed., p. 331.

35. Ibid., pp. 332–33.

36. *MEGA* II, 3.1, pp. 252:9–254:31.

37. Ibid., pp. 262:4–24, 262:1–3, 263:28–36.

38. Marx, *Das Kapital,* 1st ed., p. 335.

39. Ibid.

40. "This division proceeds from the separation of the various types of professions up to that division where many workers take part in the production of one and the same product [*produit*], as in manufacture." Marx noted, "He should not call it product, rather commodity [*marchandise*]. Also in the other division of labor different labor for the same *Product.*" *MEGA* II, 3.1, p. 266:8–12. Compare this with Storch's original French text (*MEGA* II, 3, p. 2867) and with the quotation—which is not completely accurate—in *Das Kapital.* Marx, *Das Kapital,* 1st ed., p. 335 n50; cf. *MEGA* II, 5, p. 805.

41. *MEGA* II, 3.1, p. 266:6–7.

42. Ibid., pp. 266:19–267:12, 248:15–249:19.

43. Marx, *Das Kapital,* 1st ed., p. 335.

44. *MEGA* II, 3.1, p. 266:33–34.

45. Marx, *Das Kapital,* 1st ed., p. 335.

46. The first part of this section in the 1861–62 manuscript is as follows: "Hodgskin remarks correctly that the division of lines of enterprise, thus the social division of labor, in all countries and under all political institutions establishes itself. It exists originally in the family, where it emerges naturally [*naturwüchsig*] from physiological differences, sex differences and age differences." *MEGA* II, 3.1, p. 266:30–35.

47. Ibid., pp. 266:35–267:2.

48. Ibid., p. 249:4–12.

49. Marx, *Das Kapital,* 1st ed., p. 336.

50. Ibid., pp. 336–37.

51. *MEGA* II, 3.1, pp. 268:29–370:22.

52. Ibid., p. 265:11–13. The emphases are Marx's, although he dropped them when using the quotation in *Das Kapital* (p. 337 n2).

53. *MEGA* II, 3.1, pp. 260:1–268:27.

54. Ibid., p. 265:4–13; see Mill's comment to this effect.

55. Ibid., p. 267:4–8.

56. Ibid., pp. 268:41–269:2, 10–11.

57. Ibid., pp. 238:10–41, 241:1–242:4, 242:28–34, 244:19–30, and 246:20–28.

58. Ibid., pp. 242:37–243:2; Marx, *Das Kapital,* 1st ed., pp. 337–38.

59. *MEGA* II, 3.1, p. 242:34–37.

60. In *Le capital* (p. 134), Marx used the verb *infesta,* but in the second German edition (p. 366), he changed the verb to *seizes* (*ergreift*).

61. Marx, *Das Kapital,* 1st ed., p. 338. The sentence from Ferguson is found in the 1861–62 draft notebook; see *MEGA* II, 3.1, p. 251:3–11. Marx cited Ferguson several times in 1861–62 and featured him as an important critic of Smith; ibid., pp. 249:20–251:16, 279:32–280:21. In *Das Kapital* Ferguson's role changed considerably. By 1867 he is used sparingly to substantiate Marx's points even though he could have used many of the references included in the 1861–62 manuscript. Because the changed use of Ferguson is most evident in section 5 of *Das Kapital,* I will discuss it at that point.

62. Marx, *Das Kapital,* 1st ed., pp. 338–39. This idea is found on manuscript page 151 of notebook 4 in the 1861–62 draft manuscript; *MEGA* II, 3.1, p. 244:3–15. Marx supported the idea in *Das Kapital* with footnote 57 (p. 339). All of the material presented there is found on manuscript pages 173–74 of notebook 4; see *MEGA* II, 3.1, pp. 270:38–271:41. Thus ideas that were widely separated in the 1861–62 draft are brought together by Marx in this part of *Das Kapital.*

63. Marx, *Das Kapital,* 1st ed., p. 339. Marx supported this last point with a footnote reference to *Labour Defended Against the Claim of Capital,* which he had also cited in 1861–62. The quotation at that time came in the midst of an analysis of what precisely was contained in the division of labor in manufacture. "With the development of the division of labor, every individual product of labor—which with the merely formal subsumption of labor under capital was still possible—disappears. The ready commodity is the product of the workshop, which itself is a mode of being-there of capital. The exchange value of labor itself—and the labor, not its product—becomes through the mode of production itself, not only through the contract between capital and labor, the only [thing] that a worker has to sell. Labor becomes, in fact, his only commodity and the commodity overall, general category, under which production is subsumed. We begin with the commodity as the most general category of bourgeois production. It became such a general category first through transformation which the mode of production itself is subjected through capital. 'There is no longer anything we can call the natural reward of individual labour. Each labourer produces only some part of a whole, each part, having no value or utility of itself, there is nothing on which the labourer can seize, and say: it is my product, this I will keep for myself' [quotation in English]." *MEGA* II, 3.1, p. 265:14–29.

64. *MEGA* II, 3.1, pp. 244:28–245:10, 269:18–23; Marx, *Das Kapital,* 1st ed., p. 340. See also *MEGA* II, 3.1, pp. 238:10–41, 241:27–242:4.

65. Marx, *Das Kapital,* 1st ed., pp. 339–40; see also, *MEGA* II, 3.1, pp. 285:35–286:15.

66. Ibid., p. 284:5–6.

67. Ibid., pp. 267:46–268:27.

68. Marx, *Das Kapital,* 1st ed., pp. 343–44; cf. *MEGA* II, 3.1, p. 245: 10–14.

69. Marx, *Das Kapital,* 1st ed., p. 344.

70. See, for example, *MEGA* II, 3.1, pp. 244:16–18, 270:23–274:3.

71. Marx, *Das Kapital,* 1st ed., p. 344. This is the combination of two ideas found in the 1861–62 draft manuscript; see *MEGA* II, 3.1, pp. 285:35–286:15, 263:3–10.

72. See ibid., p. 270:4–15 for the same idea.

73. Marx, *Das Kapital,* 1st ed., p. 345; see also, *MEGA* II, 3.1, p. 274:6–13, where Marx draws upon Ure's work for this idea.

74. For major references to alienation, see ibid., pp. 252:8–254:30 and 288:1–289:38; the theme also appears on, pp. 245:2–10, 246:29–34, 262:12–25, 264:10–30, 275:24–276:17, and 285:35–286:15.

75. Ibid., p. 289:24–39.

76. Ibid., pp. 252:13–16, 20–23, 253:2–4.

77. Marx, *Das Kapital,* 1st ed., p. 345. In the French edition, Marx shortened the passage slightly but made its point more forcefully. "It [manufacture] cripples the worker, it makes of him something monstrous, it quickens the artificial development of his dexterity in detail, it sacrifices a world of the producer's aptitudes and instincts just as in the states of La Plata, one immolates a bull for its hide and tallow. It is not only the work that is divided, subdivided, and distributed among diverse individuals, it is the individual himself who is broken up [*morcelé*] and transformed to an automatic spring of an exclusive operation, which realizes the absurd fable of Menenius Agripa representing a man as a part of his body." Marx, *Le capital,* p. 156.

78. *MEGA* II, 3.1, pp. 253:29–254:6, 254:8–22.

79. Marx, *Das Kapital,* 1st ed., p. 346. Marx supported this claim with the following citation (p. 346 n65) from Storch, a citation not located in the 1861–62 manuscript. "The worker who is the master of a whole craft can carry out his work and find the means of subsistence anywhere; the other (the manufacturing worker) is nothing but an *accessory* who separated from his fellows, has neither the capacity nor independence, and finds himself forced to accept any law it is thought fit to impose."

80. *MEGA* II, 3.1, p. 253:9–17.

81. Ibid., p. 254:3–31.

82. Marx, *Das Kapital,* 1st ed., p. 346.

83. Ibid., p. 347; cf. *MEGA* II, 3.1, p. 250:19–26; see also Smith, *The Wealth of Nations,* p. 782 n48.

84. *MEGA* II, 3.1, p. 250:12–13.

85. Marx, *Das Kapital,* 1st ed., p. 347, all Marx's emphases; cf. Smith, *The Wealth of Nations,* pp. 781–82.

86. *MEGA* II, 3, p. 3146.

87. Marx, "Die Resultate," p. 162.

88. Marx's use of *The Wealth of Nations* in *Das Kapital* is extremely complex. For example, in note 57 in the first edition (p. 339), he referred to the English edition—"(A. Smith Wealth of Nations, b. I, ch. I.)"—although the quotation was paraphrased from the French translation of Garnier in 1844 (*MEGA* IV, 2, p. 335:37–39) and excerpted more fully in 1861–62 (*MEGA* II, 3.1, p.

271:2-14, see especially lines 2-5). In addition, in the 1861-62 citation, Marx excerpted the full comment by Mandeville that pre-dated Smith's ideas (ibid., p. 271:19-41).

In *Le capital*, there are a number of places where Marx changed his use of *La richesse des nations* for the French edition in comparison to the first or second German editions of *Das Kapital*. Compare, for example, *Le capital*, p. 234 n1 with *Das Kapital*, 1st ed., p. 528, and 2d ed., p. 560; *Le capital*, p. 248 n3 with *Das Kapital*, 1st ed., p. 556, and 2d ed., p. 591 (note added to the third and fourth German editions; see Karl Marx, *Das Kapital*, 4th ed. [Berlin: Dietz Verlag, 1961], pp. 596-97); *Le capital*, p. 273, notes 1 and 3 with *Das Kapital*, 1st ed., pp. 608, 609, and 2d ed., pp. 647, 648; and *Le capital*, p. 274 n1 with *Das Kapital*, 1st ed., p. 610 and 2d ed., p. 649.

89. Marx, *Das Kapital*, 1st ed., p. 348; see also *MEGA* II, 3.1, p. 274: 24-27.

90. Cf. Marx, *Das Kapital*, 1st ed., p. 348 and *MEGA* II, 3.1, p. 275: 9-23.

91. Marx, *Das Kapital*, 1st ed., pp. 348, 349 n73.

92. Ibid., p. 350.

93. Ibid., p. 351.

94. *MEGA* II, 3.1, pp. 246:35-247:40, 254:36-39, 256:33-38, and 261: 17-42.

95. Ibid., pp. 246:29-37, 247:26-248:14, 256:32-38, and 261:17-42.

96. Marx, *Das Kapital*, 1st ed., p. 351 n76.

97. To show how Marx excerpted from and arranged his 1861-62 material for *Das Kapital*, it is possible to indicate the sources for most of the material in the text and footnotes. Unfortunately, merely citing page and line references to the 1861-62 manuscript does not convey very well how Marx selected some ideas from a lengthy argument, although I have noted this on occasion. The first sentence and footnote 76 involve material from *MEGA* II, 3.1, pp. 246:35-248:14, 254:36-39, 256:33-38, and 261:17-42. The question from Beccaria in footnote 77 is from ibid., p. 260:35-40, and the one from Harris in the same note is from ibid., p. 256:35-37. Footnote 78 is excerpted directly from pp. 254:41-255:2. In footnote 79 Marx supplied the textual quotation from Thucydides that he had explained, but not quoted, on p. 255:3-7. Footnote 80 draws material from a number of places; the first sentence is discussed at greater length in 1861-62 (p. 259:24-37), and the second sentence is a condensation of Marx's discussion and excerpts found on p. 257:1-30. The quote from *The Republic* is excerpted from p. 258:4-7, although in 1861-62 Marx had set out a fuller quotation (pp. 257:33-258:37). The Thucydides quotation is from p. 255:8-14, and the final part of the footnote where he shows how English bleachers used a Platonic idea against a clause in the Factories Act is taken from an addendum to the division of labor section of the 1861-62 manuscript (p. 290:14-40). Footnote 81 is drawn from pp. 255:32-34 and 255:36-256:18, where Marx wrote out the entire quotation in Greek. There are some minor differences between Marx's German rendering of the quotation from Xenophon's *Cyropaedia* in *Das Kapital* and the German rendering of the

Greek supplied by the *MEGA* editors (Apparatus, p. 136). The quotation from Isocrates' *Busiris,* footnote 82, is not contained in the 1861-62 manuscript, and p. 259:10-23 presents the quotation from Diodor's *Historische Bibliothek* that is referred to, but not quoted, in footnote 83.

98. Ibid., p. 259:24-37.

99. Marx, *Das Kapital,* 1st ed., p. 352.

100. See *MEGA* II, 3.1, pp. 257:1-259:6 and pp. 78-81 herein.

101. Marx, *Das Kapital,* 1st ed., pp. 352-53; *MEGA* II, 3.1, p. 255:14-31.

102. Marx, *Das Kapital,* 1st ed., pp. 353-55.

103. One can see the evolutionary influence in a number of places within the division of labor section of chapter 4. Consider, for example, Marx's analysis of the internal and external sources for the development of the social division of labor and his contrast between heterogeneous and homogeneous sources for the division of labor.

SIX

MARX'S DIALECTIC

Before 1844, Marx had completed a doctoral degree in philosophy, studied Hegel both formally at university and informally within the "Doctors' Club" in Berlin and as a member of the Left-Hegelians, and written several critical pieces from within a largely philosophical, speculative framework.[1] In other words, before his entry into political economy, Marx had a firm background in abstract, systematic, dialectical thought.

Despite this background in theory, Marx was actually drawn into political economy by his work as the editor of *Die Rheinische Zeitung* where, for the first time, he had to take into account some concrete, historically unique events.[2] But his entry into the study of political economy was not very concrete. Marx's first study of political economy, as one might expect in view of his previous academic training, focussed upon the classic treatises in political economy—the works of Adam Smith, David Ricardo, Jean-Baptiste Say, James Mill, and others—at a largely theoretical level. In fact, in the case of *La richesse des nations*, Marx only excerpted summary and theoretical statements while passing over all Smith's concrete examples and historical detail. At the same time, Marx demonstrated little historical expertise when he read through some of Smith's more questionable historical claims and generalizations, despite the fact that Marx included critical commentary in his study notebooks drawn from *La richesse des nations*.

Confident in his ability to analyze political economy critically, and with the encouragement of Engels, Marx began to draft the manuscript for a pamphlet [*Broschüre*] that would discuss political economy.[3] He

161

carried the same theoretical emphasis of his early reading in political economy into the draft manuscript.

In the Paris manuscripts of 1844, Marx broke new ground by drawing from, and developing, the conception of mediated human development found in Hegel's *Phänomenologie* by interpreting Hegel's ideas through the framework of production and labor found in political economy. This perspective let Marx turn Hegel's abstract notion of *Veräusserung* to the somewhat more concrete conceptions of *Entäusserung* [estrangement] and *Entfremdung* [alienation].[4] With a reworked formulation of Hegel's conception of alienated human action, Marx could then use that perspective as a vantage point from which to reexamine political economy. Even though this approach allowed Marx to address political economy in a new manner and develop new insights, the analysis was incomplete in two respects.

On the one hand, Marx's understanding of political economy was too narrow and superficial. On the division of labor question, for example, his whole argument centered completely on the aspects of the division of labor that he had excerpted from *La richesse des nations* and placed in his 1844 study notebooks. Thus, in the Paris manuscripts, Marx began his critique of the division of labor with an implicit reference to Smith's utilitarian notion that the pursuit of individual interests—the real basis, according to Smith, behind the propensity to truck, barter, and trade that led to the division of labor—works to advance the interests of all. But, Marx noted, the *"division of labor* is the political economic expression of the *sociability of labor* within alienation [*Entfremdung*]"* and because labor is an "expression of human activity within estrangement [*Entäusserung*], of the manifestation of life [*Lebensäusserung*] as the estrangment of life [*Lebensentäusserung*], so too is the *division of labor* nothing other than the *alienated* [*entfremdete*]*, estranged* [*entäusserte*] positing of human activity as a *species activity."*[5]

Marx continued his argument by indicating that even though political economists saw the division of labor as "the prime mover of the production of wealth," the "political economists are very unclear and contradictory about its character [*Gestalt*]."[6] To prove the point, he presented Smith's conception of the division of labor in juxtaposition to differing statements by Say, Frédéric Graf von Skarbek, and James Mill. But this was all Marx could manage on the basis of his background in political economy in 1844. In effect, his critique of the division of labor did little more than re-present, within a specific context, his criticisms of alienated labor found in other parts of the Paris manuscripts.

The second way in which Marx's analysis was incomplete concerns the unfinished state of his emerging social ontology, a problem that he himself realized. Thus, despite the fact that Marx had signed a contract for the two-volume *Kritik der Politik und Nationalökonomie* with Carl Leske in February 1845, he wrote to Leske on August 1, 1846 to explain why he could not draft the *Kritik* as originally planned.

> It seems to me that it is very important to produce a polemical piece against German philosophy and against the prevailing *German socialism* in *advance* of my *positive* development. This is necessary in order to prepare the public for the viewpoint of my Economy which directly opposes the hitherto existing German scholarship [*Wissenschaft*]. It is, moreover, the same polemical piece about which I have already written to you in one of my letters [and] which has to be completed before the publication of the Economy.[7]

Die Deutsche Ideologie represents a significant stage in the development of Marx's conception of the division of labor and an important dimension to his method for four reasons. First, by beginning *Die Deutsche Ideologie* with a statement of their premises, Marx and Engels created a textual context that almost required them to demonstrate the validity of those premises through a general, historical overview. Despite the general nature of this overview, it led Marx and Engels into the division of labor issue from a different perspective than that of Marx's 1844 study notebooks or draft manuscript. Consequently, Marx and Engels discussed aspects of the division of labor that Marx would not have considered had he relied solely on treatises in political economy, issues like the concrete conflicts surrounding the social division of labor, the impact of large-scale industry on culture, and the division of labor and social relations. Second, Marx and Engels developed the alienation theme in terms of more concrete examples. Finally, they began to deal with the division of labor with greater historical specificity—in terms of manufacture and large-scale industry—and this differed considerably from Smith's transhistorical conception of the division of labor.

The second point of methodological importance related to *Die Deutsche Ideologie* is the insight it provides into how the writing and elaboration process influenced the development of Marx's concepts. The exercise of producing the Paris draft manuscript made Marx aware that his ontological premises needed clearer formulation and that his linkage between the division of labor and the alienation theme was incomplete. The first realization encouraged him to establish his premises clearly in *Die Deutsche Ideologie,* and the production of that draft manuscript involved Marx in some concrete, historical analysis and commentary. The resulting clarification of his premises and the use of concrete, historical material had a far-reaching impact upon how Marx would link the division of labor to the alienation framework from 1846 onward.

In the Paris draft manuscript, Marx's conception of alienation was heavily influenced by Feuerbach's materialization of Hegel's philosophical anthropology. As a result, Marx tended to link his idea of alienation to the separation of humankind from some ahistorical notion of species–being. With the drafting of *Die Deutsche Ideologie,* particularly the section on Feuerbach, and the more concrete mode of presentation, Marx began to present the alienation theme in far more concrete, historically specific terms although a conception of human possibility that some might claim had an ahistorical, species–being-like quality remained as part of his problematic. In any event, in *Die Deutsche Ideologie* there is a decided shift of emphasis from a speculatively based telos to a far more concrete, empirical conception of alienation. Thus, Marx and Engels contrasted the relationship that exists between the worker and his or her product, from the medieval crafts worker to that of the "modern worker," and they discussed how "the productive powers appear as totally independent of and divorced from individuals" as the "totality of productive powers" assume a "thing-like character and are for the individuals themselves no longer the power of the individuals, rather of private property and therefore of the individuals only insofar as they are owners of private property."[8] In other words, there was a change in the referent for the alienation theme; alienation in *Die Deutsche Ideologie* was a much more historically concrete conception than in 1844. Although I would not see this as the epistemological rupture that Louis Althusser did, the shift of the referent for the alienation problematic is certainly a marked change in Marx's work and allowed him to develop the idea far more fully than if he had left it within a conception of alienation rooted exclusively in the philosophical conception of species–being.[9]

The third point of methodological importance is Marx's move to study history. The recurrent pattern in Marx's methodology is that he would work through his ideas initially at a theoretical level until he had exhausted the explanatory power of his model. He would then examine the resultant questions through the pursuit of empirical information. This return to empirical study would then permit Marx to develop his abstract conceptions further. The movement from the study notebooks and draft manuscript of 1844 to *Die Deutsche Ideologie* in 1846 is only the first of several instances where he moved from theoretical elaboration to empirical, historical analysis to gain greater insight into the political economy as he exhausted the limits of his abstract conceptions of the political economy.

The final point of methodological importance about *Die Deutsche Ideologie* concerns Marx's desire to grasp the political economy comprehensively. The letter to Leske is just one of many indications that although he had decided political interests in his public life, Marx the *Wissenschaftler* was motivated by a deep-seated desire to comprehend political economy in its totality. There is little doubt that he could, on a number of occasions, have yielded to Engels's pressure and written a critique of political economy long before 1867, yet Marx did not. He knew that he had not yet mastered the discipline of political economy or its empirical referent. In producing the definitive critique of political economy Marx, it seems, was motivated as much by the intellectual challenge that the task presented as he was by the political considerations that coexisted with his critique. This intellectual challenge kept him focussed on his critique of political economy at the expense of other writing projects and certain political activities.

Marx's 1847 polemic against Proudhon's *Philosophie de la misère* is significant on several accounts. On the one hand, *Misère de la philosophie* reflects Marx's return to theoretical material. Aside from re-presenting some of the historical material on the division of labor found in *Die Deutsche Ideologie,* Marx included references to Adam Ferguson, Pierre Lemontey, and Andrew Ure. Ferguson is important because for the next twenty years Marx would use him as a major critical weapon in debates with Smith over the division of labor, although this changed decisively in *Das Kapital.* Ure is noteworthy because the reference to him, to refute Proudhon's position that machinery could reconstitute the community lost through the division of labor, meant that Marx had considered, for the first time, an issue related to the technical division of labor, the dimension of the division of labor question that he would develop most over the next two decades. Finally, the text is a mixture of approaches, with Marx adopting a classical Greek, dialectical mode of presentation in the first part and a more straightforward, historically based critique in the second. This mixture of styles represents a chronic tension in Marx's work. He was most comfortable, it seems, as the gadfly of others and preferred to debate at the theoretical level of analysis, yet that approach had severe limitations. Ferdinand Lassalle, in a letter to Marx on May 12, 1851 spurred by exaggerated rumors that *Kritik* had been published, indicated the limits inherent to the role of the critic.

> I hear that your Political Economy [*Nationalökonomie*] now finally sees the light of day [*sic*]. Three thick volumes at once. I have been ravenous for them, one waits no longer. . . . [Y]our pamphlet against Proudhon is

quite suitable to have inspired in one the greatest interest for your positive achievement. Because it fully demonstrates an actually astonishing literary-historical erudition and a most penetrating understanding of economic categories. But it limits itself—which was after all quite appropriate there—to refuting Proudhon without developing the questions according to your positive side, which, as was said, could not be otherwise in this pamphlet. But just for that very reason I have awaited to see on my desk the three volume monster of Ricardo turned socialist, of Hegel become economist—since this must unify both and you will unify both.[10]

The problems inherent to a critique of categories would only become fully apparent to Marx as he worked through his massive notebooks of 1857–58 and in a series of exchanges and discussions with Engels and Lassalle during the same period.

While Marx seemed to prefer working at the level of theory, his method continually forced him to return to empirical material in an effort to overcome the gaps in his arguments as they arose in the course of his work. In the fall of 1857, he began the massive, seven-notebook work that its first editors entitled *Die Grundrisse der politischen Ökonomie: Rohentwurf.*[11] What is most significant about these notebooks for this discussion is that in compiling them Marx was carrying out three tasks simultaneously. First, he was drawing together, and setting out before himself, considerable information on political economy, both empirical and theoretical. His overall order—a chapter on money leading into a chapter on capital—represented a straightforward logical progression. Yet within that minimal framework, Marx conceptualized and reconceptualized his project several times, the second noteworthy feature of *Die Grundrisse.* When one takes into account the plans outlined within the seven notebooks, in the indexes, the plans Marx constructed after he had completed the text, and his correspondence during 1857 and 1858, it is apparent just how much he was wrestling with the problem of how to order the wealth of material he had for his critique as well as the form of his argument.[12] Finally, as Marx wrote, the context of his arguments influenced how he developed many of his insights.

For Marx, *Die Grundrisse* was, on the one hand, a logical extension of many of his early critiques, although it was a critique of the whole of political economy at once rather than just one, or a few, of its leading thinkers. On the other hand, it represents a significant strategic break from Marx's earlier work in political economy. Within *Die Grundrisse,* he was establishing the text and context of his own, full-length, critique of political economy. Consequently, it and its associated indexes are major experimental externalizations of Marx's critique.[13]

Even though Marx wrote little on the division of labor itself in *Die*

Grundrisse, there are sections of the text that reflect some of the methodological themes outlined previously. First, within a discussion of value, Marx noted that Smith's conception of the division of labor was associated with a natural conception of surplus value creation; humankind's propensity to truck, barter, and trade gives rise to the naturally bountiful practice of the division of labor. Thus, for the first time, Marx linked the division of labor to theories of value. His later analyses of the division of labor as a source for increasing relative surplus value have their origin, to some extent, in this part of *Die Grundrisse.*

Methodologically, this raises an important point. Although Marx had already determined the unique product sold by the worker to capital in an earlier section of *Die Grundrisse,* he did not yet link that insight, nor the way in which surplus value was produced, to all parts of his 1857–58 text. Those linkages would occur after he had gone back through the text, created an index, and then constructed his position systematically as he followed through the new outline established after the completion of the seven notebooks. Thus, Marx's conception of capital in general developed its full relational character on the basis of the practical act of setting out ideas, reassessing their form, content, and order, and then placing them within a more comprehensive framework. On many occasions this process involved the use of new empirical information to further develop some of the relations within capital in general.

In *Die Grundrisse,* Marx continued to develop his use of the alienation theme to address some of the central problems associated with the division of labor in manufacture. At the same time, he also brought out the dimension of human self-actualization through labor, a dimension of the alienation theme he had not addressed since 1844. Finally, Marx developed within *Die Grundrisse* the theme of historical specificity by distinguishing more fully between the division of labor within manufacture and the use of machinery in large-scale industry.[14]

When writing for popular consumption, Marx's style was more concrete but much less economic in terms of space and time than when he covered the same ideas in his lecture notes or drafts. Other than time and space considerations this type of praxis has another dimension. Marx, it seems, continually returned to his early philosophical training when working through complex issues. By working abstractly, with a specialized vocabulary, he could develop a theoretical skeleton with which to detect areas that needed further theoretical or empirical development, or aspects of his work that needed empirical illustration. The relationship between theoretical elaboration and the subsequent movement to empirical material is a continuous theme in terms of how Marx developed his critique of political economy. Furthermore, the relationship was central to the method he employed in the development of his ideas throughout the twenty-three-year production process of *Das Kapital*.

Finally, the 1857–58 period represented a watershed in the production of Marx's critique because although he had the opportunity to publish its first part and had a definite outline in mind, Marx did not proceed with his *Kritik* in 1859 as he had envisaged it in 1858. The exchanges of correspondence with Lassalle and Engels, plus the visit to the latter in May of 1858, led him to reconsider the form in which he would present *Zur Kritik*. The decision, taken in May 1858, to be less abstract had several repercussions on the eventual publication of *Das Kapital*.

First, the development of Marx's position on capital in general, within the new format, meant that his text expanded well beyond the originally envisioned length. At the same time, he was unable to prepare the third chapter for publication along with the first two chapters in 1859, and this significantly diminished the impact of *Zur Kritik*. The text was largely ignored by bourgeois and socialist reviewers alike.

The volume's failure posed a problem and a blessing for Marx. There is no doubt from his correspondence that Marx felt some of the burden of uncertainty when the product of fifteen years' work caused scarcely a ripple in the academic or political community. At the same time, however, he must have also realized that his text did not represent the apogee of his work on political economy. His best material still lay in the notebooks on his writing desk, and he had yet to conceptualize and synthesize completely all major aspects of the production process of capital. Thus the blessing was that the change in plans during 1858 gave Marx additional time to conceptualize his work more fully and return to empirical material to develop some of his insights further. He carried out some of the conceptual work on the division of labor theme in the draft for the third chapter of *Zur Kritik* that he worked on between August 1861 and March 1862.

Marx's 1861–63 Notebooks

The five notebooks that Marx produced as a draft for the third chapter of *Zur Kritik der politischen Ökonomie* contain a number of features characteristic of how he developed his concepts. First, it is apparent from the section on the division of labor that, following *Die Grundrisse*, where he dealt only implicitly with the theme in sections on the labor process, machine production, and within the issue of alienation, Marx turned to a number of treatises in political economy concerning the division of labor. In view of the topic's contrast between *Die Grundrisse* and the 1861–62 notebooks two points are particularly noteworthy.

First, as in the past, in the process of working through his critique of political economy in 1857–58, Marx realized that there was a major aspect of the issue he had not considered fully: the technical division of labor. Why he would write extensively on the technical division of labor in 1861–62 rather than in 1857–58 is hard to substantiate although two possibilities suggest themselves from the way Marx worked. One concerns his reading interests. It is possible that while reading a number of treatises in political economy in preparation for drafting the third chapter to *Zur Kritik,* Marx began to note the full significance of the technical division of labor for an understanding of the issue. As a result, he began to include considerable material on that aspect of the division of labor in his notebooks.

The other possibility—to which I would accord most emphasis—concerns Marx's post-1858 knowledge interests.[15] Following the drafting of *Die Grundrisse,* he established, in the same notebook as the proposed introduction to the text, an "index to the 7 notebooks (the first part)."[16] This index indicates an intention to move beyond *Die Grundrisse* on the basis of a consciously developed outline that differed, in many ways, from the original progression found in the notebooks themselves. Sometime between January 1859 and October 1859, Marx established another draft plan, this time "To the Chapter on Capital."[17] He decided to analyze the production process under the following major headings: "Transformation of Money to Capital," "Absolute Surplus Value," "Relative Surplus Value," "Original Accumulation," and "Wage Labor and Capital." Under the first heading, he included "Exchange between Commodities and Labor Capacity," "The Labor Process," and "The Valorization Process." Under "Relative Surplus Value," Marx had headings for "Cooperation," "The Division of Labor," and "Machinery," although he had only one reference from *Die Grundrisse* under the division of labor heading.

Thus, following 1858, Marx set out a series of plans for the development of his critique and then went through the notebooks that comprised *Die Grundrisse* to note relevant material for each heading of his plan. It seems logical that these plans provided definite knowledge interest reference points for any further reading Marx did in political economy. His work on his approach to the critique of political economy did not stop in early 1859. At some point in that year, Marx placed a number of excerpts from all of his available study notebooks into a citation notebook.[18] The index to the citation notebook contains a relatively large section devoted to the division of labor issue, although even it does not contain all of the material that Marx would include in his 1861–62 discussion of the topic.[19] In view of his overall outline for the third chapter on capital and his attempts to prepare a draft of that chapter, Marx had become increasingly aware of the need to deal more fully with the division of labor issue than he had previously. This insight was probably heightened as he compiled an index to his *Grundrisse* notebooks concerning material for the third chapter and found only one reference to the division of labor issue in that text.[20] Thus, as a result of the progressive conceptual development of the chapter on capital that Marx achieved from the series of indexes, he became progressively aware of the significance of not only the division of labor in general, but the technical division of labor in particular. That aspect of the division of labor relates most closely to the relative surplus value theme within which the study of the topic was located.

A study of the indexes, citation notebooks, and the 1861–62 draft indicates something more. Although Marx had included several references to the division of labor in the index to his citation notebook, the bulk of the authors cited in the 1861–62 draft were not listed in the index although they were included in the notebooks used to compile the citation notebook. This suggests that right up to the writing process, Marx was still thinking about the division of labor issue and that he used more than his citation notebook as a source for the draft manuscript.

The second major point in a comparison of the 1857–58 notebooks with those of 1861–62 is that although Marx used material from *La richesse des nations, Élémens d'économie politique,* and *Essai sur l'histoire de la société civile,* the bulk of the material on the technical division of labor in the 1861–62 text comes from treatises Marx read after 1859. Thus he cited material from works by Charles Babbage, Cesare Beccaria, Louis Blanqui, George Harris, Alonzo Potter, Dugald Stewart, Francis Wayland, and Xenophon, all listed in the seventh of the 1859–62 study notebooks. The timing and the nature of the material Marx turned to in his study of the technical division of labor should both be emphasized.

In response to his growing awareness of the significance of the technical division of labor, Marx first turned to largely theoretical sources. On the basis of these works, he formulated his own initial insights as far as his sources allowed. In other words, the same pattern, although at a different level of understanding of the political economy, occurred in 1861–62 as in 1844. Marx turned to theoretical work in political economy to gain an initial insight into the technical division of labor. Only later would he develop his grasp of the phenomenon through empirical study once he realized the limitations of the primarily theoretical insights.

The 1861–62 notebooks hold additional insights into Marx's method. For example, he was most likely led to his study of the technical division of labor because he had finally established his own framework for analyzing the production process under capital. This merits emphasis in part because of Marx's struggle between 1857 and 1859 over the actual order and form his critique would take and also because of the contrasts of the 1861–62 text to many earlier statements on the division of labor. In 1861–62, for example, Marx opened his analysis with themes that either relate directly to the technical division of labor, polemically confront those who failed to distinguish between the social and technical division of labor, or directly emphasize that it is the technical division of labor with which he is primarily concerned.[21] At the same time, the most sustained analyses of the division of labor within the 1861–62 notebooks proceed from aspects of the technical division of labor and link those to the formal subsumption of labor under capital and aspects of the alienation theme.[22] Thus, the entire thrust of the most significant dimension of the division of labor changed significantly from the pre–1858 conceptualization to that found after 1861. This conceptual development took place on the basis of Marx's struggle to order his critique satisfactorily. The resulting knowledge interests that emerged guided his reading and writing from 1859 onward.

In addition to the insight into how his knowledge interests influenced how Marx developed his ideas, the 1861–62 notebooks also provide two instances where ideas are developed on the basis of reading interests during the 1859–61 period. These examples also document Marx's practice of systematically pursuing references or issues to their primary sources.

While reading Stewart's *Lectures on Political Economy*, Marx found a reference to Xenophon's *Cyropaedia*. Rather than relying on Stewart's English citation, however, he traced the reference to the Greek original, read through it, and made notes from sections of the *Cyropaedia* related to the division of labor. Among the differences between Stewart's citation and the material Marx excerpted is the latter's attention to Xenophon's insights into the division of labor within the workshop, a topic related to some of Marx's knowledge interests at the time.

In addition to locating material in Xenophon relevant to the technical division of labor, which he would not have otherwise found, Marx also followed a reference in Stewart to Harris's *Three Treatises*.[23] Harris noted that he had derived his ideas from Plato, so Marx turned to the *Republic* in the Greek original and excerpted material relevant to the division of labor. Thus, on the basis of reading interests related to Stewart's *Lectures,* Marx developed an entire section of his analysis of the division of labor related to the work of the ancients. Moreover, he subsequently included that work in his analysis of the division of labor in *Das Kapital.*

The 1861–62 notebooks provide further insight into how Marx externalized his ideas. In the draft to the third chapter of *Zur Kritik der politischen Ökonomie,* he experimented with different styles of presentation. In some sections of the text, he carried and developed the argument himself. At other points, he juxtaposed statements from a variety of political economists, whereas in still other places, Marx blended his ideas with those of others into a conventional academic presentation. At no point in the chapter, however, did he present any detailed, empirical account of the division of labor to illustrate, in a wholly concrete fashion, his main theoretical points about the division of labor. This absence is consistent with the entire draft manuscript of the third chapter for *Zur Kritik.*

In contrast to *Das Kapital,* which has several lengthy, concrete, illustrative sections in the text, Marx did not include detailed accounts of the working day, for example, or the empirical examples found throughout the analysis of machinery and large-scale industry in 1867. Thus, despite his movement in 1859 away from a totally abstract presentation, or a critique of economic categories, the envisaged length of *Zur Kritik* still kept Marx from including extensive empirical illustrations in his 1861–62 text.

Another aspect of the externalization process found in the 1861–62 draft is Marx's practice of placing ideas loosely associated to one another in various parts of the text. The 1861–62 manuscripts represent a rough draft and indicate how the elaboration process proceeded when Marx was trying to settle on a final selection of material.

Two final features of the draft manuscript are worthy of note. The first concerns the alienation theme, which is developed twice within the draft. First, it is linked to the relatively concrete conceptions of the formal subsumption of labor under capital and the idea of products, once produced, standing in opposition to workers. The division of labor is then linked to the alienation theme through a discussion of the division of labor within the context of value and the emerging theme of the fetishism of commodities. Although not fully developed, the section indicates Marx slowly working toward a full incorporation of all his major themes within the framework of value.

Finally, in the 1861–62 manuscripts, Marx closed his discussion with an explicit account of the contradictions inherent to the division of labor. This section represents an advance over a similar attempt made in *Die Deutsche Ideologie*. At the same time, however, it was a mode of presentation from which Marx was moving away as he abandoned *Die Kritik der ökonomischen Katagorien* in favor of *Zur Kritik der politischen Ökonomie*. By *Das Kapital,* he would feel no need to systematically indicate the logical or historical contradictions found within the political economy because his more concrete form of presentation made the tensions self-evident.

Following the analysis of the division of labor in the 1861–62 manuscripts, Marx proceeded to discuss machinery, but his analysis was far from exhaustive. On manuscript pages 190 to 211, he organized a large collection of excerpts from treatises in political economy and a limited number of factory reports to indicate how "machinery as the basis of capitalist production intends in no way to lighten or shorten the day's toil of the worker."[24] Despite the presence of some of the major themes on the machinery issue that would appear in *Das Kapital,* the analysis in 1861–62 was limited by Marx's restricted background in the history of the machine. Following a nine-month excursus into theories of surplus value, he returned to the machinery question in January 1863.

Marx's study of machinery in 1863 illustrates two fundamental aspects of his method. The first is his use of history and empirical analysis. Between 1844 and 1846 Marx exhausted the limits of his theoretical understanding of the political economy and turned to historical analyses. As his overall theoretical framework was nearing completion in 1863, Marx again turned to historical study, the nature of which required highly specific and focussed empirical information. As a result, it is apparent that at no time in his study of political economy did he withdraw totally from empirical analysis to an exclusively theoretical mode of elaboration. On the contrary, the more his intellectual conception of capitalist production developed, the more Marx was dependent on specific historical information. As his abstractions became more developed, he was dependent upon specific, detailed historical material; abstract and concrete, to be fully related in a dialectical unity, required comparably exact information and detail.

This trend leads to the second aspect of Marx's method that the end of notebook 5 and notebook 19 document: the relationship of his concepts to the empirical information he gathered and the textual context in which he developed his ideas. Although Marx's study of machinery was designed to increase his knowledge of machinery itself as well as answer the question of how to distinguish a machine from a tool, the answer to both questions provided the key to the dynamic linking cooperation, the division of labor, and machinery (or the transition from manufacture to large-scale industry). While studying the history of technology and industry in *The Industry of Nations,* Marx discovered the argument that "In all machines there are certain parts which *actually do the work for which the machine is constructed.*"[25] Recognizing that it is "the *working machine* . . . [which] is the decisive factor," Marx could then identify the dynamic.[26] The focus of analysis had to center on the simplification of work tasks, the specialization of tools, and the ability to create production processes in which numerous specialized tools could function in large numbers, and in a sequence, to produce certain commodities. Grasping this dynamic empirically led Marx to reconceptualize the division of labor process. Thus, among other developments, he introduced two new terms—*Gesamtarbeiter* and *handwerk-mässig*—during the post–1863 period to represent conceptually the tendencies leading from manufacture to "machinofacture."

Although Marx used the term *handicraftlike* in the 1861–62 manuscripts, he used it at that time to describe the work process before its decomposition into detail tasks in manufacture.[27] Following his study of machinery and his discovery of the "working machine" as the link between manufacture and large-scale industry, Marx employed the term to represent a fundamental theoretical distinction. He wanted to emphasize that even though manufacture represented the breakdown of handicraft and guild production and resulted in the simplification of tasks, manufacture was still dependent on human labor power and labor capacity.

Gesamtarbeiter seems to have a more complex developmental history. The raw material for the concept existed in Marx's work in 1861–62, but he did not use the term until "Die Resultate des unmittelbaren Produktionsprozesses" and even then he developed the term within an excursus on productive and unproductive labor found within some "Additional Comments on the Formal Subsumption of Labor under Capital."[28] One can tie the development of the term quite directly to Marx's work on machinery. His reading on the history of machinery and technology influenced his thought in two major ways. First, he began to view the production process in more mechanistic and evolutionary terms. Second, and related to the first point, as Marx began to understand machinery concretely through his reading of *The Industry of Nations* and the works of Johann Poppe and Babbage, he could more clearly conceptualize the linkages between manufacture and large-scale industry. He identified the processes of the simplification and specialization of tools, as well as the possibility of changing the source of motive power from human to some mechanized form as centrally important. The term *collective worker* appears to have its origin in these realizations and is tied to the historically concrete process of the increased application of instrumental rationality to the production process to extract greater amounts of relative surplus value. Consequently, the term encapsulates an important theoretical development in the emergence of large-scale industry. Marx has moved from his empirical information back to the development of his theoretical framework.

The Division of Labor in *Das Kapital*

One of the least examined aspects of any scholar's method is the impact that the planning and concrete writing processes play in the development of his or her ideas. A close reading of the division of labor section in *Das Kapital* documents the importance of both processes in the development of Marx's ideas and concepts. If, for example, one combines the material of 1861–62 and 1863, then it is apparent that almost everything found in the 1867 discussion was present in the earlier period, but the whole of the later text is not equivalent to the sum of the parts found in 1861–62 and 1863. One of the major dimensions to Marx's method—how his concepts and ideas developed—centers on the organization and elaboration processes, which are demonstrated in *Das Kapital* as much as any other place in his work.

In terms of ordering his material, Marx made some fundamental decisions by 1867. First, his critique would begin with an analysis of the production process. This meant that some aspects of his 1861–62 study, especially the social division of labor, were excluded from the 1867 account because they related to the sphere of circulation. Second, the discussion had a more evolutionary, mechanistic tone, largely the result of the influence of Darwin and Poppe. Third, because of the focus on production, and the inclusion of the division of labor analysis in the section on relative surplus value, Marx focussed on the technical division of labor rather than the social division of labor. Finally, he adopted an order of progression found in Hegel's *Wissenschaft der Logik,* that is, a progression from the simple and immediate to the complex and mediate. In terms of the extraction of relative surplus value, this meant, at one level, moving from cooperation to manufacture to large-scale industry and machinery. At another level, it meant moving within manufacture and the division of labor from "The Double Origins of Manufacture" to "The Detail Worker and His Tools" through the "Two Basic Forms of Manufacture," as well as "The Division of Labor within Manufacture and within Society" to "The Capitalist Character of Manufacture."

175

The first level of development was enabled and structured by Marx's reading of the empirical history of machinery in 1863. This enabled him to recognize the dynamic link, centered on the "working machine," that drew these three loosely related means of production into a dynamic whole. The development of Marx's insight into the common dynamic between these three means of production was a major accomplishment because it enabled him to identify the dialectical tensions that created the movement from simple cooperation to the far more complex structure of large-scale industry. This discovery was developed even further in the production of *Das Kapital,* where Marx first introduced his terms *handwerkmässig* and *Gesamtarbeiter* to represent concrete conditions and relationships abstractly. As a result, the overall development of the chapter from the origin of manufacture to its capitalist character enabled Marx to organize his mass of material into a far more persuasive and focussed argument than ever before.

The second level of development, the movement from the origin of manufacture to its capitalist character, provided the perfect framework for Marx to present the fundamental characteristics of the division of labor analytically and build toward a more complex, synthetic totality at the end of the third section of chapter 4. This framework organized the wealth of material at Marx's disposal to deliver its full impact.

The development of a new organizational framework led to considerable reorganization and regrouping of material. The fourth part of section 3 of chapter 4 shows the greatest change in strictly quantitative terms. The greatest change in qualitative terms centered on the use of Smith, and to a lesser extent the use of Ferguson. In the case Ferguson, Marx demoted him to a minor role in 1867 from a relatively major role as a frequently cited critic of Smith. This change in status was directly related to the changed use of Smith in 1867.

In *Das Kapital,* Marx first used Smith implicitly in the section on "The Detail Worker and His Tools." In 1867, with the technical division of labor receiving more attention than ever before, Marx finally dealt with Smith's arguments in favor of the division of labor. At the same time, although Marx did not reference the ideas to Smith, he wove a critique of each point into the text. This critique, on the one hand, reduced the need for Ferguson as the critic of Smith and, on the other hand, enabled Marx to present the concept of the division of labor in an elaborated form of dialectical contradiction that emphasized some of its antagonistic relations in ways that he had never achieved before.[29]

In the section on "The Division of Labor within Manufacture and within Society," Marx presented his arguments against Smith for failing to distinguish between the social and technical divisions of labor. The differences between 1861–62 and 1867 are twofold. First, in 1867, Marx drew all of his material into one section rather than the dispersed form present in 1861–62. Second, and more significant, although Marx had commented several times in 1861–62 that Smith failed to distinguish between the social and technical divisions of labor, he only made the point once in 1867 but located it strategically at an important part of his argument. In *Das Kapital,* Marx argued that "[i]n spite of numerous analogies, and the connections between the division of labor within society and the division of labor in the workshop, both are distinguished not only by *degree* but *essentially.*" He continued by pointing out that one could imagine with Smith that "the social division of labor distinguishes itself from that of manufacture *only subjectively,* that is for the observer who sees here [in the workshop] the diverse detail labors at a glance; while there [in the social division of labor] their dispersion over great expanses and large numbers of occupations in every particular branch obscures the interconnection." But he argued that the difference is far more essential; it relates to the fact that in the social division of labor commodities are produced, whereas in the technical division of labor "the detail worker *produces no product.*" On the basis of this major distinction, he proceeded to enumerate several others.[30]

The point is that Marx had shown that Smith, the classical interpreter of the division of labor theme, was in error in terms of understanding the issue and that the error led to the oversight of fundamental distinctions between the social and technical divisions of labor. This is important because the process of developing a concept is more than just the positive elaboration of one's insights. It is necessary to show the weaknesses of the major competing conceptions and, in the case of the division of labor, Smith was the major exponent of the bourgeois understanding of the idea. In *Das Kapital,* Marx had developed a context of analysis that highlighted his own positive conception of how one should grasp the division of labor while refuting, through excellent textual developments, the conception present in Smith. In the final section of the discussion of the division of labor in manufacture, Marx explicitly used Smith in connection with the alienation theme. The presentation of alienated labor in 1867 is the third aspect of the difference between the 1861–62 manuscripts and that of *Das Kapital.*

Marx's discussion of alienation and its relationship to the division of labor is also shaped and developed by its context in *Das Kapital.* In the 1867 text, he presented several points found in the 1861–62 manuscripts, for example, the inversion of subject and object, the fact that it is the workers' products that stand in opposition to them, and the hierarchical structure that results from commodity production in manufacture.

In contrast to 1861–62, however, Marx refined the text of his 1867 presentation so that it made his points more precisely and forcefully. For example, he emphasized that "[t]he worker originally sold his labor power to capital because he lacked *the conditions for the production of a commodity,* his *individual labor power* exists now only when and insofar as it is purchased by capital. It functions only in an interrelation which exists after its sale, in the workshop of the capitalist. In accord with his natural conditions, unable to produce some independent thing, the manufacturing worker develops his productive activity only as an appendage in the workshop of the capitalist."[31]

Marx not only tightened his discussion more fully in 1867, but he also subtly directed it to a particular dimension of the alienation theme concerning the consequences that the simplification of tasks had on the intellectual development of the workers. Thus even though he was still concerned about how alienated conditions of production prevented the full development of human potential Marx could use this more focussed issue to exploit Smith strategically. Following the use of Ferguson as a critic of the division of labor, Marx developed the following paragraph linking Smith critically to the division of labor.

> "The spirit of the greater number of men" says *A. Smith* "develops necessarily from and in their daily work. A man who spends his whole life in the performance of a few simple operations . . . has no opportunity to exercise understanding. . . . He becomes in general as stupid and ignorant as is possible for a human creature." After Smith described the stupidity of the detail-worker, he goes on, "The uniformity of his stationary life naturally ruins also the *courage* of his mind. . . . It destroys even the energy of his body and disables him, his power can be expended fully and lastingly only in the detail employment to which he is raised. His skill in a particular trade appears to be gained at the cost of his intellectual, social, and martial virtues. But in every industrial and civilized society, this is the condition in which the laboring poor, that is the great mass of the people, must *necessarily* fall."[32]

As a result, in 1867, Marx had not only organized his material far more advantageously, eliminating repetition, building an argument synthetically, and including more information than in 1861–62, but he also developed his conception in his own terms while simultaneously undermining the classical proponent of the division of labor: Adam Smith. This is noteworthy because it represents an aspect of concept formation frequently overlooked in establishing the persuasiveness of individual positions and concepts. With these changes between 1861–62 and the presentation in *Das Kapital,* Marx constructed his most comprehensive, focussed analysis of the division of labor and had set the stage for the ensuing critical examination of machinery and large-scale industry in section 4 of chapter 4.[33]

In the Introduction, I cited Bertell Ollman's statement that method involved five components: ontology, epistemology, inquiry, intellectual reconstruction, and exposition. The majority of work on method has focussed on the first two points to the neglect of the latter three. On the basis of this study, it becomes apparent how misleading that practice can be. Not only are all five dimensions of Marx's method closely interrelated in a complex, nonlinear manner, but the last three elements, despite their neglect, are highly significant components in the development of his critique of political economy.

Marx's ontology in particular, and his epistemology to a lesser extent, have roots in his 1844 and 1846 expositions of the political economy, and he developed them over the next dozen years as he wrestled with the substance of political economy and how to order and present his critique of the discipline and the phenomenon.

Marx's concepts are the result of a complex dialectic between his own mental apprehension of ideas as they developed over the twenty-three years considered in this study and the actual sources of information available to him as he developed his ideas, as well as the actual elaboration processes he employed in trying to organize and present his insights between 1844 and 1867. This dialectic can be seen in a number of ways, ranging from the excerpting of material from treatises in political economy to the collection of empirical, historical material. It is visible in the development of new outlines and changed modes of presentation—both of which influenced the form and content of Marx's arguments—and the production of such new concepts as "collective worker" and "handicraftlike" to encapsulate particular relationships within the division of labor characteristic of manufacture. Most important, it is apparent how Marx's concrete production process led him to a variety of intellectual obstacles. As he overcame each, he developed a more comprehensive grasp of the division of labor up to 1867, when Marx was able to weave classical arguments skillfully into his analysis in favor of the division of labor while simultaneously using either Smith or his own resources to undermine those very arguments. The result was a richer concept of the division of labor than he had begun with initially in 1844; it was also a far more comprehensive conception than could be found in the literature on political economy.

All of these developments were the result of the relational totality of inquiry, intellectual reconstruction and exposition at the heart of Marx's method. Although I would not argue that the study of Marx's ontology and epistemology are insignificant in terms of understanding his method, I would maintain, on the basis of this work, that when he wrote in the afterword to the second German edition of *Das Kapital* "the means of presentation must be distinguished formally from the means of investigation" and that "[i]nvestigation has to appropriate the material in detail, to analyze its different forms of development and to trace out their inner association" he indicated the concerns most central to an understanding of his method.[34]

NOTES

1. Karl Marx and Friedrich Engels, *Historisch-kritische Gesamtausgabe* [hereafter cited as *MEGA*¹], ed. David Ryazanov and Vladimir Adoratsky (Berlin: Marx-Engels Verlag, 1927-32, Moscow-Leningrad: Verlagsgenossenschaft Ausländischer Arbeiter in der UdSSR, 1935), I, 1.1, pp. 5-83; David McLellan, *Karl Marx: His Life and Thought* (London: Macmillan, 1973), pp. 16-61; Franz Mehring, *Karl Marx*, trans. Edward Fitzgerald (Ann Arbor: Ann Arbor Paperback, 1962), pp. 9-43.

2. Karl Marx and Friedrich Engels, *Gesamtausgabe: Werke, Artikel, Entwurfe* [hereafter cited as *MEGA*] (Berlin: Dietz Verlag, 1975ff), II, 1.1, p. 99:23-26.

3. *MEGA* I, 2, p. 314:20-36.

4. Ibid., pp. 236:37-237:15, 284:32-285:28, and 292:18-21. See also, Herbert Marcuse, "Neue Quellen zur Grundlegung des Historischen Materialismus," *Die Gesellschaft* 9, no. 2 (1932):136-74, esp. 136-52.

5. *MEGA* I, 2, p. 309:11-16.

6. Ibid., p. 309:20, 23-24.

7. *MEGA* III, 1, pp. 23:34-24:3. The text referred to is, no doubt, *Die Deutsche Ideologie*.

8. *MEGA*¹ I, 5, pp. 41:30-42:3, 56:39-41, 57:5-8.

9. See, Louis Althusser, "On the Young Marx," and "Marxism and Humanism," in *For Marx*, trans. Ben Brewster (London: New Left Books, 1977), pp. 51-86, 221-47, especially p. 227.

10. Ferdinand Lassalle, *Der Briefwechsel zwischen Lassalle und Marx*, vol. 3 of *Nachgelassend Briefe und Schriften* [hereafter cited as *BZLM*], ed. Gustav Mayer (Berlin: Springer Verlag, 1922), pp. 28-29.

11. The commercial crisis of 1857 is often cited as the stimulus that encouraged Marx to set out his critique at that time. See Marx to Engels, December 18, 1857, Marx to Lassalle, December 21, 1857, in Karl Marx and Friedrich Engels, *Werke* [hereafter cited as *MEW*] (Berlin: Dietz Verlag, 1956-90), 29:232, 548. In *Marx's Method* (Oxford: Basil Blackwell, 1975), p. 27, however,

Terrell Carver has pointed out that Marx had predicted economic crises many times before 1857; the years 1850, 1851, 1852, 1853, 1855, and 1856 are mentioned. Carver maintains that the chance gift of Bakunin's copy of Hegel's *Wissenschaft der Logik* was a more important factor in Marx's work on *Die Grundrisse;* see Marx to Engels, January 16, 1858, *MEW* 29:260. Given the nature of the *Die Grundrisse,* I would agree with the importance that Carver puts upon *Die Logik.*

12. The continual struggle with the form and order of *Die Grundrisse* is apparent in the text. In addition to the four variations for the overall plans found within the text (*MEGA* II, 1.1, pp. 43:1-13, 151:26-152:3, 187:13-33, 199:16-204:30), there is a fifth suggestion by Marx that the order could not be determined until after he had written the text completely (p. 237:17-29). The text is also replete with asides about ideas that belong elsewhere, or that will be developed later in the text (pp. 92:6-8, 95:33-34, 112:28-31, 126:4-5, 130:11-14, 194:33-34, 196:23-25, 197:36-37, 206:27-29, 210:9-10, 210:10-11, 217:36-40). For examples of the correspondence concerning the plan and order of *Die Grundrisse,* see note 13.

13. Writing to Engels on May 31, 1858 (*MEW* 29:330), Marx pointed out that "the reading of my own manuscript [that is, *Die Grundrisse*] will cost me nearly a week. The devil is, namely, that in the manuscript (a thick volume if it was printed) everything jumbles together like beets and cabbages, much that is only determined for much later parts. So I must make an index in which notebook and which page number the shit appears in the course [of the notebooks]." On February 22, 1858, while working on the final part of notebook 6 or the beginning of 7, he pointed out to Lassalle that "the thing [*Die Grundrisse*] proceeds slowly because objects [*Gegenstände*] that one has made for many years the main object [*Hauptobjekt*] of one's studies, as soon as one finally should be settling accounts with them show new sides again and again and solicit new considerations." Ibid., p. 550.

14. See, for example, *MEGA* II, 1.2, pp. 377:31-378:27, 476:26-477:26, 499:3-17.

15. Of course, Marx's reading interests and knowledge interests did not operate separately or independently of one another. The two constitute a dialectical relation, but it is still possible, as in this case, that one would have more influence than the other. In this particular case, it seems likely that Marx's knowledge interests played the more significant role.

16. *MEGA* II, 2.1, pp. 3-14. Marx made two drafts of the index for the first part of his critique. In the first index (pp. 3-7), he developed a general topic outline for his discussion of value, money, and capital in general. The second draft (pp. 8-14) contains a more detailed set of references for the topics "Money as Measure," "Money as Means of Exchange," and "Money as Money." The indexes are located on pages 23-33 of notebook M. In "Siebzig Jahre 'Zur Kritik der politischen Ökonomie,'" *Archiv für die Geschichte des Sozialismus und der Arbeiterbewegung* 15 (1930):23, David Ryazanov dates the indexes about the same time Marx wrote to Engels concerning the outline of *Zur Kritik* and focussed on value, money, and capital in general; see Marx to Engels

April 2, 1858, *MEW* 29:315–18. The editors to *Die Grundrisse* (p. xii) suggest mid-May 1858 as the date of the indexes.

17. *MEGA* II, 2.1, pp. 256–63. The editors to *Die Grundrisse* (pp. xii–xiv) date this index February-March 1859. They argue that Marx had completed his indexes to the seven notebooks between mid-May and the end of August. Although poor living conditions kept him from working in the summer of 1858, he wrote the original text to *Zur Kritik* from September to November and in November finalized the first two chapters that Jenny Marx copied out so they could be sent off to Duncker on January 1, 1859. The foreword was sent in on February 23, 1859. Thus, the editors argue, Marx began his "Draft Plan to the Chapter on Capital" in the February to March 1859 period, although he could have constructed it in late January 1859. See Marx to Engels, January 21, 1859, *MEW* 29:385.

18. *MEGA* II, 2.1, pp. 264–71; *MEGA* II, 2, pp. 414–43. The editors of the new *MEGA* point out that a water mark "Etowgood 1859" on a page of the citation notebook indicates that the work could not have begun before 1859. In compiling the notebook, Marx apparently began with the eighth of his 1851 London notebooks and proceeded through them before citing from the Paris, Brussels, and Manchester study notebooks of the 1840s and finishing with the seventh notebook of his 1859–62 London study notebooks. In compiling the index to the citation notebook, he was not guided by his draft plan to the "Chapter on Capital," but rather set out headings on the basis of key ideas in the first citations. He compiled the index to the citation notebook in January and February 1860.

19. *MEGA* II, 2.1, p. 268:6–18.

20. Ibid., pp. 272–86. The "References to my own Notebooks" was originally dated by the first editors of *Die Grundrisse* as February 1859, but because this index occurs in notebook B'' on pages 28–36, thus following the index to Marx's citation notebook, he could not have developed the index before 1860. The editors of the new *MEGA* argue it was probably compiled in June or July 1861 following a long period of ill health and the Herr Vogt affair.

21. Ibid., pp. 237:29–242:7.

22. See especially *MEGA* II, 3.1, pp. 252:12–254:35.

23. Marx made excerpts from Harris's work and included them in notebook 7 of the 1859–62 London study notebooks; *MEGA* II, 3.1, Apparatus, p. 158. He included a section in his citation notebook (p. 136).

24. *MEGA* II, 3.1, p. 292:6–8.

25. *MEGA* II, 3.6, p. 1949:3–4, Marx's emphasis.

26. Marx to Engels, January 28, 1863, *MEW* 30:320; *MEGA* II, 3.6, p. 1947:17–41.

27. *MEGA* II, 3.1, p. 252:8–11.

28. Karl Marx, "Die Resultate des unmittelbaren Produktionsprozesses," *Arkhiv Marxsa i Engel'sa* 2(1933):100–18.

29. Karl Marx, *Das Kapital*, 1st ed. (Hamburg: Otto Meissner, 1867), pp. 321–24.

30. Ibid., pp. 338–40.

31. Ibid., p. 346.
32. Ibid., p. 347.
33. Ibid., p. 355.
34. Marx, *Das Kapital,* 2d ed. (Hamburg: Otto Meissner, 1873), p. 821.

BIBLIOGRAPHY

Adoratsky, Vladimir, ed. *Arkhiv Marxsa i Engelsa,* vols. 1–2. Moscow: Partiyanoe Isdatelstvo, 1932–33.

———. ed. *Arkhiv Marxsa i Engelsa,* vols. 3–4. Moscow: Partisdat tsK VKP, 1934–35.

———. ed. *Arkhiv Marxsa i Engelsa,* vol. 5. Moscow: Gosudarstvennoe Isdatelstvo Politiceskoya Literaturu, 1938.

———. ed. *Karl Marx: Chronik seines Lebens in Einzeldaten,* Moscow: Marx-Engels Verlag, 1934.

Althusser, Louis. "Marxism and Humanism." In *For Marx,* translated by Ben Brewster, pp. 221–47. London: New Left Books, 1977.

———. "On the Materialist Dialectic." In *For Marx,* translated by Ben Brewster, pp. 161–218. London: New Left Books, 1977.

———. "On the Young Marx." In *For Marx,* translated by Ben Brewster, pp. 51–86. London: New Left Books, 1977.

Babbage, Charles. *On the Economy of Machinery and Manufactures.* Philadelphia: Carey and Lea, 1832.

———. *Traité sur l'économie des machines et des manufactures.* Translated by Edward Benoit. Paris, 1833.

Carver, Terrell. "Editor's Preface." In *Marx's Method,* pp. 3–45. Oxford: Basil Blackwell, 1975.

Ferguson, Adam. *Essai sur l'histoire de la société civile,* 2 vols. Translated by M. Bergier. Paris: Veuve Desaint, 1783.

———. *Essay on the History of Civil Society.* 1776. Reprint. New York: Garland Publishing, 1971.

Gambel, Andrew, and Paul Walton. "Marx, Adam Smith and Political Economy." In *From Alienation to Surplus Value,* pp. 143–57. London: Sheed and Ward, 1972.

Gerth, Hans, and Charles Wright Mills, eds. *From Max Weber: Essays in Sociology.* Oxford: Oxford University Press, 1949.

Gide, Charles, and Charles Rist. *A History of Economic Doctrines.* 2d English ed. Translated by Robert Richards. Toronto: George Harrap, 1948.

Glucksmann, André. "A Ventriloquist Structuralism." *New Left Review* 72 (1972):68–92.

Gould, Carol. *Marx's Social Ontology.* Cambridge: MIT Press, 1978.

Grossman, Henryk. "Die Änderung des ursprünglichen Aufbauplans des Marxschen 'Kapital.'" *Archiv für die Geschichte des Sozialismus und der Arbeiterbewegung* 14 (1929):305–38.

Hall, Stuart. "A 'Reading' of Marx's 1857 Introduction to the *Grundrisse.*" Occasional paper distributed by the University of Birmingham through the Centre for Contemporary Cultural Studies, 1973.

Hegel, Georg Wilhelm Friedrich. *Enzyklopadie der philosophen Wissenschaften,* vol. 1. Frankfurt/M.: Suhrkamp, 1970.

———. *Wissenschaft der Logik,* vol. 1. Frankfurt/M.: Suhrkamp, 1969.

Hutton, Charles. *A Course of Mathematics.* London: Blane Brothers Printers, 1841.

Israel, Joachim. *Der Begriff Entfremdung: Zur Verdinglichung des Menschen in der bürokratischen Gesellschaft.* Hamburg: Rowohlt Taschenbuch Verlag, 1985.

Kaiser, Bruno. *Ex Libris Karl Marx: Schicksal und Verzeichnis einer Bibliothek.* Berlin: Dietz Verlag, 1967.

Kolakowski, Lezek. "Althusser's Marxism." In *Socialist Register,* edited by Ralph Miliband and David Saville, pp. 111–28. London: Merlin Press, 1971.

Lassalle, Ferdinand. *Der Briefwechsel zwischen Lassalle und Marx.* Vol. 3 of *Nachgelassene Briefe und Schriften,* edited by Gustav Mayer. Berlin: Springer Verlag, 1922.

Lefebvre, Herni. "Forme, function, structure dans *Le capital.*" *L'homme et la société* 7 (1968):69–81.

———. "Réflections sur le structuralisme et l'histoire." *Cahiers internationaux de sociologie* 35 (1963):3–24.

McLellan, David. *Karl Marx: His Life and Thought.* London: Macmillan Press, 1973.

Maguire, John. *Marx's Paris Writings: An Analysis.* Dublin: Gill and Macmillan, 1972.

Mann, Julia de L. "The Textile Industry: Machines for Cotton, Flax, Wool, 1760–1850." In *A History of Technology,* vol. 4, edited by Charles Singer, E. J. Holmyard, A. R. Hall, and Trevor Williams, pp. 280–95. Oxford: Clarendon Press, 1958.

Marcuse, Herbert. "Neue Quellen zur Grundlegung des Historischen Materialismus." *Die Geselleschaft* 9, no. 2 (1932):136–74.

Marx, Karl. *Capital,* vol. 1. Translated by Ben Fowkes. Harmondsworth: Pelican Books, 1976.

———. *Le capital,* vol. 1. Translated by Joseph Roy. Paris: Maurice Lachâtre, 1875.

————. *The Ethnological Notebooks of Karl Marx.* Transcribed and edited by Lawrence Krader. Assen: Van Gorcum, 1976.

————. *Exzerpte über Arbeitsteilung, Maschinerie und Industrie.* Transcribed and edited by Rainer Winkelmann. Frankfurt/M.: Verlag Ullstein, 1982.

————. *Grundrisse der Kritik der politischen Ökonomie (Rohentwurf) 1857–58.* Berlin: Dietz Verlag, 1953.

————. *Das Kapital,* 1st ed., vol. 1. Hamburg: Otto Meissner, 1867.

————. *Das Kapital,* 2d ed., vol. 1. Hamburg: Otto Meissner, 1873.

————. *Das Kapital,* 4th ed., vol. 1. Berlin: Dietz Verlag, 1961.

————. *Das Kapital: Kritik der politischen Ökonomie,* 3 vols. in 1. Compiled by Julian Borchardt. Berlin-Schöneberg: Neuzeitlicher Buchverlag, 1919.

————. *Karl Marx: Selected Writings in Sociology and Social Philosophy.* Edited by Tom Bottomore and Maximilien Rubel. London: Watts, 1956.

————. *The Letters of Karl Marx.* Selected and translated by Saul K. Padover. Englewood Cliffs: Prentice-Hall, 1979.

————. *Misère de la philosophie.* Paris: Alfred Costes, 1950.

————. "Die Resultate des unmittelbaren Produktionsprozesses." *Arkhiv Marxsa i Engel'sa* 2 (1933):4–266.

————. *Die technologisch-historischen Exzerpte.* Transcribed and edited by Hans-Peter Müller. Frankfurt/M.: Verlag Ullstein, 1981.

————. *Theorien über den Mehrwert,* 3 vols. in 4. Transcribed and edited by Karl Kautsky. Stuttgart: J. H. W. Dietz Verlag, 1905, 1910.

————. *Theorien über den Mehrwert,* 3 vols. Berlin: Dietz Verlag, 1956, 1959, 1962.

Marx, Karl, and Friedrich Engels. *Ausgewählte Briefe.* Edited by Vladimir Adoratsky. Moscow-Leningrad: Verlagsgenossenschaft Ausländischer Arbeiter in der UdSSR, 1934.

————. *Der Briefwechsel zwischen Friedrich Engels und Karl Marx: 1844 bis 1883,* 4 vols. Edited by August Bebel and Eduard Bernstein. Stuttgart: J. H. W. Dietz, 1913.

————. *Gesamtausgabe: Werke, Artikel, Entwürfe.* Berlin: Dietz Verlag, 1975ff.

————. *Historisch-kritische Gesamtausgabe,* 10 vols. in 11. Edited by David Ryazanov and Vladimir Adoratsky. Berlin: Marx-Engels-Archiv Verlag, 1927–32.

————. *Historisch-kritische Gesamtausgabe,* 2 vols. Edited by Vladimir Adoratsky. Moscow-Leningrad: Verlagsgenossenschaft Ausländischer Arbeiter in der UdSSR, 1935.

————. *Izbrannui pisma.* Moscow: Gospolitizdat, 1947.

————. *Marx/Engels Selected Correspondence: 1846–1895.* Translated and edited by Donna Torr. New York: International Publishers, 1934.

————. *Marx/Engels Selected Correspondence.* Moscow: Foreign Languages Publishing House, n.d..

————. *Marx/Engels Selected Correspondence.* Moscow: Progress Publishers, 1955.

————. *Sochineniia,* 2d ed., 50 vols. in 54. Moscow: Isdatelstvo Politiceskoya Literaturu, 1955–81.

————. *Verzeichnis Werke, Schriften, Artikel.* Berlin: Dietz Verlag, 1968.

———. *Werke*, 43 vols. in 45. Berlin: Dietz Verlag, 1956–90.

Mehring, Franz. *Karl Marx*. Translated by Edward Fitzgerald, Ann Arbor: Ann Arbor Paperbacks, 1962.

Meszaros, Istvan. *Marx's Theory of Alienation*. London: Merlin Press, 1970.

Ollman, Bertell. *Alienation: Marx's Conception of Man in Capitalist Society*. Cambridge: Cambridge University Press, 1971.

———. "Marxism and Political Science: Prolegomenon to a Debate on Marx's Method." *Politics and Society* 3, no. 3 (1973):491–515.

Poppe, Johann. *Geschichte der Technologie seit der Wiederherstellung der Wissenschaften bis an das Ende des achzehnten Jahrhunderts*, 3 vols. Göttingen, 1807–11.

Rattansi, Ali. *Marx and the Division of Labour*. London: Macmillan, 1982.

Ricardo, David. *Des principes de l'économie politique et de l'impôt*, 2d ed., 2 vols. Translated by F. S. Constancio. Paris: J.-P. Aillaud, 1835.

———. *On the Principles of Political Economy and Taxation*. Vol. 1 of *The Works and Correspondence of David Ricardo*. Edited by Piero Sraffa and Maurice Dobb. Cambridge: Cambridge University Press, 1951.

Rojahn, Jürgen. "Marxismus—Marx—Geschichtswissenschaft: Der Fall der sog. 'Ökonomische-philosophischen Manuskripte aus dem Jahre 1844.'" *International Review of Social History* 28, no. 1 (1983):2–49.

Rosdolsky, Roman. "Einige Bemerkungen über die Methode des Marxschen *Kapital* und ihre Bedeutung für die heutige Marxforschung." In *Kritik der politischen Oekonomie Heute: 100 Jahre Kapital*, edited by Walter Eucher and Alfred Schmidt, pp. 9–21. Frankfurt/M.: Europäische Verlaganstalt, 1968.

———. *The Making of Marx's Capital*. Translated by Peter Burgess. 1968. Reprint. London: Pluto Press, 1977.

Rubel, Maximilien. "Les cahiers d'étude de Marx." In *Marx, critique du marxisme*, pp. 301–59. Paris: Payot, 1974.

———. "Chronologie." In vol. 3, *Oeuvres de Karl Marx: Économie*, pp. xcvi-cxxxi. Paris: Éditions Gallimard, 1965.

———. "Une échange des lettres entre Lassalle et Marx." *La revue socialiste*, December 1949, pp. 434–47.

———. "A History of Marx's 'Economics.'" In *Rubel on Marx*, edited by Joseph O'Malley and Keith Algozin, pp. 82–189. Cambridge: Cambridge University Press, 1981.

———. *Marx Chronologie*. London: Macmillan Press, 1980.

Rubin, Isaac. *Essays on Marx's Theory of Value*, 3d ed. Translated by Milos Samardzija and Fredy Perlman. 1928. Reprint. Montreal: Black Rose Books, 1973.

Ryazanov, David, ed. *Arkhiv K. Marxsa i F. Engel'sa*, vols. 1–5. Moscow: Gosudarstvennoe Isdatelstvo, 1924–30.

———. *Marx-Engels Archiv*, vols. 1–2. Frankfurt/M.: Marx-Engels-Archiv Verlag, 1926–27.

———. "Siebzig Jahre 'Zur Kritik der politischen Ökonomie.'" *Archiv für die Geschichte des Sozialismus und der Arbeiterbewegung* 15 (1930):1–32.

Say, Jean-Baptiste. *A Treatise on Political Economy, or the Production, Distribution and Consumption of Wealth*, 6th ed. Translated with notes by C. R. Princep.

American edition containing a translation of the introduction and additional notes by Clement Biddle. Philadelphia: Grigg and Elliott, 1846.

Sayer, Derek. *Marx's Method.* Atlantic Highlands: Humanities Press, 1979.

————. "Method and Dogma in Historical Materialism." *Sociological Review* 23, no. 4 (1975):779–810.

Schmidt, Alfred. *Der Begriff der Natur in der Lehre von Marx.* Frankfurt/M.: Europäische Verlaganstalt, 1962.

Schumpeter, Joseph. *History of Economic Analyses.* Edited from the manuscript by Elizabeth Schumpeter. New York: Oxford University Press, 1954.

Smith, Adam. *An Inquiry into the Nature and Causes of the Wealth of Nations.* Vol. 2 of the Glasgow Edition of *The Works and Correspondence of Adam Smith,* edited by Roy Hutcheson Campbell and Andrew S. Skinner. Indianapolis: Liberty Press, 1976.

————. *Recherches sur la nature et causes de la richesse des nations,* 5 vols. Translated by Germain Garnier. Paris, 1802.

Stewart, Dugald. *Lectures on Political Economy.* Vol. 8 of *The Collected Works of Dugald Stweart,* edited by Sir William Hamilton. Edinburgh: Thomas Constable, 1855.

————. *The Industry of Nations: A Survey of the Existing State of Arts, Machines and Manufactures,* vol. 2. London, 1855.

Weiss, Helde. "Die 'Enquête Ouvrière' von Karl Marx." *Zeitschrift für Sozialforschung* 5 (1936):75–98.

Zeleny, Jindrich. *The Logic of Marx.* Translated by Terrell Carver. 1962. Reprint. Oxford: Basil Blackwell, 1980.

INDEX

Adoratsky, Vladimir: as editor 25-26n1; history of *Kapital,* 58

The Advantages of The East India Trade (anonymous): on division of Labor, 81, 84, 150-51

Alienation: as abstract concept, 8, 135, 161, 164; as concrete conception, 8, 42, 45, 49, 164; and division of labor, 35, 37, 39, 41, 45, 49, 50-51, 70, 71, 75-77, 84-86, 124-25, 167, 172; and surplus value, 35, 49; and Smith, 35; in *Deutsche Ideologie,* 41, 45, 163-64; and production, 45; in *Grundrisse,* 48-49, 168-69; as objectification, 51; in *Kapital,* 54, 64, 133, 142-50; and commodity fetishism, 70, 84-86, 91-92, 135, 172. *See also* Estrangement, Paris manuscripts

Althusser, Louis: on method, 4, 5; on epistemology, 164

Ancient Greeks: on division of labor, 71, 78-81, 129, 134, 142, 150-52, 171-72; and Smith, 74; in *Kapital,* 79, 80, 171-72; Marx's knowledge interests, 93. *See also* Petty, Plato, Xenophon

Babbage, Charles: and division of labor, 39, 103, 170; on machinery, 103, 105, 111, 129, 131, 174-75

Beccaria, Cesare: on division of labor, 81, 170

Blanqui, Jérôme: on division of labor, 81, 170

British Museum: Marx's use of, 17

Capital: as alienated property, 49; in *Grundrisse,* 49, 57; productive power, 50, 82; and money, 56, 91; in general, 56-60, 65, 168; concentration of, 83; variable, 83; constant, 83; and raw material, 84

Capital, original accumulation of: in *Grundrisse,* 48; and division of labor, 48-49, 82, 83

Cherubliez, Antoine: on machinery, 102

Citation notebooks: described, 27-28n19; and Smith, 89; enduring resource, 93-94, 169-70

Class: ruling, 42; society, 45, 72

Clock: basis for machine, 107, 112, 116n33

Collective worker: origin of conception, 110-11, 112-13, 126-29; and detail workers, 111, 126-27, 130, 132; and pin-making, 130; and *Resultate,* 132; and skills, 132; and method, 179. *See also Gesamtarbeiter*

Commodity: fetishism of, 70, 84-86, 91-92, 135; and social division of labor,

Index

Traité d'économie politique (Say): in study notebooks, 15-16, 20
Traité sur l'économie des machines et des manufactures (Babbage): on machinery, 105

Umrisse zur Kritik der politischen Ökonomie (Engels): influence on Marx, 33
Ure, Andrew: and division of labor, 39, 86, 131, 165; in *Deutsche Ideologie,* 46; and Marx, 47; on Smith, 86; on labor capacity, 86

Valorization process: and alienation, 46, 49; in *Deutsche Ideologie,* 46; in *Grundrisse,* 47, 49
Value: in Smith, 48; labor as source of, 48; in *Zur Kritik,* 56; and capital, 56; and money, 56; and fetishism of commodities, 70, 84-85; mass of, 89; from machinery, 102. *See also Grundrisse*
Vogt, Karl: the "Vogt Affair": 59, 63, 67

Wade, John: in *Grundrisse,* 50; power of capital, 50
Wage labor: in *Grundrisse,* 49; relation to capital, 49-50
Wagner, Adolf: Marx's marginal notes, 2; *Lehrbuch,* 2
Wakefield, Edward: editor of Smith, 48, 64, 148
Wayland, Francis: and division of labor, 82, 111, 138, 170; and class, 82
Wealth of Nations (Smith): and division of labor 7, 37; knowledge interests, 40; and physiocrats, 48; and pin-making, 131; Wakefield edition, 148. *See also* Adam Smith, *Richesse des nations*
Wealth: growth, 89

Weiss, Helde: on *Enquête Ouvrière,* 27n15
Winkelmann, Rainer: on study notebooks, 15
Wissenschaft der Logik (Hegel): and Marx's method, 133-34, 175
Workers: and alienation, 43, 49, 76-77, 91-92; proportional allocation, 72, 83, 111-12, 131; concrete labor, 72; in cooperation, 72; and capital, 73, 74, 76-77; as parts 76; coordination, 83; conglomeration of, 83, 102; and fetishism, 85, 91-92; and poverty, 88-89; stratification of, 89; specialization, 108; See also Craft worker, Detail worker,
Working conditions: under manufacture, 88-89, 109
Working day: length of, 6
Working machine: origin, 104, 107, 176

Xenophon: on division of labor, 71, 79-80, 81, 152, 170, 171; in *Kapital,* 79, 152; and Stewart, 79, 80, 171

Zeleny, Jindrich: on method, 4
Zur Kritik der politischen Ökonomie (Marx): draft manuscript, 9-10, 48, 52, 69, 73, 101, 151, 167, 168-69; preface, 33; Duncker contract, 35, 58-59, 67n88, 93, 134-35; outline, 54-60; as pamphlets, 55, 59; length, 55-56, 58, 65n74, 134-35, 172; and Engels, 55, 57-59, 168; on value, 56, 73; writing style, 56-58, 141, 172; public response, 59, 66-67n87, 168; and Kugelmann, 59, 93, 101; errors in political economy, 73, 134; division of labor, 73; the commodity, 91; second part, 101, 141, 172; focus, 122. *See also Grundrisse,* Lassalle, Marx

About the Author

ROB BEAMISH completed his doctorate in sociology at the University of Toronto. He is an associate professor at Queen's University, Kingston, Canada, where he teaches social theory and the political economy of sport. Among his forthcoming publications are *After Ben Johnson: Drugs and Sport in Canada* and *Voices from Berlin,* an ethnographic account of how Berliners have adjusted to the fall of the Berlin Wall.